Trobriand Islands

Kuaniaga
Kanapu
Gabwina LUSANCAY IS.
Nauria Kaileuna
Tuma
Kiriwina I.
Kitava
Iwa
Muwo Vakuta
Marshall
Bennett
Is.

0   50
MILES

S O U T H

Santa Cruz
Islands

Samoa Islands   Pago Pago

New
Hebrides

Fiji
Islands   Suva

Tonga
Islands

Loyalty
Islands

P A C I F I C

North
Island
Auckland

NEW
ZEALAND

Wellington
South
Island

O C E A N

Tangaroa's Godchild

Books by Olaf Ruhen

Tangaroa's Godchild

by Olaf Ruhen

LITTLE, BROWN AND COMPANY • BOSTON • TORONTO

Published simultaneously in Canada
by Little, Brown & Company (Canada) Limited

PRINTED IN THE UNITED STATES OF AMERICA

To my parents •

Olaf Ruhen •

tangaroa's
godchild

pROLOGUe

IN A certain warm embowered island of the Coral Sea
today the fishing fleet stands by while the village magi-
cian, in defiance of an alien government, a foreign missionary and the white population, performs a simple
ceremony, addressing his actions and his words to his
ancestors.

He tells them the state of the weather, and reports
upon the repairs that have been made on the canoes since
their last venture. He describes what preparation has
been given to the nets already loaded on the thwarts, and
by name enumerates the crews standing by, ready to
push off. He names the fishing grounds to which the
canoes are bound, and prays that the ancestors will in
spirit accompany the fleet. He is meticulous in his state-
ments, in particular when he describes what precautions
have been taken to guard against any calculable calam-
ity. When the ceremony comes to an end, the men will
run the great canoes into the water, shouting and laughing, eager for the contest.

This is not religion, nor is it magic, though mission
and government consider it so and provide a penalty for

holding the ceremony. It is a simple means of ensuring that the crews will not carelessly go to sea, that their equipment will be sufficient and in order, or alternatively, that they will be aware of any inadequacies caused by previous loss or disaster. It is a reminder too of how much they owe to the discoveries of their ancestors, a thanksgiving for the wealth of knowledge with which their fathers endowered them. For a man's equipment against the sea is carried lightly, being housed, for the most part, within his skull.

This is the true belief of the adventurer at sea; his whole respect is commanded by sea-knowledge and re-source; his total ambition is to make his personality allied with such respect. It is trite to call the sea his mistress; he accepts her as such in all her moods.

Women are sisters under the skin and one ocean is very like another; a mistress may have myriad lovers, and all of them devoted. For myself I have the blood of Old World islanders in my veins; I am lonely wherever ocean waters do not reach; but it is the South Pacific to which I am committed, as a man loving all women may be faithful to one. Intellectually I am aware that the South Pacific is an ocean, that its composition may be analyzed, its bounds may be mapped, its depredations checked. I know that the laws which control it may be studied and understood, and that in the light of our twentieth-century knowledge it may be regarded as insensate and presently controllable.

But emotionally I hold it a sentient being, command-ing love and loyalty, demanding its tale of respect and attention, moody and capricious, steadfast and dependable, lightning-swift and nation-strong, muffling the thunder and stressing the whisperings of the sand-rooted she-oaks, cradling the defenseless and overwhelming the strong, halting the swift and speeding the weak, erratic as a woman, and firm as the faith in which she lives.

I hold my emotional life in a jealous regard, and make no apologies for believing as I do; at least I do not wish to. I have no desire except, as I can, to set down here (as an artist might paint the image of his love, brush-stroke by brush-stroke) the concept I have of an ocean I love. It is a debt that I owe; for I believe that the image of what I am, and of my fellows, was molded in some degree by that ocean.

ETWEEN MIDNIGHT and morning, on windless nights
under the moon, the sound of the surf is dominant,
the soft, surging, swinging rhythm of the restless edge of
the untroubled sea. The drilled platoons of an endless
army survey the objective of the beach and rise, gathering power to speed their advance. They roll majestically
into the attack, inevitably to be wasted in the maneuver
and to lower their brave plumed banners and retreat beneath the next echelon of their oncoming support.

Sometimes a campaign registers a small success in the
Sea-God's challenge to the land; such victories come in
times of storm. On nights of calm and moonlight the
flung armies are symbols only; they mark the watchful-
ness of the resting ocean. And between midnight and
morning their sound is the most pervasive of the night's

vibrations, but only because most other activities are dormant.

The beach lies vulnerable to the storms, Antarctic-born, that sweep up from the Southern Ocean. Its single shield against their fury is a pinnacle of black basalt that stands a mile and a half to sea, equidistant from most points on the curving two miles of sand. The sector of the arc runs northeast and southwest, so that except for an hour or two early in the morning, the breakers attack into the sun. But the rising moon also makes its first appearance from behind the water, and lays a golden pathway to beckon the feet of any adventurer into the sea world (and the sky world) of romance.

To the north the beach is terminated by a low cape which, at its seaward extremity, has the form of a Lawyer's Head, the nose pointing perkily to sea (or to the moonrise), the eyes cast downward upon the frothing lace that is the sea's confused commotion at his throat, the temples masked with a rocky resemblance to a solicitor's wig, with lines of artificial curls and the faintest indication of a ribbon.

Towards the south, the confusion is one of land. At first the sand runs out in a moraine of porphyritic boulders, and these in their turn give place to the basalt reef that trapped them there in bygone ages. Still farther south, and still based upon the reef, is a cliff of hardened clay, an outpost of the green and timeless hills that crowd in endless formations upon this eastern coast of the South Island of New Zealand. South again the sea has made a further indentation that may be considered as a purlieu of the beach; there is no sand here, but a waste of larger pebbles the size of bowling balls. Accumulations of them are yarded within a series of outcrops of the basalt reefs. At the end of this small bay a basalt cliff, a million million hexagonal pillars of basalt standing on end, is an abrupt termination of the area.

North and south of the beach are other islands, fragmentations of the capes they guard; and two or three of the nearest of these must be accounted as lying within the beach area. They were part of my world when I was a child, a world not limited, certainly, but dominated by the beach.

I have wider horizons now; though certainly it will take the remainder of a lively lifetime to expand them to the point at which I shall be content. As an aviator I have climbed to a vantage so high that I could distinguish, with an unaided eye, the curvature of the globe. As a fisherman I have taxed my resources, though never my will, in a probe of the ocean's illimitability. As a journalist and author I have despaired of ever recording more than a fraction of the wonderful variety of fellowmen, of their capacities and ambitions. I have marveled at the color of their dreams and the veracity of their instincts. I have been unable, in half a century, to rid myself of the sense of wonder and the joy in discovery that marks a child's life. I have looked at marvels and experienced delights; I have fought my enemies and my loves and brought them down or been myself undone; or again, in company that differed not at all, come close to Paradise.

But the world of my childhood centered upon the glory and the wonder of the barren-seeming beach.

The curved boundary of the sandy sector was marked, in the earliest of the days of which I write, by a complex of high sandhills. At the back of the sandhills lay the town, and in the second street, high-hedged, protective, weather-worn, happy and surrounded by flowers, stood the house where I first fell heir to the gifts of consciousness. At three o'clock one morning when I was five or six years old, I awakened to the command I had left with my mind the night before, in disobedience to the wish of my mother, which was that I should go to sleep on thoughts of the prayers I had said. I awoke to the sound of the surf, and the urgency of adventure, and for a while lay quiet, savoring them both and listening to the breathing of my elder brother in his bed across the room. The blind was up, the wide window open, the bedroom a harbor of the mellow light.

I came out from under the blankets with exaggerated caution, sliding a foot to the floor, getting a purchase with its ball on the cold linoleum before I sat up. I did not dare to dress; not there, not in that room with my brother asleep; he was seven years older than I. I gathered up my short pants, my singlet and my shirt, and tiptoed from the room. One of the two doors led outside to the moon-flooded garden, but its lock was noisy. I took my clothes in my arms to dress in the kitchen warmth.

No shoes, no stockings, no hat. From the bin in the

dark cool pantry, a paper bag. Out, like a burglar, to the garden, out to the gooseberry bushes ripe under the pear trees, and filled the bag, not with the big smooth-skinned berries, big as bantams' eggs, that were destined for pies and jams and stews, but with the smaller, sweeter, hairy fruits which we, in our wealth of gooseberries, selected as the only worthwhile eating.

Then at last, with emergency rations of a paper sack of berries clutched in my hand, with my heart clutching at my ribs, I was adventure-bound. I was in a world alone; no other moved. There was not an adult in the street, not a light in any window; not in my world, not before four in the morning. The streets were quite deserted; only the garbage cans were lined up in groups of two and three, all filled with coal-ash in that fire-warmed world of my childhood. No Constable Schubert, that big and ominous figure of authority. No one at all.

And the beach was lit by moonlight. The incoming waves, topped with a whirling froth, picked up the moon's illumination. When their strength was spent and they retreated seaward, the miles of hard wet sand gleamed momentarily with a cold white luminosity. But not a bird flew. The air was still, and the leaves on the trees were without a flutter.

There could have been enemies behind the lupin bushes, in the tunnels under the gorse behind the high wooden fence that marked off the playground and advertised Bulldog Tobacco and Cavendish Cigarettes. They might have lurked in the dark doorways of the few shops in the suburban streets, the mysterious dark yard of the boardinghouse that once had been a hotel. But I wanted to hide behind no brother or sister; I was by myself, alone, and the night was mine.

The Esplanade was deserted; the rows of seats where solid burghers took their Sunday afternoons and the early hours of milder evenings were ranked empty, facing the prospect of surging water. I jumped to their planked eminences one after the other and ran along each one, along the promenade, in front of the Pavilion, where children older than I could rollerskate. I was king of the night and, like a king, alive to its special dangers while I ran southeast, away from the moon, my pale shadow leaping ahead of me from seat to seat.

Near the second row of concrete steps that led from the promenade to the shore, the magic of solitude was abruptly broken. There were people on the sand, a man and a woman. They lay together on a rug, and parts of them, not ordinarily exposed in my experience, gleamed nakedly in the kindly lunar light.

Curiosity battled fear, and had to come to a victory, being supported by adventure, upon which I was bound. I watched in total incomprehension while his hands and hers, slowed and brought to tenderness, as I now imagine, by the great lassitudes and contents which follow the transports of physical love, caressed the other body. His face was to her breast, and his hair stroked the smooth pedestal of her neck. She looked up and saw me, and in the same instant grabbed for the fringed selvage of the rug, and threw it over them so that it held them in an envelope.

"Hey, Marty."

"What's the matter?"

"There's a kid. Watching us."

"Oh, Christ."

Cased in the rug, he wriggled round to look at me, where I hung over the rail at the top of the wall, fifteen feet above his head.

"Beat it, sonny. Grab your hook."

"He's awful little, Marty."

"He's big enough to hammer if I catch him. On your way, kid."

I was petrified, clinging to the rail, just tall enough to see over it.

"Too little to be out, Marty. What's he doing out? What time is it?"

"Time he was gone."

"He must be lost, Marty. Or running away. Better grab him."

I turned and ran, on towards my destination, not jumping from seat to seat now, just running. At the end of the Esplanade I jumped on one last seat, to make it four. Four was my lucky number; it went on and on if you halved it or if you doubled it; it was a magic number. I counted everything in fours, jumped on four lots of four seats, hit four successive telegraph poles with my open hand, ran my stick along corrugated iron fences in such a way that four ridges of the metal gave out with detonative responses. Long before I went to school I knew about the magic of four. I had two sisters, two brothers; that was four. If I had had grandparents they would have been four — I envied the kids with grand-parents.

When I left the Esplanade I followed the road above the boulders. It went on to curve through a cutting in the hard clay cliff and then past stone walls crowned with veronica and lupin, hugging the hill above the reef-straked pebble beach. It led eventually to the foot of the basalt, where in a quarried amphitheater a bandstand was centered for the Sunday delectation of the town's more sober citizens.

Responsible and dignified, they walked here in their Sunday best, and those who were lucky found seats for their comfort. The others remained on their feet or sat carefully upon large white handkerchiefs spread on the grass. It was a beautiful place; the floor and one wall of the amphitheater were covered with a thick growth of cocksfoot; the basalt pillars of the cliff were overgrown with great hanging screens of giant mesembryanthemum, and when the autumn colorings were set against the white and blue of sea and the black rocks there was a glory there.

I went up when I came to the cliff, round the back of the amphitheater and across above the sea's edge, cling-ing like a small fly against the perpendicularity of the cliff and round, and over to its crest, staying on the ocean side of the fence, two strands of wire that had been erected for safety.

To me the fence represented safety indeed, for in the wide fields on its other side was danger: horses and cattle at pasture. Such enormous beasts conducted a life that was on the ultimate edge of my experience; I had some slight acquaintance with the great and slumbrous dray-horses that accompanied the men who worked on the road, the sleek fat happy horse that drew the springcart of the sleek fat happy Chinese who sold vegetables, the saddle horse of the butcher's boy, and the old worn plug that drew the baker's van. But I knew these animals in the confinement of traces and harness; they moved under restriction; and while I might be game enough, for a dare, to run under their bellies close to their huge hoofs, I was by no means inclined to meet them at their freedom.

So I moved like a ghost from bush to bush between the fence and the verge of the precipitous cliff, going roundabout to my objective, which, not to make a mystery of it, was a certain tableland where mushrooms grew.

Far out to sea the eastern sky was lighted, and in my ignorance I thought the dawn must be at hand; that the sun would soon come thrusting above the waves and dispel the chill and the mists of night. From this height the island seemed close under the cliff, only halfway to the horizon and guarded by it instead of crowning it. To both north and south I could see new capes and bays, and other tiny rocks protruding from the sea.

The wet grasses, timothy and rye and cocksfoot, clung against my legs; their seed was ripening, and some stuck to my skin. In a week or less I could come and cut the cocksfoot heads with a pair of ancient scissors, carry my harvest home in a sugar bag, and when it would be all collected, flail and winnow the seed and sell it to the grain merchants. That was how the children in my family made their spending money for the last half of summer. But the beginning of the mushroom season was more exciting.

Lights flickered on when I passed Cargill's castle, where the colony's first leader had chosen a solitude to build in grandeur; lights sprang up in the farmhouse half a mile inland; the grazing cattle had turned their heads in the direction of their barns; the day was beginning. An occasional mushroom gleamed white against the grass, one here, one there. And after half an hour I came across a fairy ring of them that I gathered apologetically, for I believed in fairies, and trusted them, and hoped for their friendship. I filled my paper sack and started for home.

Below the castle I met the Major, walking at a great rate on his early constitutional. He looked at me curiously, but said nothing. He knew me by sight, but I was beneath his notice, and consequently, in the tradition of my family, he was beneath mine. But it was true that to a boy from another district I could retail long stories of the Major's prowess; they went back into the mists of history, to the Boer War and the Zulu War before that; tales of derring-do and feats of horsemanship, with drawn sabers and pennants flying from the lances.

The sun came up as I passed along the Esplanade, a blinding sun at eye level in a tracery of golden-penciled horizontal clouds that promised a fine day. The man and the woman had gone from the beach; the mark of their blanket had blotted out a square of the pattern of foot-steps above the tide mark.

Down at the edge of the sea Margie-Bargie was doing her morning exercises to the rising of the sun, her angular body cloaked from neck to knee in a swimming costume of rusty black bordered with circles of white. There was a complex of white, with circles about her upper arms where the short sleeves ended, circles just above her modestly revealed knees, a circle about her erect and wrinkle-riven neck, another around her waist, the largest circle of all marking the termination of her skirt three-quarters of the distance down her thighs.

Sometimes I got up early just to see Margie-Bargie at her exercises. She rose before the sun and, her costume hidden by an ankle-length raincoat, her hair caught up in a rubber bathing cap, her feet in ankle-hugging carpet slippers, her hands clutching a bag and a scanty towel, she hurried to the seashore for her morning devotions. Usually she performed alone; some mornings she had an embarrassing, exasperating audience of small fry. She didn't usually notice them; she would have carried out her performance in front of the world.

Her arms behind her, tense and outflung, she breathed deep of the fresh salt air, standing exactly at the point at which the incoming waves would run to cover her ankles and raising herself rhythmically on her toes.

As though she gathered momentum from this begin-ning, she brought her arms next into play, raising and lowering, up . . . down . . . up . . . down. Then her feet joined the dance, skipping, jumping, together, apart, in,

out, one . . . two . . . one . . . two . . . to the command
of some long-dead instructor. Looking at Margie-Bargie
you could take his place, deliver his commands: "Hands
on hips . . . *hup* . . . two . . . three . . . four. . . . *Hup*
. . . two . . . three . . . four." On and on and on, through
waist-bending and head-turning and knee-bending and
head-throwing-back and head-turning and once again
skipping, feet together, feet alternate, right-foot-raised
and skipping, left-foot-raised and skipping, arms swinging, knees rising until the sun was high above the water.

Then came a timid onslaught on the waves, a splashing
of water on the skin, a toe-raising approach towards the
rolling surf, and finally, with hands clasping opposite
shoulders, with elbows shielding her unnoticed and un-
noticeable breasts, she would turn her back to a comber
and be thrust beneath the scud.

Then scampering away out of the water she would
dab herself with the towel, assume her raincoat and her
carpet slippers, and scurry back to the little shop wherein
she helped a pair of aged parents, a little mouse of a
woman, incapable, one would say, of standing out from
the crowd in any way, except for those early morning
devotions on the shore.

This morning I watched poor Margie-Bargie through to
the end of her exercises and, a little warmed now by the
sun's promise more than by its rays, made my barefoot
way home, carrying my paper sack of mushrooms. I encountered the O'Brien girls heading for the water. They
were wearing nothing but their knitted swimsuits, in a
scandalous new fashion that was lately come to our prim

little suburb; such wear, as I knew from my father, was not for the street, however well it looked upon the sands, and I hurried past them, ignoring the polite surprised compliments they paid me on my wealth of mushrooms.

Besides, I wanted to hurry, for the total success of my enterprise as I had planned it demanded that I should be home in time to waken my parents with a morning cup of tea, and as I turned into the street I was overjoyed that the kitchen chimney carried, as yet, no plume of fresh morning smoke.

I built up the fire and boiled the water and made the tea and buttered scones and showed my father the mushrooms, which he always loved, and my happiness was complete.

If my mother thought I had been abroad too early, she said nothing then. But the next time I crept from beneath the covers at a comparable hour she intercepted me and sent me back to bed.

2

RISING SEAS heralded the most terrible of the storms. Long before the winds whipped them to a savage frenzy the combers grew in magnitude, and as their strength and size increased, so likewise did the speed of their advances; they came racing into the beach, sweeping up the long, inclined shelf of sand, on and up by their own inertia until being spent at last they had raised themselves so high above the level of the waters from which they came that, returning, they piled up new strength and went speeding back to sea, to meet their advancing fellows in an upsurge of power that sent the spray a hundred feet in air.

In the quiet house, two hundred yards from the limit of the beach and separated from it by the steep and significant sandhills, the sound of the waves would subtly change from sibilance to an ominous and muttering guttural, swelling and diminishing but always impinging upon consciousness.

"The seas are big tonight," my father would say, working on his accounts at the table or, more rarely, seated with a newspaper or a book before the fire, his family around him engaged upon their own pursuits.

And I would glow inwardly, for I loved the storms, being assured of this safe haven.

Then the wind would come to unleash a tireless fury upon the coast, and sooner or later, next morning perhaps, I would go to see the magnificence of the Sea-God's battle.

I believed with an unquestioning faith in the God of my Presbyterian Sunday school; I had no shadow of doubt but that He and He alone had reigned since before creation's dawn; this was the tenet and the mainstay of my entire existence. Yet in a way that admitted of no reasonable explanation, there was a Sea-God too in a contemporaneous and unrelated sphere, and I adored him without subtracting from the total of my real and overriding faith. The quality of that faith is still unchanged today; the Entity to which it fastens is an enlarged Entity, enlarged to the extent that my capacity for undersanding has increased. My God differs somewhat from the God of my childhood, but still demands a total belief.

Yet when I was small I believed also in fairies; there was one frequently within my room, a tiny being who loved to pose in the morning reflection of the window transmitted by a porcelain doorhandle. And when I went to watch the storm, as I went to watch every storm that whipped the beach, the shrieking Oceanides rode the waves, their wet and wind-whipped hair lank and olive-green and studded with misty pearls; a triumphant crew that gloried in the power of racing wind and water.

I liked best to go with my father; in his company I had nothing to fear. In winter, when we turned the corner to come upon the deserted Esplanade, the chill wind whipped my breath away, stilled it in my throat and left me gasping. I would turn to him and walk half-sideways, burying my face in the skirt of his coat. To the equinoctial storms of spring I would face out, head back and chest up, as my teachers unsuccessfully tried to make me drill at school.

I liked too to go there by myself, racing down the sandhills towards the oncoming surf, leaping for the cross bars that linked the lines of piles driven in to save the sand, and hanging there to look down upon the water boiling beneath my feet, racing the waves and defying their power.

But my father's own joy was communicated to me in understanding. Sometimes the breakers were so high that in their violence they covered the total beach, mounted the fifteen-foot wall of the Esplanade, and roared a hundred yards down the street, coming to a bewildered end in the ambush of storm drains where the tram tracks ran parallel to the shore.

Opposite the boulder beach the sea roared with the voice of an angry and a waiting crowd. Between the reefs of rocks the round boulders rattled one upon the other in the suction of the water's return; they roared and shouted and cracked and groaned until their protests were muffled beneath the surge of the next great wall of water. The cliffs echoed their cries, the skies imitated them with the roll of thunder.

At the foot of the cliff at the southern end of this beach, the basalt was honeycombed with water-driven tunnels; and at the toe that extended farthest a small basalt island, that never in my experience was blessed with a name, took the first shock of each oncoming wave, and initiated, by its obdurate obstruction, a magnificence never to be equaled.

These were not ordinary waves, as I have said. On a calm day, on this beach, they might perhaps have been a mere six or seven feet high; in the storm they would have overwhelmed a two-story house; and indeed, as a man much acquainted now with heavy weather on a wild ocean, I can testify to this. And a wave of thirty feet in height from trough to crest, on becoming a breaker, rears up to a height more than half as much again, and crashes down like the Hammer of Thor, with the power of a god, and a god's carelessness of what might lie beneath.

At the cliff's edge in the storm, each such wave, in process of becoming a breaker, struck the thirty-foot high obstruction of the island on its upward surge, obliterating it entirely from view and throwing a fan of white water hundreds of feet into the air, where the wind caught it and whirled it through the eddies created in its own attack upon the cliff, and carried it far inland.

And simultaneously the wave was chasing upon the foot of the cliff itself, from where the water, driven with unimaginable power, raced through the tunnels and emerged in a great white blasting fountain that exploded from the more sheltered side of the cliff, while the contrary backwash raced upon itself for a new commotion at several points with the waves that followed. In the boiling white of the sea near the cliff, writhing tentacles of bull-kelp were flipped in the air; a child could visualize the agonies of a monster imprisoned and wakened to torture.

The flying spray glistened, even under the dark clouds, upon the black basalt of the cliff; above the rock, high, high up, the grass and withered mesembryanthemum glowed green and gold, red and orange. The skies above raced in driving patterns. It was all a glory, and a spectacle of ordered confusion, never following exactly the same pattern twice. It used to hypnotize my child's eyes and I would watch for hours, with a red and frozen nose peeping out from the mufflings my mother contrived for me if it was winter, with bare legs and my throat open to the weather in any other season.

If I was with my father we halted only momentarily, for he loved action, and we walked up and down the beach front braving the stinging spray until the cold on our faces turned to a burning, and we would go home to the fire. At such times I would reach up and take his hand; he did not make many displays of affection, though he was a man much influenced in his actions by his love of his fellows, a fraction of his love for all the fabrications of his Creator.

His love was of that quality which did not demand recognition; he never cared that it was not made visible to others, and perhaps he closed his own inner eye upon it. But it was the outstanding quality of his life: his love with his honesty; for in all things great or small he was the most honest man who ever drew breath.

It was in the days of storm that the sea disclosed its living personality to me; it was then that I believed most passionately in the beings who rode its crests and reveled in its extravagances; and of the Nymphae that peopled my beginning world, it was the Oceanides I most loved.

When I was a little older, maybe twelve, I was helped to a greater understanding by a forester friend who used to watch these waves with me, for he told me the stories he learned from his Polynesian ancestors; men of the brown, courageous race who understood more than any others the humors and the occasions of the sea, and personalized them to pass their understanding on.

Hoani told me of Tangaroa, the ocean, and his brother Tawhiri-Matea, the wind, the Maori Aeolus, and that other brother Tane-Mahuta, who is the forest and the things of the forest, the birds and the trees and the flowers. And how these brothers are constantly at war with each other, in constant changes of alliance, in a constant harmony of conflict.

The brothers were three of six that were born of the mating of Rangi, the Heavens, and Papa, old Mother Earth, and lived in the cave of darkness between the breasts of mated bodies until, in dawning consciousness, they thrust their parents apart in the struggle for light; and with the light the world began.

Only Tawhiri-Matea, the wind, had argued against the struggle; light is not necessary to the wind. Only he had not plotted to divide the wife from the husband, the mother from her man; and when the others went against him he made the unalterable resolve that there should be no peace, not anywhere, not in all the long unwinding of days. He bred children that were numerous and strong and irresistible in their might: the East Wind and the West Wind and the South Wind and the North Wind and the Tornado and the Hurricane and the Storm. From him descended the days of drizzling rain and the obliterating mist, the lightning and the thunder were his, the gale and the whirlwind.

And in command of these his children he made war, first upon his brother Tane-Mahuta, who was the forest, and then upon Tangaroa the sea. And some of the children of the forest took refuge in the sea; some of the sea's children ran to the forest; and for this there has been unceasing war also between forest and sea.

So when Man in his time challenges the sea, if he is a man of understanding (and no other can successfully wrestle Tangaroa of the many weapons, the many eyes, the many resources) he allies himself with Tane-Mahuta; and with the products of the forest — the ships, the masts, the sails, the nets of cord, the ropes and anchor stones — he is armed for the struggle.

Even the mighty Tumatauenga, the God of War and

the Father of Men, finds both ally and adversary in
Tangaroa and Tane-Mahuta his brothers (for he also
was given birth between the hot moist bodies of the
Heaven and the Earth).

It was the mind of man that created and occupied that
natal cave; it was his awakening consciousness that admitted the light in the turmoil and conflict that he attributed to the gods. For gods have their birth and their
being in the mind of man; the continued existence of any
god anywhere is a testimony to the strength of human
consciousness — that human consciousness which, in the
Christian religion, under the name of the Holy Ghost, is
given equality with the Creator of all things and the
Savior of humanity, and identification with them in the
Trinity.

No man can deny the gods without denying the minds
of men. And of course it is true — it is more than true:
it is essential and just — that the minds of men should be
at variance; but gods are born upon reasons, and reason
is the miracle of the conscious life of humanity. Look at
a man's gods and you understand his motives and his life:
the Polynesian was the greatest seaman who ever looked
to a star. So that even a slight, unsatisfactory knowledge
of the Polynesian gods could help my understanding of
the sea. It helped, moreover, my understanding of other
gods and, I hope, my understanding of other people.

But when I was small and heard the stories, they
showed me vividly the nature of the ocean.

The wide expanse of sand that was the beach sometimes afforded evidence of unsuccessful struggles that

man had waged against the ocean. One morning when I came for my swim there was the housing of a small boat's cabin; once there was a lifebuoy so long in the water that weeds and barnacles had encrusted it, and when I pulled them off to discover the name beneath, the rotted canvas came away with them in fragments.

Less recognizable relics of the storm came often. At almost any time some ancient beam was to be found upon the beach, studded with twisted and broken bolts, and pitted with holes wherein still lurked the tiny crabs that had joined it in its voyage through the waters, bearded with weed and bearing a cargo of mussels and barnacles, and seeming to belong by rights to the sea that had rejected it.

Such evidence was far outweighted by constant testimonies to man's victories — in the ships, for example, that plumed the horizon with an infrequent smoke, and the fishing vessels which passed far out to sea beyond the island, tiny dots of white upon the white-flecked ocean.

But there was one area where man had never won a victory, and that was on the shelving beach itself. At one time a house had been built there; it was battered by a storm or two and then broken up in a fury of waves. Another man made a like venture; his house was not there long before he made a tactical retreat and had it hauled by teams of massive Clydesdales to a site a quarter-mile on the other side of the sandhills. Even the piles set up in long groynes and planned to hold the shifting sand in place were often uprooted by the waves; the brush fences, higher up the beach, would last a season or two and then the waves would take them away. Any construction of man's verging on the beach seemed to constitute a challenge to the living ocean; sooner or later a strength of waters would undo, in a matter of an hour or two, the work of men.

A road was formed, running along the crest of the sandhills to make a pleasance for the town; the sea licked in and undercut the hills, and the road was totally destroyed.

The townsmen had difficulty comprehending the lesson. Their answer was another road: a strong, well-founded road that ran along the foot of the sandhills, a few feet only above high water. The sea let it stay a season or two and then, in a night, eliminated it. It became a battle between obstinacy and obduracy: the road was rebuilt a little higher. In the tactic of another sport the sea answered with new hills of piled-up sand that buried it many feet deep. A new road was built on top of this sand; the sea came in and took both roads together.

Eventually a little track was built that stayed. It was not established till the children of men sought help from the children of Tane-Mahuta, and planted marram grass and lupin to protect the stronger-seeming road. It stays today, winding between the sandhills now, scented with lupin all spring and summer long, and often lashed with spray.

Beneath the clay cliff between the sand and the boulder beaches, the reef was riven in a cleft deep and wide enough to form a swimming-hole; and in the days when sea bathing was still a medication and not a pleasure, the people completed the enclosure with concrete walls, raising them only to that height at which the sea, twice a day, would flush out the pool. A rope spanned the pool at a suitable depth; a springboard overhung it. A fence kept the less venturesome children from entering except at the turnstile where they paid their pennies; on crowded days the poorer children and the wilder scrambled round the surf-lashed cliffs.

Beyond the cleft in the reef was a wide expanse of black rock; and in time, upon this, was built a wooden house that quite overhung the sea and was surrounded by it on three sides. The house was filled with freckled, red-haired Celts; they were as hardy a breed of children as it is possible to raise. They lived for years in that cottage of which the foundations were fronded with kelp and seaweed; the red paint was scoured away by every storm; the nightly sounds of screaming rock and thumping timber did not disturb the artless children's sleeping confidence; and we others envied them their place of residence, as wild as any eyrie of cormorants.

The seas tolerated the house for years; when the eldest children were in their adolescence it struck. That was the wildest afternoon that I have ever seen. Great combers lifted the roof of the house and began to tear it from the top down. Each wave struck and raced on; when the height of the storm coincided with the top of the tide the inmates of the house came to safety, carrying a pitifully few belongings; and the house fell behind them like a house of cards.

Its components littered the beach for months; a wrack

of red-painted timber lying among the heaps of bull-kelp
that the storm had tossed up on the sand.

Children took it home. Their fathers built the better
planks into dog kennels and chicken houses; the shorter
ones and the broken ones were burned to warm the
winter houses.

For we lived a great deal on the offerings of the beach.
We bagged the sand and took it home to spread daily
upon the dropping-boards beneath the perches in the fowl
houses; the round boulders we collected, two or three at
a time, made field drains across and across the water-
logged earth of our back gardens; the giant kelp and the
bull-kelp became fertilizer for our orchards; the shells
and shell-sand were ground in noisy mills to make grit
for feeding chickens. We lugged the very water from the
surf to be heated for medicinal baths for rheumatic old-
sters; we had good meals from the shellfish that lived
among the rocks.

Then was the time of the Great World War — the first
of the Wars, the War to End War; and small as I was I
learned that the seas could help as well as destroy. In
those days it was not easy to live in such a community,
narrow and isolated, when you had, as we had, a German
ancestry. There were some children forbidden to play
with us; there were louts who sought, in the covering
darkness of night, to make sport with us, knowing they
would have some community support.

So that when I was small I often started from my sleep
to the sound of stones being rained upon the roof; I often
woke to see my mother's grief at finding her flowerbeds

destroyed; her lawns, that cost her weeks of back-breaking work, spaded up; her loved bushes broken. But there
was a fixation of the louts, evolved from what beliefs or
superstitions I do not know, a fixation that amounted to
a habit: they used to lift our gate from its hinges and
carry it to the ocean and cast it away.

"The gate has gone."

My father would be furious.

"Just never mind. The boys will get it," my mother
would reply.

And sure enough, we always found it on the beach; an
offering rejected by the sea that stole so much, and cast
up on the sand; not always in the same place, but always
in a place that could be estimated by someone who knew
the set of the currents and the state of the tide. I was too
small to be of much help in bringing back the gate; my
brothers unfailingly managed it. The gate disintegrated
long since and is replaced by another; but it died of age
and dry rot. The sea to me and to my family was as help-
ful as it was destructive of the property of others.

I often think about that gate. The war, with the local
feeling, had other effects, and perhaps they were far-
reaching. It controlled my choice of companions: I used
to run with the rebels and the rejects. There were one
or two exceptions among close neighbors.

But for a great deal of my childhood my choice of
friends was limited — to Jews and to Roman Catholics,
both rarities in this Protestant neighborhood. They were
unchancy friends; their choice was as limited as mine,
and we ran together not from affection but in mutual

protection; making, of deliberation, enemies among the others.

The circumstance may have been good or bad; I would not know. It tended to thrust me all my life upon the side of the underdog, yet I would not have had that otherwise. It tended even more strongly to make me walk alone, to work alone, and to think alone. I do not know whether that is good or bad, but I am happy in my destiny.

And I do not remember too much about these narrow enmities; I remember with great and singular clarity (in consideration of my years at the time) the friendliness of the wanton sea that always thrust our gate back on the beach.

3

I N THE great segment of a circle represented by the arc of the beach and the radii linking this to the island at the central point, the territory covered by the sea might be reckoned uncommonly barren. It consists almost in its entirety of a level stretch of the whitest sand imaginable; the same sand, in the same quality, as that of which the beach is composed.

Under the clay-topped ranges that encircle the town itself, and lead back from the sea to the high volcanic peaks, are great deposits of a diatomaceous earth. But at the beach, removed in distance from the nearest part of the deposit less than a mile, the diatomaceous content is not great, despite the continuous falling of the shells of the dead diatoms. The water is too shallow, and at the same time too disturbed, for any great accumulation of them.

The sand here is composed mainly of grains of quartz, and in its never-ending circulation it has been abraded by the wind as frequently as by the underwash of the sea, so that the microscopic pebbles are smooth and rounded.

They are so round, indeed, that during the land-based cycle of their interminable travel, if they should come under the influence of the drying winds from the north, they become sonorous, and sing to the friction of feet, making a screech like seagulls at play at the first disturbance, but rapidly losing the power to produce a noise. When I was a child I learned to know the weather in which the sands might be expected to sing, and coursed down the seaward range of the sandhills, waiting till the bare soles of my feet evoked the pleasing screech of quartz. I knew how the sand felt: a delicious sensation of vibration was transmitted from the source of sound to my own skin and traveled upward through my body till it tingled the tips of my ears and the hair on my head. And the speed with which I scraped my feet over the loose surface of sand decided the pitch of the transmitted note. It was a joy to be alone when the beach was singing, and to run with the dry wind in my face and the treble of the sand combining with the rumbling bass of the crashing combers.

But if the air was damp, or the sand had been disturbed, or the sun had not come out, the sands would not sing.

Few creatures live beneath the sand, and those few are seldom to be seen. There are the sandhoppers, tiny crustaceans like great gray fleas, forever burrowing and traveling beneath the surface in spite of their capacity to leap with great agility through the air, which they will do if they are uncovered. Near the edge of the water, below the line of high tide, there are a few cockles, buried deep. And farther still, at the line of the tide's deepest recession at new moon or full, and in a small area near the southern rocks, a type of swimming crab in summer seasons buries itself and waits for night.

Far out in deep water, over the sand, there is a more abundant life. A few worms protrude their heads from their tunnels of sand to salvage the food washed to them by the tides that forever sweep up from the south. Living on the worms is a scanty population of English soles, so-called; and overlooking this population from time to time come those marauders which venture into shallow waters; for even as far out as the island the water over the sand is no more than six or seven fathoms deep. Overlooking in their turn these marauders — ling, and in the summer-time, small gropers — the sharks come cruising from time to time; there are frequently sharks in the bay, and some are of types dangerous to humans; but for some unexplained reason there are, in these waters, no shark tragedies.

Flounders of two or three varieties inhabit the bay in small numbers: the sand flounder, the greenback, the black, and very rarely, the yellowbelly. The megrim ranges from top to bottom of the waters, hugging the sand with other flatfish for its rest. In seasonal swarms, the red cod sweep into the bay in great numbers, but stay briefly; the barracouta and kahawai range through the waters in close-packed, uncountable herds in summer months, but keep on the move. Porpoises and, more rarely, whales invade the bay; the large black porpoise with the falcate fin is the commonest, but a smaller, whiter dolphin appears and plays happily on the outer edge of the surf.

Near the rocks at Lawyer's Head, and at the cliff towards the southern end, brill and turbot swim, always in pairs, the male and the female, separated by more than a yard or two only in death; the most devoted of lovers, the closest of companions. Here too, lurking in a nest of coiled and rotting stems of seaweed, the hagfish, the most loathsome of all the sea's creatures — and at the same time one of the most resourceful — lies in wait for any kind of prey.

South of here is a formation of slaty rock, covering the bottom for several square miles; and on the rock is anchored a forest of giant kelp. Each single trunk of the weed is, from top to bottom, never as thick as a man's finger; yet it reaches up thirty or forty feet; almost, but not quite, to the surface of the sea. Perhaps it is more true to say that it reaches the low troughs of the waves at low tides; at most times of the day it is invisible from the air or from the nearby cliff, but its presence may be recognized in calm weather always by the oiliness of the surface above the groves.

The single stems of this forest grow two or three feet apart, each twining pillar decorated with leaves and fruits in an old bronze; and this concentration offers reasonably safe haven to an army of fish. They are safe

3 7

here especially from the fisherman, who is rash indeed, or inexperienced, if he drops a line into the forest.

So here the animal life is abundant: blue-cod and leatherjacket, rock-cod and parrot fish, moray eels and octopuses, crustaceans in hordes and battalions, crayfish and crabs and prawns. The leftovers from the daily meals should enrich the northern sand until it could support communities far more numerous than it does, but a trick of the tide sweeps the debris of the forest life to seaward of the island and away from the sandy sector adjacent to the beach.

Sometimes when I was a child and came to the beach early in the morning I was the recipient of the ocean's gift of a frostfish. On a frosty night in autumn this mystery of the sea casts itself ashore to take its own life. It has suffered from no illness, unless the fish world has its neurotics too. It is not chased ashore by enemies, unless they are ghosts of its own spirit world. It comes at speed, leaping eagerly on the crest of the wave and committing itself to destruction.

The best way to catch a frostfish is with a fast horse, on a cold and frosty morning. Put the nag to a canter and range the beaches till you find your quarry, a four-foot length of silver, toothed like a barracouta, fleshed with meat no epicure could refuse. The horse is desirable for frostfishing; it gives you an advantage over the many who walk abroad on cold clear mornings looking for the fish. And there's the wind in your face, and the splash of water beneath the hoofs and the thrust of muscles under the saddle. And there's no need for a gamebag if you ride a horse; you find your fish and bend him about your horse's neck with his tail through his gills into his mouth. And when your horse is thus collared, you jump to his back again and ride off for another.

I had no horse, not then. I dragged my rare finds home over the sand, struggling against the weight.

I've only known one man to make the gesture of refusing this gift of ocean. He was a scientist, and in the interests of science he took the newly stranded fish to sea again, only to see it leap straight for the shore as soon as it was liberated from the boat. Again and again he tried to save the frostfish from its fate; but it was a determined suicide and finished up, as a good frostfish should, upon a breakfast plate.

Once or twice, in that child's lifetime of mine, the sprats, pursued by barracouta or perhaps red cod, cast themselves upon the sand in such great numbers that the local population, armed with buckets, basins, washtubs or flour bags, could not cope with the harvest.

But in general the population of the marine hinterland converging on the beach was a meager and scanty scattering. It was for this reason, among others, that the sand was so white and fine; only now and again was the beach briefly tinted, after a fresh of the tide, with the golden hue of shell-sand; and shells themselves were rare and only of common varieties.

Consequently a small boy, investigating the life about him, normally spent his time on rocks and reefs where available animals could be studied at close quarters. On many and many a day I went to the reefs when I knew that the tide was retreating. There I would squat by some available pool for hours.

The skin on the soles of my feet was so tough that I could jump from rock to rock, and run over the myriads of small, inch-long mussels that crusted their crowns, without sustaining an injury, though their shells were sharp as knives. I learned to achieve a sense of balance, to walk firmly on wet weed or smooth stone, and lightly on the pitted basalt. And I found more treasure than Aladdin in his cave.

There were anemones, clustered thickly in all the crevices where water was retained when the tide had gone. They were not the proud and glorious animals, flaring like flowers, that inhabit warmer waters; they were small and drab, gray and green and brown, and the largest of them was the size of the ball of my thumb. But it was a thrill to poke them with a questing finger, and feel the tentacles pulling on my skin; or to wait and watch them erupt, and throw out the grains of sand caught in their last closure.

There were the angels' trumpets too, much like anemones, but in actuality small worms that lived in shell tunnels of their own building, shaped like cornucopias and colored all the same, in bands of red and white and green, like the flag of Heligoland. I used to repeat the old jingle when I saw them:

> *Red is the land,*
> *And white is the sand,*
> *And green the strand*
> *Of Heligoland.*

From the open end of each horn flared out a brave fringed scarlet banner; when the water receded and left them stranded it appeared only as a mass of jelly, like the red currant jelly my mother made from the many bushes in our garden.

There were chitons, and sometimes among them the King of Chitons, a shellfish, but a shellfish clad in rich brown leather, with veins of smoke blue. His shells were inside his body; I found them sometimes in little drifts of debris among the boulders, shaped like small butterflies but disappointingly pale. In piles of rotting kelp were enough periwinkles to fill bucket after bucket; they lay without movement, waiting for the water to return. In dozens of experiments I found that out of water they could walk with the greatest difficulty; in water their muscles became adequate to locomotion.

When I told my mother she explained about specific density, and I learned how Archimedes, pondering on the problem of detecting and exposing the fraudulent goldsmith who coated lead with the royal metal in work so fine that none wished to mar it by investigation, thought of the solution in his bath; and in a shocking state of nudity ran home through the populous streets, crying: "Eureka! Eureka!" I thought the situation had its humor; my mother found an application for the story in explaining the immobility of periwinkles in the atmosphere. She had a remarkable mind, pertinent always to my own problems.

Seeing my interest, she bought me books. We were always short of money, but books were necessities and not luxuries in our house. And from the books I discovered the names of the animals I daily watched.

Under the rocks were suckerfish; little fish like tadpoles three or four inches in length, and never seen except when clinging to the rock. The ventral fins were modified into suckers; when the fish relinquished one position it was to move with the speed of a lizard to another, seeming to slide over the rock rather than to swim. They could withstand the heaviest crash of breakers; their habit was to occupy positions where the surge and play of troubled waters reached its zenith. The females were rose-pink; the smaller males came in a variety of colors.

When I was a child I confused them with the much larger and more adventurous remoras; the suckerfish that travels the world taking passage on a shark or a sword-fish, the fish that lost the Romans the battle of Actium by fastening to the keel of Antony's ship and slowing it down. And it was not till I saw the remora used for turtle fishing that I knew my mistake.

In many corners of the world the natives keep a remora clinging to the canoe hull. It is made captive by a line fastened to a ring around the tail; and when a turtle is sighted the remora is removed from the hull by pushing forward on the sucker that in this instance is a modification of the dorsal spine at the top of the head. The remora is thrown near the turtle, to which it immediately fastens, and the quarry is then hauled in by the line on the remora's tail.

Hearing of this, or reading of it, I used to experiment

with my suckerfish; but all they could catch were the sea-girt rocks.

There were cockabullies in the pools, and sometimes a thornfish, brown and pink and white, and difficult to see against the anemones. Again and again I ripped my hand upon its spines. And out beyond the farthest rocks it was sometimes possible to see, and even at the bottom of a king tide to catch, the pauas, sliding two by two on their great black single feet among the weeds.

The paua was the sea's great treasure. Its flesh made soup or rissoles of an exquisite flavor; its roe was a delicacy more rare than peacocks' tongues; and the peacock itself could not rival the blue and green colors of its inner shell. I keep some of the shells by me today; their colors and textures satisfy some longing towards perfection.

I was seated one day, crosslegged upon a boulder, watching angels' trumpets as the sea immersed them and flooded back again, when two men came clambering, more awkwardly than I, across the rocks.

They stopped, and one said, "Do you know if there are pauas here, on this beach?"

The presence of elders always confused me.

"Out there," I said, pointing with my chin in the Chinese way I had acquired from heaven knows where.

"Where?"

"Just the end of the reef here."

They made to walk past me, and I added, "But you can't get them now."

They stopped.

"The tide will be right out soon," one said, consulting his watch.

"Saturday week," I told him. "Not till Saturday week."

"They come in by the calendar, do they?"

"They're there all the time. But there's a new moon Saturday week. That's the next king tide. And you must come early in the morning then, around six. It will be too dark to see pauas on the afternoon tide that day."

"You know a lot about them," the first man said, and that pleased me.

"Anyway, they're too deep to get except on a king tide," I told him. I could have added that the seas ran too awkwardly through the creviced channels.

"We'll just go and see," he said, disbelieving.

An hour later, when the rising tide drove them back again without their pauas, they stopped by my pool and talked awhile. I showed them the chiton that threw the butterfly shells and the crab that planted seaweeds and sometimes anemones on his own back. And then was overwhelmed with confusion to find they were scientists who worked at the museum.

"You'll make a zoologist when you grow up," one said, but I shook my head. I would see lions and tigers, that I knew; but I would walk among them.

Where the seas rushed through the tunnel on the face of the cliff, the bull-kelp grew in such wild profusion that there seemed no room for water wherever the growth was enclosed, or partly enclosed, by rocks. Each tree of the bull-kelp grew from a trunk as thick as my thigh, and flowered out in great spongy fronds, wide at first, then

4 4

narrowing and lengthening into snakelike tentacles, each frond a honeycomb of air spaces covered with a brown sea-leather. It grew so thickly that in later years I several times put my schooner against the rock of a small island at half tide, and with confidence, if I knew the slope of the rock, for the elastic kelp fended it off in safety.

In the enclosed places, the kelp writhed and moved with life, sensitive to every touch and pressure, the long fronds intertwining, making a sinuous pattern of moving lines, always in curves, always thick and touching one another. The pattern, in deep browns and blacks, was bordered always by the white of disturbed waters and then the green of open ocean; and it fascinated me as it moved incessantly in regular sweeps as though the synchronized legs of a thousand octopuses searched in unison for quarry never to be found. I would sit for hours upon the basalt steps above, among the flowering mesembryanthemums, and stare into the brief quick patterns traced out upon the water.

On the rare occasions when, as lads, we lit fires upon the evening beach, we always enlivened them by the burning of the dried kelp fronds. The honeycombs of air kept up a constant series of machine gun explosions until the piece disintegrated; the iodine smell invested the smoke with sea-character; and when the flames had burned down, the last remaining flickers were colored orange and yellow and a soft and luminous violet.

And every day upon the beach we cut balls from the rounded trunks for our games of cricket or rounders, or just for bouncing in solo play. When they were fresh the kelp stems had the qualities of cured rubber; the balls bounced high and satisfactorily, and the exercise of cutting them from the trunks trained our eyes to know the balance and conformity of a true sphere.

One of my constant tasks when I was young was to drag a great bundle of the kelp down the dusty metaled roads to my home. A tree, weighing much more than myself, could be handled quite easily, for it offered little resistance to the irregularities of the road. Day after day I dragged the kelp, sometimes several pieces each day, if the storms had cast it up on the beach in quantity.

Once home, in the big yard filled with flowers and trees, the kelp was wrapped about the roots of a certain apple, and when it was heaped high, up to the spreading branches, was covered with a light coating of earth, while the new consignments were placed elsewhere. Under the earth the kelp rotted and fed the tree — we had apples as big as my head, apples that made pies for a family of seven, apples weighing a pound and three quarters each.

And after the season the enriched earth was spread elsewhere in the garden, to feed all other growing things.

The fronds of the kelp made bags. Filled with the prepared carcasses of mutton birds and sealed with fat, they were found in the food markets; the bull-kelp was a useful growth. But I learned to treat it with respect.

One morning, when I was late upon the beach, I found the sea baths watched by a curious crowd, and grave and sober men walking about the rocks where the bath house had once stood. In the water beyond these rocks was another ocean-grove of bull-kelp that writhed and twisted forever and ever with the surging breakers.

The bull-kelp here sheltered a colony of butterfish, sweet and toothsome; black torpedoes of fish that differed from all others in that their bones shone silky green beneath the white flesh. An expert could fish for butterfish where the rocks met the sand. He must be expert, and he must use two rods, the second to extricate the hook from the kelp.

I don't know how young I was when I learned that kelp was dangerous stuff; I regarded the rock fishermen as examples of inexcusable foolhardiness; not for daring the breakers, for there was a reward in that, but for daring the churning forest of the kelp.

But I must have been nearly ten years of age when I arrived at the beach this day in midmorning, and saw the curious crowd, and heard why they were there.

There had been a swimmer in the baths early in the morning; and he had been so delighted with the water that he resolved, as people often did, to take a spell in the surf along the beach. Other people walked; perhaps this fellow's girl was watching, or perhaps he was contemptuous of the dangers he must have heard about. Whatever his reason, he walked as far as he could out upon the rocks and dived into the sea; estimating, I suppose, that he could clear the kelp.

The inevitable old bystander had seen it.

"It was a beautiful dive," he said. "I never saw a better."

But the kelp had held and swamped the flying body;

he was somewhere close to the rocks, beneath the writhing stems.

There was a great to-do about finding the body. A few
swimmers swam as close as they dared to the rocks.
Constable Schubert, aided by all who had time loose on
their hands, patrolled the surface of the shelf. The baths
manager, a physical culturist whose uniform was a neck-
to-knee swimsuit with a badge upon the chest, bustled to
and fro, confiding what details he could muster to the
group of bystanders.

At the end of the day the swimmer had not reappeared,
and that night there were lanterns on the rocks.

On the second day the little crowd had thinned till it
included only two or three besides the constable. They
watched in vain. The waves increased in strength towards
the afternoon, and by night were so high that no continued watch was possible.

On the third day I happened early on the beach, and
for a few moments watched the group now hopeless on
the rocks. And by the sheerest chance was there when the
miracle happened.

From the swirling weed a hand thrust up, clear of the
sea from elbow to outstretched fingers, and within a yard
of the good constable's feet. He bent to clutch the hand,
and in a moment it had drawn him under; helmet and
uniform and all.

Horrified, I turned and ran, and did not see the sequel.
The weed, that had retained its first prisoner more than
two days, rejected the constable on the next swell; hands
caught at him and hauled him back on the rocks. And

4 8

he still kept a tight grip on the wrist of the luckless swimmer; his duty was well done.

But I was running for the open beach in panic at this close approach of death's mystery; it was my first sight of death. And after that day the patterns of the kelp portrayed for me a more sinister design.

4

TWICE A year the sooty shearwaters moved across the bay, flying low against the water in the fashion that has earned them their name, yet flying too in so great a company that the upper levels of each flock were as high as the peak of the island. So great a company, indeed, that they passed without any sensible diminution of their numbers for three or four days, in a tireless free movement that had carried them all the way from Alaska.

From the beach it seemed as though a thousand million mites were drifting in a speedy current of air; the remorseless flow of airborne bodies was an awe-inspiring phenomenon never to be overlooked or disregarded. There was a majesty in the birds' obedience to the will of their tribe, to the strict and never-changing discipline, to the seasonal call of the breeding places.

Between the migratory flights of spring and autumn

the birds, though rarely, appeared again to forage for
their food; this especially when the krill, the red crusta-
cean that is the food of whales in southern oceans,
darkened the water.

The phenomenon of the krill must be accounted even
greater than the phenomenon of the birds; the tiny red
shrimps move with apparent aimlessness in masses so
vast that description becomes impossible. Once my
schooner plowed fourteen sea miles through a school of
krill that must have been equally as wide, perhaps wider;
the water was red, bright red, and there were no gaps in
the color. The inch-long shrimps swam close together;
not in a sheet, but in a body. Twenty fathoms down, at
the bottom of the sea, the fish had bellies crammed with
krill. At the top the shearwaters, the mollyhawks, the
albatrosses, the petrels and the gulls had eaten to such a
repletion that they had to regurgitate to fly. Often the
effort was beyond the birds; the planks of the schooner
pushed them aside as they drifted in the sea.

Sometimes an accident of wind and tide leaves the
edge of such a school of krill stranded on a beach; you
can walk for miles over foreshores knee-deep in the
brilliant red crustaceans. Such accidents never happened
on the beach of which I write; the krill appear in a season
that is short in these latitudes, and the tendency of the
tides, particularly of the great Antarctic Drift that sweeps
up from the Pole, is to hold them offshore at this point.

Between the fish below and the birds above, the krill
are slaughtered in uncounted millions. Around the edges

of the red mass the cetaceans cruise, the whales and the porpoises. And deep below, but still haunting the edge, the sharks are lively, waiting to feed, not upon the krill but upon their predators, stuffed to sluggish content and for once unwary. But the sharks and the porpoises never meet; except that the thresher sharks sometimes harry the red-blooded animals.

The season in which the krill, on their northward drift, came in the vicinity of the bay would normally coincide with that in which the infant shearwaters were large enough to leave their nests, and their parents had more freedom of range; so that although the vast breeding grounds of the birds lay, in general, a hundred and twenty miles to the south, an influx could sometimes be expected.

Frequently enough the season coincided also with that in which, armed with scissors and sickle, I would climb the cliffs to harvest the heads of the ripened cocksfoot grasses; the heads only, for I had to carry my harvest on my back home to the winnowing. Some years I made a few pounds at this ploy; enough to pay for schoolbooks and give me spending money equal to that carried by the sons of rich fathers, of whom there were a good many in the district. And when I saw the birds, that was an invitation to sit down and, with my back pillowed against my sack of cocksfoot heads, my feet propped against some outcrop of the cliff's rock, to give myself up for an hour or two to the worship of movement.

Even the shore birds were there, the little gray gulls, and the noisy robbers, the black-backed gulls; there were terns of several varieties, and fluttering flocks of Cape pigeons, and sometimes gannets and cormorants. But the shearwaters constituted the mass of the wheeling, screaming flocks. Then there were the mollyhawks, and the booby birds, and the best sight of all, the albatrosses.

After I grew to manhood and learned the ways of the sea I became familiar with the great birds, and I am not among those worshipers who see them as the epitome of all that is noble, all that is exquisite in flight. Time was when no ship's complement, it seemed, was without some embryo poet or novelist or autobiographer leaning over the taffrail and watching the albatrosses, lingering until the moon had ceased to illumine the wake, and rushing off to his cabin to set the oil lamp in its gimbals and write eulogies to that effortless flight.

According to such observations, the enormous birds followed the ship day after day, week after week, month after month, with scarcely the flicker of a wing tip; for the poets ignored completely those less aesthetic moments which followed the tipping of galley refuse over the lee rail.

Some writers still follow a comparable practice, but those who do so and travel with the great liners have to lean heavily upon their imaginations. Except for brief and unimpressive periods, albatrosses no longer follow ships, not for lack of refuse to tempt them, but simply because they haven't the speed to keep up. The albatross, in spite of its camouflaging beauty, is one of the most awkward and underpowered birds to travel the larger oceans. As a navigator it is superb, and it can hold its place as an opportunist, but as an aviator it simply isn't in the race.

The habit of following ships ended, for albatrosses, when speed increased to more than sixteen or eighteen knots. The albatross can hold a steep and screaming glide of perhaps thirty knots and more; but its ancient joy was to ease along at six or eight knots behind the old windjammers. In this habit it showed poor judgment and bad flying sense, for the low speeds kept it perilously on the brink of stalling; a risk increased because of its position in the superstructure-turbulence of the ship.

The bird loved this hazardous turbulence, and used it to maintain altitude; and with its frequent proximity to the stalling angle, often fell into a low-speed stall and dropped squawking into the water, or hit the deck with a wet-sounding flop. It matched this performance very often by attempting to utilize hot air rising from funnels of slow streamers for a lift, for it is the laziest of birds.

Yet when it is in a braggart mood it will perform what airmen call "Rate Four" turns, maintaining an incredibly steep angle of bank, and rippling the water surface with a wing tip feather as it swings. On these occasions it never comes to grief, for it performs this, its only aerobatic maneuver, at a safe high speed.

A petrel, smart and efficient on the wing, can outfly an albatross in distance, speed and aerobatic ability. And that silly-looking clown the pelican, with more than twice the weight to lift, is superior.

The stalling angle of the albatross is encountered at a speed of below six knots of level flight; yet he cannot

take off without some fifteen to twenty knots of wind, or
the additional aid of a peaked wave crest, or a sustained
taxi-run. When the wind is below ten knots he tries to
run along for ten or twenty yards, his flat feet flailing the
water clumsily, until he can lunge off the top of a wave.
Only when the wind is raising white horses can he sit
where he is, spread his long slim pinions, and rise unaided. If there is no wave and no wind, he sits alone and
hungry until the right conditions come along.

The truth seems to be that he raises his wings initially
in such an awkward way and at such an acute double-
dihedral angle that he reduces the lift area, putting the
wing-loading up to an absurd height just when he should
most reduce it, and presenting such an acute angle of
wing chord to the airstream as to necessitate an expendi-
ture of several times the amount of effort that should be
necessary to make him airborne.

His use of flaps and air brakes for landing is un-
polished; and as often as not the landing gear of his feet
(locked for impact both geometrically and mechanically,
as in the heavy transports) trips him into an undignified
plunge into the fortunately yielding water. He has never
learned from the huge and heavy swans, who come to a
slick landing on any sort of water surface by a pro-
nounced use of the inner primaries of their weight-carry-
ing wings as zapp flaps, and modify the angle of approach by using tailfeathers as combined elevator and
air brake system. A still more skillful use of such elemental flying controls is practiced by the gannets, who

can fly into a vertical cliff face at speed, to land lightly in a couple of inches of space.

Were he a good aeronaut, the albatross need not descend to the depths in which he wallows at feeding time. Except when he is subsisting on the krill or any of the other forms of manna which the sea provides in their seasons, the albatross lives by grabbing a well-fed smaller bird by the neck and shaking him until he has disgorged his most recent meal.

To a certain extent, this habit is practiced by lesser ocean birds, so that it is not unusual to see a shearwater, for example, pass his meal to a black-backed gull, who delivers, under menaces, to a mollyhawk, who is himself victim to the albatross.

This system would, of course, mean the total extinction of all smaller birds unless they were blessed, as they are, with greater powers of flight. It is an act of mercy that the albatross is as clumsy as he is. Any smaller bird is safe from him until it has gorged so heavily that it finds it difficult to fly, and at this stage the loss of a meal does it no harm.

But there are days upon the open sea when your mast is tracing its mysterious script against the vellum of a cumulus-filled sky and the albatrosses are following in the pattern of a dream, the royals and the wanderers. They lift and lilt, playing in the turbulence, and they are the most beautiful birds under heaven.

To a lad sitting in the cocksfoot on the cliff, drenched in the scents of autumn tanged with sea salt, himself a dreamer and already in love with beauty, the appearance of the albatross was enough to fill his hours with song, his mind with poetry.

And before I learned for myself, in the wide spaces of the sky, the elements of airborne locomotion, I looked to the albatross as to the assurance of a beauty-loving God; it was at once a pledge and a challenge, and I knew that some day I must ally myself with the sea and the air, and the freedom of space.

I do not know how often I watched the miracle of a wheeling gull, suspended for the fraction of an instant as though its lower wing tip were embedded in a pedestal of air, the fine clean line of its tensed and confident pinions superbly related to the proportions of the body enclosed between them, and responsive as of the instant to the dictates of the brain informed by those sharp and questing red-rimmed eyes. Sometimes, at the most critical juncture of an aerial maneuver, the gull would spy a new tidbit requiring its instant attention, and on the instant would adjust its attitudes, never for a second relinquishing its strong sure control of air.

And seeing some such marvel, I understood from an early age man's primal necessity to capture the elusive, vibrant and never static instant of beauty, and to give it concrete form, so that he might transmit to others not only the moment of beauty but also his emotional responses to it. For me all of beauty is exemplified by a gull wheeling against the sky, above the white and boiling line of surf.

Sometimes in the nesting season I climbed the cliff to settle myself in a cranny of the rocks in the sunshine and look at gulls and dream of beauty; and I would stay there for hours, watching the birds beneath posture against the wild cliff and the angry water. I could clamber round the cliffs with considerable agility at this time; I had just about reached the stage of going bird-nesting when our little seaside suburb was visited by tragedy.

Its adolescents were a reasonably adventurous lot; they came in the main from families well, but not abundantly, supplied with riches. About twenty of them, for example, had a regular weekly meeting in a hilly pig paddock, where they played, to the accompaniment of an intense hilarity, a form of football on motorcycles. The pigs and the muddy slopes were additional hazards; not a few arms and shoulder blades were broken before the contest was prohibited by the good Constable Schubert.

Among these older lads, Norman Boult and David Harp were prominent, for differing reasons. Boult was from one of the best families in the district, a sixteen-year-old lad who showed promise of early talent in the arts, and was as handsome as he was talented, tall and straight and well-featured. He lived in a two-story house staffed with servants and set well back in impressive grounds; and much was forgiven an errant lad if his companion in mischief had been Norman.

David Harp, from one of the poorer families, was also influential, but only among his own age group. The parents of other lads deplored his talent for leadership and the hero-worshiping which it evoked. When David rode a borrowed horse in and out of the Sunday school hall; when he incited a group of friends to lift a baby car into the church porch while the community was at services; when, after a prohibition of Sunday cricket on the beach, he produced an effigy of the local councilor and burned it on the street in front of the bandstand — his escapades nearly brought him into serious trouble, averted because of the influence of his companions' families. The community's tolerance for him was stretched to breaking point about the time he and Norman skipped their Sunday afternoon obligations and went bird-nesting on the cliffs.

They took with them a too-light, too-old rope that belonged somewhere or other in the Boult ménage. And during the course of their adventures they came at last, that sunny Sunday afternoon, to a section of the cliffs we called the Funnel Drop.

At this point a cleft divided the face that reared ninety feet above the crashing waves. The cleft continued into the sea; at its foot a deep and narrow pool was banked by rising jagged rocks, so that the surf boiled furiously there, unhindered in the center of the formation and at the verges forced into unimaginable turmoil; a confusion bad enough in the calmest days, but in rough weather magnificent in its storming violence.

The cleft on the cliff face, twenty feet or so across, was almost, but not quite, a sheer drop. There was an overhanging shelf near the top, and another perhaps fifteen feet from the bottom. Between the two shelves, but nearer the upper one, were rock crannies, and these sheltered the nests of birds. One or two windblown and battered shrubs clung with the strength of the desperate to the upper rock faces; but between the upper shelf and the lip of the cliff was a section that no climber could negotiate with hands and feet alone.

They were these nests in these crannies on the mid-section of the Funnel Drop that Boult and Harp decided to rob.

David Harp, the instigator — he was always the insti-gator — lay on the top of the cliff, with a purchase of the rope round the trunk of a bush behind him. Norman Boult, the lighter and more agile of the two, tied the rope around his waist and worked his way down the rock, carefully and without incident until he went over the upper overhanging shelf. He lowered himself carefully over it, and from then on was aided by the rock crannies beneath. There was a good nest within easy reach — I knew the birds which occupied it almost as individuals; from the other side of the cleft I had watched them by the hour until I knew all their habits and could distinguish them, even on the wing, from others of their kind, or so I imagined.

Norman lowered himself until he was level with the nest. There were fledglings there, instead of the eggs he had expected to find, and he stayed, swinging in the rope, one hand grasping, safely, as he must have thought, a good handhold at the edge of a cranny.

But the rope above him, straining against the con-centrated thrust of a corner of rock, parted, and he fell. His foot caught against a protruded knob, he turned over in the air, struck the ledge below with his head, and can-noned off into the deep and narrow basin in the sea.

I cannot of course reconstruct just what were David's immediate reactions to the sudden cessation of strain on the rope in his hands. A week or two afterward I went to that place, and lay where David must have lain. There were marks on the trunk of the bush still, from the abrasive rope where David had payed it out; but there was a welter of footprints all about by that time, and I could fit none of them to the circumstances of that afternoon as I had heard them.

From where he lay he could not have seen Norman swinging on the rope beneath the shelf — but he could command a view of the pool where Norman fell. And he must have lain there a minute or two, in that position, aghast at what he saw: Norman's body floating, entirely without conative movement, in the troubled swirl of waters, and the blood staining the blue-green sea, and the white froth of the pool. And all at the bottom of the perilous dizzy drop. He must have known that Norman's only chance, and a slight one at that, would lie in being rescued immediately from the water which even then must have been dashing him against the craggy edges of the pool.

David anyway could not have hesitated long. He stripped off all his clothes, flinging them away from him in his haste. He jumped over that fearful edge and moreover planned his jump so that his feet hit purposefully against the upper overhanging shelf on which the rope had broken. From there he dived about eighty feet into the pool, the thrust against the shelf giving him the outward impetus necessary to clear a ledge of rock at the bottom. In his free fall, Norman's collision with the lower shelf had performed a like function.

For man's most splendid feats there are no witnesses. There were none for David, and this reconstruction of mine developed through by intimate knowledge of the scene. Once in the water, and recovered from the shock of his dive, David found the body of his friend. It was lifeless; but he was not, for some time, to know.

Like all the rest of us who lived near the beach, David had had a cursory training in lifesaving methods; therefore he turned the body to bring the mouth and nostrils into the air; and for a moment or two tried to combat the ceaseless plunging of heavy water in that narrow channel. He was aware — were we not all aware? — of the necessity of fighting with and not against the waves; somehow he managed to bring Norman to the ledge at the cliff end of the pool; no haven this, for it was ever washed by a compelling, scouring surge of white water muscled with a power that would have brought great constructions to quick disaster.

About eight feet above the ledge was a smaller and triangular shelf, the slightest possible promise of refuge; and somehow, with his adolescent strength, David gained this, and pulled the body of his friend up with him.

He had no room to move, barely enough to ease his muscles. He got there in the last of the afternoon; the sun was behind the cliff and could not search him out, but the sunshine still danced upon the sea. He huddled there, naked and cold against the stone, and clinging to the clothed but freezing body of his friend, his back against the bare, jagged rock.

But if his body was tortured, that was nothing to the tortures of his mind. He was the elder of the two, he had instigated the expedition; yet he had held the safe place at the top of the cliff. He had the reputation of a daredevil and that of a ne'er-do-well; the tragedy was undoubtedly to be sheeted to his account. But he had done what he could in amendment, and now continued to do it.

About eleven that night the tide reached its greatest height, and at this stage every incoming wave, thrust skyward by enormous constricting pressure from the two parallel reefs acting upon the initial inertia of the landward-sweeping swell, washed over him green in such quantity that he was hard put to retain a hold on the body, now frozen into a stiff immobility.

It was impossible for him to change his position much beneath it. Caught between the structure of the rocks and the stiffened body, he suffered dreadful cramps, his jaws ached from the cold, his whole being became no more than a preposterous artifact of pain. His hands would barely operate; he was not able even to sob.

About this time a full-scale search was under way. In the families of some of us, a late arrival for the evening meal was nothing to become concerned about; we were out upon our own occasions, and though we would have to provide an explanation upon our eventual appearance, and undergo some form of punishment as like as not, we did not cause much worry.

In the Boult family things were different. When Norman did not arrive home by afternoon's end, his father made inquiries. By nine o'clock he was thoroughly frightened. He had established, at that time, that Norman's companion was David, and that David too was missing from his home. When some lad, interviewed in his bed, volunteered that David and Norman had gone bird-nesting on the cliffs, the search was begun.

Constable Schubert was technically in command; actually he took his orders from almost any of the party and became merely the axis round which the search was established. The searchers were all middle-aged and solid citizens of the town; when, next morning, I heard their names I was astonished (after the manner of lads of my own age) at the composition of the group. They were bankers, lawyers, an editor and businessmen of such remote austerity that I could not imagine they would ever find their way round the cliffs.

At three in the morning, John Sampson, whose establishment of blacksmiths, employing forty men and at that time altering its character to fit the increasing trade in car repair, found the clothes of David Harp at the top of the Funnel Drop. It was five, and the sun was up, before he had gathered the other searchers and sufficient rope and gear to make a descent of the cliff.

By that time the figures on the triangular ledge were visible from the other bank of the cleft; there was no movement in them, and with heavy hearts the searchers presupposed their deaths. Sampson himself, a big man and, one would say, a man unused to exercise, went down the cliff and fastened his rope, first about the body of Norman, and secondly that of David, who reached the top without regaining consciousness. Bringing up Sampson was the hardest task. It took them half an hour, and he collapsed on the cliff top.

David was a month in the hospital; and when he came out he made only one or two brief appearances near his old haunts. He was quiet, almost morose, and soon afterwards disappeared, having left both family and district with the purpose, as I suppose, of making his fortune. His reputation was worse, thereafter, rather than better; he was always cited as the instigator of the events which led to tragedy. Had he remained, I suppose he might have regained his old eminence in the adolescent community, but the matter was never put to the test.

Nevertheless, he became a boyhood hero of mine; he was never to know it, and I do not know of others who shared my admiration.

5

THE DETRITION of the cliffs and their stubborn deflec-
tion of ocean currents through long ages had brought
about the birth of the sandspit which, reaching out and
out, had touched a hilly island and converted it into a
peninsula; and then through ages more had grown into
this beach which was my world. The isthmus of this
peninsula had strengthened until the beach fronted a
swamp a mile in depth. Then in an older country, the
first pioneers had, on the barest of reports, preselected an
adjacent site for their proposed city; and when they came
they drained this swamp to convert it into fields of uncommonly rich potential. These fields their sons had covered with a checkerboard of small houses set in neat sub-
urbs, each barely distinguishable from its neighbors, yet
each possessed of local pride and tradition.

On the seaward edge of this human fastness which had

lately been a swamp, the beach with its high, steep guardian dunes became a challenge and an irritation. For while the swamp had offered few problems, and the clay hills that flanked it to north and south had been readily adapted to human concepts of desirability, and the quiet harbor to the west could be firmly controlled, the beach and the dunes were not so readily tamed. A hole dug there filled itself in within a day or two; a wall would be smothered with a hill of sand, or else have its foundations, however deeply planted, undermined so that it collapsed.

The sandhills themselves were forever on the move; their peaks might rise one day a hundred feet from the vanished eminences of yesterday. Boundary markers and pegs, the very beginnings of control, vanished overnight. Opposed to the persistent might of sea and wind, the efforts of man in this area seemed doomed to frustration.

There was a rhythm and a purpose in the movement of both beach and dunes, a rhythm of satisfying permanence. When the wild weather from the south, the southeast and the southwest swept in, the sand was resistant to the winds, for they were dampening or soaking winds that cemented the surface down and held it close. In these seasons, though, the same winds, pushing the tops of the waves ever more masterfully towards the beach, and angling their direction somewhat, promoted a faster underflow and scour; so that whatever sand was covered by the reaching combers was scooped up in tremendous quantities and carried far into the bay. There it was subjected to a tidal movement, itself a complicated one.

On the flood tides, the gentle three-knot current from the south, the Great Antarctic Drift which is one of the world's important ocean movements, was augmented by the moon-guided twice-daily tide to increase its speed to four or five knots northward. On the ebb this lunar tide negated the influence of the Drift, so that at times the water of ocean stayed in the one place, at times it moved almost imperceptibly southward, and at times it continued to move north, but at a reduced pace. At new moon or full, when the lunar pull was strengthened by the circumstance that moon and earth and sun were all in a line, the effect was exaggerated, but never sufficiently so that the southward movement became an effective carrier.

Throughout the period of storm, whatever sand was carried to sea during the ebb tide was deposited as soon as it reached water deep enough to simulate a calm at lower levels; but in the flood it traveled northward to be built up in undersea dunes near Lawyer's Head. Such undersea dunes, being lately formed, were soft and a menace to trawlermen; the nets cut into them and were broken away from the steel warps and the footing chains and lost forever. But from this reservoir of sand, the normal seas built up the northern end of the beach, and eventually the material of the undersea dunes became the material of the exposed sandhills.

When the winds came light and dry from the north, however, the picture changed. Such winds carried the sand from the hills, shifting it in great bulk to the depleted southern end of the beach. Moreover, by slowing down the motion of the waves, racing the upper volumes of the water back faster than those beneath, they permitted the sea to bring back the sand stolen in past southerlies and build up the beach at the surface.

After such days there was often a sprinkling of yellow color, signifying shell-sand from the depths, upon the white surface of the beach. The windblown sand moved always southward, but it was met by this offering of ocean sand; and moreover, when it reached the wet surface from which the waves had lately withdrawn, it was deposited securely before it could blow away out to sea.

Such conditions prevailed in the fair days of summer.

The process brought about a constant sifting and movement of sand that tended to ensure the continuity of the beach, the dunes, and the sand below the water in the bay. And as the weather of the district was highly variable, so the beach itself had a continuity of change.

Within a single week it was possible to see an infinity of variation. On the first day, level sand. On the second, with a blustering south wind, the beach divided laterally into two — a great bank sometimes six or eight feet high marking the height of the tide and the edge of the depredations of the sea. On the third day, a drying north wind, and a breakdown of the steepness of the bank. On the fourth, a continuing wind shifting the sand, so that a bar appeared, which at mid-tide was as high as the still-remaining bank. On the fifth day, the ends of the bars closed in and a series of lagoons in mid-beach, reflecting the blue skies and the white flying clouds brought by the north wind. On the sixth day the lagoons, that were traps for the scud and flying sand, filled to the original level; and on the seventh destructive seas again, rising under the influence of a wind backed round to the south once more.

Such mutability, while it added to the delights of childhood, was not to the liking of a human community, and the community made attempt after attempt to contain the sand in a changeless pattern. The successful solution was to hold the dune sand in position with plantings of marram grass and lupin. Windblown sand was caught at the beginning of its journey by leaves and branches; the roots, making a network beneath the surface, held moisture high and inhibited movement. Additionally, the nitrogenous compounds introduced to the soil by the leguminous lupins encouraged the growth of softer grasses like Yorkshire Fog, and bushes of native solanums and veronicas.

The plantings were successful to the point of containing the dunes, but they had merely interrupted one phase of the total sand movement. The windblown sand no longer moved in any quantity from north to south, but there was only a slight interference in the waterborne movement from south to north.

The southern end of the beach, therefore, where people were in the habit of seeking their weekend relaxation, became denuded of sand, and the great black boulders, never seen before, began to show through the surface. The human answer to this was to build long groynes out to sea; pile drivers appeared on the beach, and the lines of stripped tree trunks, adzed to conformity and tipped and ferruled with steel, marched towards the island, as though to form foundations for amusement piers or ill-placed wharves.

They were only partially successful in countering the sea drift and eddying the northbound tide so that it relinquished its cargo of sand. The detrition of the beach continued, but at a slower pace; and in its progress it removed the groynes, one pile at a time, and carried them off to sea. The piles were replaced in the stubborn contest, and a further system of brush fences, constantly renewed, supplemented the containment system on the higher part of the beach.

At the same time the hollows in the dunes were filled with the ashes from the town's fireplaces and the garbage from its tables. The landward slopes were leveled by teams of men and horses, and spread with a thin covering of clay and earth, and planted with groves of maritime pines, so that the great reservoirs of sand were covered, and could no longer fly in the wind to supplement the beach. Later still, flower gardens banked the pine groves, and tennis courts and bowling greens and football grounds were established.

But the beach continued to waste at the southern end until it established a new rhythm. The widening of the northern end by the natural processes formed new areas for the wind to plunder, and the beach settled, in never so pleasing a form as before, to a new movement based upon its altered shape.

The courts and yards into which the beach was divided by its groynes and fences, no less than the forests of shrubbery established at such an aggravated cost in labor, created a playground for the children and the adolescents of the district. The children's play was more innocent than that of their seniors; sometimes the one impinged upon the other, with unforeseen results.

Thus, once, an Indian upon a secret scouting trail, I came on hands and knees to a vantage point among the bushes to see a strange tableau. A pretty girl with a red cascade of hair sat stripped to the waist among the marram grass, the wind fondling her locks with the same light persistent touch as bent the stiff grass blades to a pattern. The fingertips of both her hands caressed the back of her neck beneath her hair, her head was lifted to the sky as, under the influence of the straining back of her body, were her generous pink-tipped breasts; and she smiled at a cloud.

With his back to me, a photographer leaned over his tripod in front of her, and near the photographer another girl, fully dressed, stood smiling as though nothing untoward were afoot. I held by breath; not from the beauty of the scene (which impressed itself upon me only afterward), but because I knew that these were illicit proceedings, and but for the precarious privacy of this small valley, much to be condemned.

But I was already interested in the illicit, fascinated by it; and almost stopped my breathing to watch. I had seen pictures furtively circulated of women without their clothing; now I was seeing them in the making, and an oppressive delight, close to horror, possessed me. I forgot my imminent danger from the cowboys of my imagination; I forgot the afternoon and the scent of golden lupin and the swelling diapason of the surf, and looked.

The girl relaxed; the photographer attended to his camera and said something to the other girl beside him. To my fascinated amazement she quietly and calmly removed her clothes until she stood without a stitch. She was a brunette, and I remember my amazement at seeing her body hair, a curved black shield that daintily hugged the molding of her lower body and her thighs, for in the pictures I had seen circulated there had been no trace of such a capillage.

The photographer walked up to her, posed her by the grass-crowned sand peak, arranged her loose hair, pushed her arms into position; while the redhead stood by, draped from the waist down in the largest towel I had ever seen, and not in any hurry to resume her clothes.

I must have been a good Indian scout; I watched them through several poses and remained undiscovered until after the photographer and his girls had packed and gone away. Then I ran home all the way, trembling with the excitements of my new knowledge.

I was much older, thirteen or fourteen perhaps, when with Buster Cade, a frequent companion, and a couple of others I walked one Sunday morning along the sand. Behind the last brush fence we came upon two girls, acquaintances of ours, lying on the sand with a rug pulled up to their chins. I knew them as Gladys and Phyllis; my father had hinted that I should avoid their company. They were much upon the beach, especially in early evening, for they worked throughout the day at a match factory in the town.

We were all of us at the stage when the acquisition of a suntan as deep and extensive as possible was a prime ambition. The lads of the district had no problem; above the surf bathing sheds was an open roof, made specially for sun bathing and guarded with five-foot wooden walls, so that in the games of French cricket and the quieter activities in which we indulged there, our naked bodies would not offend outsiders.

Girls, though, had to provide their own opportunities for exposing their skins; and we were sure, when we saw Gladys and Phyllis under the rug, that before our arrival they had been out in the irresistible sun. The inference was that they were undressed, or dressed so lightly as to arouse an adolescent curiosity; which, of course, being lads, we at once determined to assuage.

"Get away," said Phyllis. "Go on, now, on your way."

"Get spent, small change," supplemented Gladys, who frequently sought and found companionship with American sailors, when they were available.

"Yeah, scram," said Phyllis.

But we were hungry-eyed little louts and would not go, for we were certain they had been basking "in the altogether," as the phrase of the day went, and hopeful that sooner or later some disarrangement of the rug would disclose illicit treats.

Finally Buster tried subtlety, as he knew it.

"I'll bet you won't go in for a swim just as you are," he dared. "Real money," he added, as an incentive.

Phyllis snorted, but Gladys came up on her elbows, in a movement too controlled to be rewarding.

"How much?" she asked.

Buster searched his pockets.

"Two bob," he said, and Gladys relaxed.

"Try betting real money," she advised.

We held a hurried conference and pooled our resources.

"Five and fourpence," Buster announced.

"I'll take it," Gladys said.

She looked carefully round to note that none of the Sunday morning strollers were closer than a quarter-mile or more, and even at that distance were headed in other directions, and then threw the blanket aside and without the vestige of a covering jumped to her feet and ran a hundred yards to the water. We gasped, and did not move, and Phyllis looked frightened.

Gladys stayed sporting in the waves a good while; so long indeed that there was time for a group of elders, two solid citizens and their wives, to approach; and then came bursting happily out of the water, running up the beach towards us with one hand covering her sex and the other arm clasped across her breasts. Later I realized I had never seen her look less of a trollop; she was a pretty girl and rewarded inspection until she was clothed and painted.

The family group was staring as though it could not believe its eyes. Gladys shot under the blanket, wet as she was, without waiting to towel; her hair plastered lankly about her face. The moment she was covered she said, "All right. Give. Five and fourpence."

"Ow," squealed Phyllis. "Gladdy, you're freezing. Move over. Get away."

"Five and four," Gladys demanded, unheeding, and Buster handed it over.

"That was really good," she said, as her hands disappeared with the money. "It really was."

Our forbidden cigarettes for the week were now a lost cause, and we would have no small change for sweets or ice cream, but still, at that stage, we thought it was worth it. We lingered a little, brazening out a resistance to the girls' protests, and then wandered away, and as we topped the sandhill looked back to see the rug thrown back, and two golden figures lying on their towels. It was too far away to be certain they were not wearing flesh-colored swimsuits; but we knew.

It was strange that I had been a party to that little incident, for I was girl-shy, in spite of having two well-loved sisters, and was consequently the butt in a never-ending series of staged embarrassments designed to trap me.

I was enamored, about that time, of a lovely redhead for whom I entertained, but secretly, emotions of the tenderest kind. I used to sit behind her in school, where I sometimes demonstrated my interest by dipping the tips of her Titian pigtails in my inkwell and then giving them a tiny tug, so that in the resultant flirt of her head the ink-laden tresses splashed on her freckled nose or brushed the cheek of her neighbor. Some such attention was my nearest approach to a declaration.

But my inner feelings were detected, apparently, by Long John Saunders, the tallest kid in the school, and the oldest. One evening after dark he met me, having prearranged an appointment with my inamorata, quite without my knowledge, in a lonely place much frequented by lovers.

We met Beryl, and I was immediately stricken dumb. And a few minutes later, without warning, John gave a wild cry and bolted off into the night, pushing Beryl into my arms.

She would have stayed leaning against me, I think, but I disengaged myself as quickly as I could. Why? I couldn't have told. I had dreamed of finding myself in situations such as this; and in such dreams I had acted manfully and with infinite resource, like Douglas Fairbanks, for example.

Instead we walked, wordlessly and four feet apart, back to where street lights lit a familiar scene. I was trembling with my ineptitude, frightened that if I spoke my voice would break into the childish treble it had recently forsaken, and altogether conscious of having missed my opportunity.

Beryl was nice. She spoke of familiar things in sentences to which I answered in monosyllables, hating myself and my embarrassment.

Two years later, when I was sixteen and nearing the end of my school life, I met a girl named Kathy. She had a companion, Jessie, and they spent the whole of the long

summer holidays lying with three or four of us in one of
the brush-fenced enclosures on the sand; surfing and
swimming and sunning, and talking.

Kathy was a tiny girl, perfect in her slight proportions.
Her bronzed skin had a texture that made it seem she had
been encased in silk; her hair, naturally waved, was cut
close about her well-shaped head; her hands and feet
looked delicate, but they were capable. Her erudition was
considerable; the gaps in it were concealed by a vivid
imagination which leaped to theory and circumstance
that might prove indicative of the missing information —
or slant the subject another way. She could cap a couplet
of doggerel as adequately as she could produce verses,
which excited those of us in the group who were en-
tranced by the imagery of words.

Her voice was not a singing one, but she could imitate
the throaty, hoarse delivery of the torch singers then
coming into fashion. She dressed with imagination supplemented with a fair family fortune; her best swimsuit
of that season had been sent her by some relative traveling in France. It had been cut on the bias — I had to ask
what that meant, beyond the obvious fact that it caressed
every entrancing curve her neat little body possessed.

I fell in love with Kathy; a calf-love certainly, though
I knew about calf-love and was sure that I had expended
mine upon Beryl's intangible beauties years before. This,
I was certain, was the real thing. But I could not let her
know; we were always, or nearly always, surrounded by
our companions. When, after a bout with the surf, we
ran along the beach together to restore our frozen circu-

lations, I was at the end of my run before I decided on the approach I would make; and then it was too late. The subject was changed and we were back at our enclosure.

It was bliss when she took a grain of sand from my eye; it was a privilege to be touching her towel as I lay beside her on my belly, my head pillowed on my other arm, my eyes devouring her. I began to plan excursions that would separate us from the others.

In a fold of the hill, which protected it from the roaring, blustering southerly winds and exposed it to the full beneficence of all the summer sunshine, an old orchard, long abandoned and belonging to my family, was concealed behind a thick grove of high, dark cypresses. With a long-planned cunning I began to tell Kathy about this retreat and to enlarge upon its undoubted beauties, its privacies and its glades of sunshine.

The first day I embarked upon this campaign, she caught me with my sails aback by proposing an immediate expedition, to which I could do nothing but consent. I in my shorts and sandals, she with a skirt buttoned round her swimsuit, we climbed the flight of three hundred and twenty-three steps that spanned the steepest fall of the hillside there, pushed a creaking gate aside, and entered upon my secret and well-loved haven.

In its orchard days, the owner had taken most of his financial return from the members of weekend excursions, who, basket-laden, paid an entrance fee and were permitted to take away however much ripe fruit they could carry. Therefore it had been planned as pleasure garden and orchard combined, and there were still walks lined with camellias, hedged with overgrown laurel and laurestinus, escallonia and olearia, picked out with red-flowering may and Australian black wattle. This last, finding the atmosphere on that sun-blessed hillside to its liking, had run riot, and at one place formed a feather-leaved shrubbery, spring-colored with masses of golden blossoms. Other parts of the domain had been taken over, in small patches, by golden broom, smelling, as I thought then, of heaven; and there were tiny glades among it all, outlined with enormous clumps of blue-flowering aga-panthus and the scarlet torches of red-hot-poker.

The apple trees had withered and shrunk and died a little from lack of care; the pears had thrived with neg-lect, and grown into giants. The plums were spiky groves; sloes had escaped into profusion, as had the Kentish cherries; there was a small wilderness of blackberry; a single peach remained, and two apricot trees; but their offerings of fruits were scanty.

To this place, then, I brought my Kathy, proud to share with her and eager to show her all its treasures. She shared them to a degree; but half was still undis-closed when she sat herself down in one of the sweetest retreats, spreading her skirt over her knees among the cocksfoot heads, with her own head on one side smiling in appreciation. Or was it invitation? The necessity to know became so urgent it choked all communication.

The glade was one surrounded with blue agapanthus. I never see the flower now without an awareness of the desirable heats of summer. The air was loud with insect song — the bass of bees, the treble of crickets — and fragrant as an herb garden. Wrens went about their busy minutes with only a side glance for intruding humans; the bellbird down near the blackberries was concerned only with his song. And I lay down in the sun a yard from Kathy, and fought my inclinations.

Oh, we talked. We talked the afternoon away. I remember that I had recently discovered Browning and Fra Lippo Lippi; on art therefore I had become an authority incontrovertible, having a good memory, and an apprehension of forthcoming conversational dangers lively enough to permit me to change an awkward subject in time.

But of love we said nothing; and the thoughts that were boiling in my head bubbled away until the pot was empty.

Nor did we leave there till the sun was behind the hill and the air was chill. Kathy, rising from a long stillness, fell against me on the steep hillside; I restored her tenderly to a balance and took her home.

And, home myself, split like the amoeba into two. My evening self, reliant and cool, flailed my afternoon self with clubs of recrimination. The glade where she had stopped was made for love — of course; that was why she had stopped. The conversation — had it not several times approached subjects that could be treated both personally and intimately, and had not Kathy led it there? The slip on the hillside — was it not calculated to throw her into my arms? Her relaxation in a world that contained only the two of us: was this not designed to bring me to her?

I was a fool; I had muffed my chances. I was an inveterate fool, to be stricken dumb and powerless all my life. It was unlikely that I would ever retain the gift of tongues when moments became crucial. Therefore I would write her a letter.

I could write. I could express with a pen what my tongue could never encompass. My eloquence was inhibited by no reactions of eyes and fingers; it was only my tongue that became inoperative in moments of emotion.

And so I wrote. It was a beautiful letter, as I thought; but in spite of my confidence I could not bear to read it through. It covered twenty-one pages in my stiff, upright, formal hand; twenty-one pages, written close, in a secrecy which I ensured by locking myself in my room, and doubly guarded by encircling the paper with my left arm as I wrote. It contained quotations from Lyly and Shepherd Tonie; but it was more eloquent, I thought, in passages that sprung full-armed from my fever-amorous convictions, long contained, and therefore released in a flood, without restriction.

I finished it after midnight, let myself out of the French doors that opened directly on the lawn from my bedroom, and walked a star-flushed mile to Kathy's house to drop it in the letter box.

Next morning, when I came down to the beach, she and Jessie were giggling over something they hastily concealed on my approach. It couldn't be my letter; it just couldn't be. I prayed that it would not be; that letter was for one pair of eyes alone.

But Jessie, the imp, couldn't contain herself; and in a

little while came out with some phrase or other taken, as I could not help but recognize, from some more impassioned extract from my twenty-one-page declaration. I jumped up and ran into the surf. There was only a day of the vacation left; and I used it to go fishing from the cliffs. When next I saw Kathy, years later, she was wearing mink on her back and rings on her fingers.

6

O F ALL the resorts to which the citizens on high days and holidays repaired, the beach alone had one peculiar quality. It was a parade ground, sharply divided into two contiguous but barely related areas.

Where the promenade and the roads lined its borders the citizens came attired in Sunday best. They sat for hours in parked cars and on the Council-provided benches displaying themselves to their fellows. Mr. Devenish, in spats, accompanied by his comfortable wife in a flowered and fruited hat, appeared every fine Sunday afternoon at precisely three-fifteen, and walked twice along the full length of the promenade, his head high, his manner graciously deferential to acquaintances, and quite remotely distant to all others.

He was preceded and followed in a never-ending procession by others of his kind; whole families of others: daughters in white dresses, with white-gloved hands holding correct little handbags; sons brushed and shined, with stiff white collars and gleaming shoes.

Such people were like marker buoys in the human tide ever flowing back and forth along this showplace of the town. You could, with reasonable accuracy, isolate the elements of the flow and put them in their places: the professional men, the tradesmen, the skilled laborers, the clerks, the petty officials of government, the laborers and, among the juniors, the students, the apprentices and the factory hands.

On the sands below the green painted railings, however, the parade assumed a character entirely different. They all came here too: the professional men and the laborers, the students and the ne'er-do-wells; but isogenic distinctions, categorizing in any way the components of the crowd, would have taxed the capacity of the most acute of sociologists. It was not that the beach, with its uniform of swimsuits, had a leveling capacity; it was that on the sands a different set of standards was established.

Here the factory lad could look polished and complete, and meet on equal terms the scion of wealthy stock. The polished banker, so suave and dignified upon the promenade, but here befurred with coarse and grizzly hair, here supported on bowed legs furnished with awkward, knobby joints, here in the pitiless sunshine shown to belong to a lesser breed altogether, could not comand the respect to which his social achievements entitled him: such achievements did not exist on the neutral ground between land and sea.

Pride of place belonged here to the beautiful and the

well-formed; the stars of the gathering here were seldom those that shone on the promenade above; the standards were upturned. And this was not a democratic process at all, but the temporary evanescent establishment of a new aristocracy, whose leaders owed their prominence to fate and fortune.

In the parade on the promenade, the classification from high to low, based upon the prosperous appearance of solid and significant citizenship, was paralleled, not quite exactly, by another breakdown applied in a more penetrating analysis. Mr. Devenish, with cane and spats, was greeted with a becoming deference; his banker, less admirably tailored, commanded a greater respect.

Jimmy Stevens, the bootmaker, might look no better than Watson Prand, the journeyman printer. But Stevens owned his own shop and paid no rent; Prand was known to spend an evening once a week in a drinking-house in the next suburb; and the nod that Mr. Devenish, say, bestowed on him was a degree more curt than that awarded to the less pretentious Stevens.

And on the beach front too, the dual standard applied. The handsome, well-muscled lads, square of shoulder, fleet of foot, skilled in beach gymnastics, were the kings of the place, but only if they combined their good looks with an ability to swim, to battle the surf, to play Rugby and generally to back up the promise of their appearance. In general they did. For an adolescence spent on the beach seemed to favor them physically at the same time it increased their skill in the water.

The Valhalla of the beach gods was the battered shed

which went under the title of the Surf Life Saving and Sea Bathing Club. It comprised club, gymnasium and dressing-sheds for the district's beach-bound youth, and sheltered the beach equipment — the reels of rope and lifesaving harness, the surfboards on which all self-respecting lads had learned to ride the long boiling combers from the point at which they lifted lazily far out at sea until they spent their last energy on the sand, and the canoes that brought teamwork to ocean sports.

In all seasons except the blustering months of winter it housed a platoon of muscled youths, and smelled of old timber impregnated with salt and sweat, of the tar with which its flat roof was seasonally treated, of coconut oil brought ceremonially to the daily anointing of the worshipers of sun and sea, of the odors of athletic humanity, all intermingled with the beach smell.

The tarpaper floors were invariably sprinkled with sand brought in on towels and swimsuits and heads of hair; the darkness emphasized by the unpainted walls was vibrant with voices and the pad of unshod feet. On the big board-room table, which was the only conventional furnishing, some groups were always demonstrating handstands or more complicated tumbling acts. It was a tribal house for young men; the elders took no interest in the activities there, the children were chased from its doors.

On the face of the building a bell was installed; it was rung when swimmers were observed to be in trouble, and its clamant jangle brought people running from houses near the beach to watch the lifesaving teams in action. It served as a shark alarm as well; all swimmers left the

water when it rang, even though shark attacks were unknown.

When the rip carried some weak swimmer beyond his
depth and out to sea, the pride with which we watched a
team go into action was more far-reaching than just a
warranty of local interest. It was a pride in the whole
quality of the human at his height; sometimes, indeed,
when the victim being rescued had taken a tyro risk in
seas no expert would have challenged, as was frequently
the case, the stars of the team displayed a most creditable
courage, hardly to be excelled in any field.

The beltman, hampered by the drag of up to eight
hundred feet of cotton rope, would be lost from sight for
most of his journey as, painstakingly and surely, he challenged the sea, diving deep beneath the oncoming waves
into the assisting undertow, employing a slow, sure
breaststroke. Ahead of him an unhampered swimmer
raced to the victim, to hold him up and prevent, as much
as he could, his seaward progress. As often as not his
simplest course was to make the man unconscious; the
sharp blows of fist or knee were much practiced in the
clubhouse gloom.

The battle required knowledge as well as persistence;
the rescuers often began their swim in a contrary direction to that in which the victim lay; their knowledge of
rips and currents brought them to him, and it was rare
indeed for the rescuers to be unsuccessful.

The promenade would be crowded by the time the
swimmers came to their mark, and you could hear the
sigh of communal relief above the crashing of the seas,

though the danger was not past; the victim was not safe until the linesmen, pulling rope with a rhythmic efficiency, brought the three men to the sand. Their task too required knowledge; it was easy to pull the men under water, and their energy was controlled therefore by signals from the beltman.

Day after day, with no reward, the lifesavers patrolled the beach, confining the swimmers to a safe area marked with flags, and hour after hour going through their drills: mock rescues and resuscitations, a soldierly marching with the gear, an exact and precise forearming against tragedy.

There was no lad on the beach who was not eager to be called up into one or other of the teams; called or not, he practiced voluntarily with his mates until he was at least proficient. And no matter how good his physique, how handsome his features, how bronzed his body, he could not join the elite until his capabilities matched his appearance. The standards of the promenade above were unallied to those prevailing upon the sands or in the clubhouse.

But the responsibilities of the volunteers were separate altogether from the joys of battling the waves: the long struggle out to where the greenbacks rose ponderously, gaining strength, from the ocean depth; the waiting for a wave that must be joined at a precise moment, a precise stage of development; and then the screaming triumph of the ride to shore, the capacity for power that precariously harnessed the surge of the restless sea to the ends of a pleasure-thrill; the poise, the constantly shifting balance, and then the feeling of the water's relinquishment of strength, the end of the experience.

Even in summertime the pleasure could not be maintained for long; the water temperature was a tingling forty-six degrees at best, and only a fool or a beginner stayed in so long that the cold penetrated deep below the skin. A strenuous thirty minutes was as long as most would endure, to be followed by a run along the wet and sparkling sand for a mile or more, and a final submission to the sun-rays. We lay drenched in sun, relaxed and immobile, for hour after hour, with the surf-song drumming in our ears and the shouts of playing children.

Sometimes, though rarely enough in those latitudes, there was a gentle surf, a slow, lazy roll of the water; and on most of those days we gave ourselves entirely to the sun, contemptuous of the easy sport the sea offered.

Sometimes, on red-letter days, the porpoises played in the surf. Once I swam with them, unknowing at the start. I rolled against the blue-black body in the waves, frightened out of my wits at the contact lest it be a shark. The porpoise in his mischief rolled away, turning back to take another wave; and then I saw the school, playing like boys, catching the breakers and riding them a little way towards the sand; not far, for the land was their enemy as the sea was ours, and they had not the taste for danger for danger's sake, or so I imagine.

I went back for a second wave, and felt the stinging in my side. When I had ridden it to my knee's depth, I stood up and looked at the patch beneath my arm that was bleeding; the rough hide of the porpoise had stripped the epidermis over my ribs in a hand-sized graze. But the salt and the sun healed it; in three or four days there was no slightest mark.

On days of carnival the beach and the promenade, with all their denizens, became an entity, and were variously occupied by the same pushing, thrusting throng, eager to be entertained. Showmen came and set up their merry-go-rounds, their mechanical horse-races, their wheels-of-chance, their checkered targets for darts and wooden balls and tossed pennies.

In the season following the one I spent with Kathy — for my mind had drawn me, in the interval, from the outskirts of her court, where I had been tolerated, to its center — the carnival came early in the year, in the uncertain springtime, for its purpose was to raise funds to replace the deteriorating gear of the lifesavers.

It was a day as gala as the community could devise; and even the weather was as perfect as any we had known. In countries where good weather is normal, no day is ever as glorious as those which come, surprisingly and rewardingly, to the battered southland. The air is flavored — "air like wine," they say, but that is untrue; it is like nothing else unless it be that sensation that comes when a refugee from the city, after a long abstinence from pure water, drinks from a mountain stream and savors its quality as of some rare beverage, unable to put a name to its especial particularity and unwilling to dub the water flavorless.

The beach was in the process of rebuilding; its sand was heaped high near the promenade, and a long level stretch reached to the water. The sea was regular, with waves large enough to promise excitement in the contests to follow, but free of the snarling rips and tides, born of an irregular beach, that sometimes broke the continuity of the surf and endangered swimmers.

The crowd, freed most wonderfully from the toils of a long winter and a hitherto meager spring, was in the best of holiday moods, from the children, scampering with their spades and pails like sun-excited insects, to the elderly, who with shoes and socks removed were venturing their ankles in the edge of the sea.

Just back of the highest reach of the water ponies and donkeys, with attendant grooms recruited for the occasion, stood and waited — never long — for hire. A flag marked the end of the course to which a coin would entitle a young rider, and the donkeys stood with heads down watching it with a kind of morose acceptance of the day's fate.

South of them a course had been marked out for the foot races, and out at sea, three men in a canoe were anchoring the buoy round which the swimming races would pass. Right under the shadow of the promenade a screaming gang of children vied for positions in the bun-and-treacle race; tough buns were threaded on long strings and hung from a rope stretched horizontally eight feet or so above the ground. The buns were freshly dipped in a basin of cane syrup till the sticky sweetness dripped in threads to the sand beneath; then boys and girls with hands tied behind their backs struggled to be first to eat them down.

The rope swayed back and forth, the buns danced and jumped on their strings, each bun responding to bites farther along the line, and each smearing its cargo of syrup over faces and heads of hair and holiday clothes. The prize they struggled for was worth little more than the entry fee; the contest was the thing. And if they had to go into the sea to rid themselves of syrup, that was small matter on such a day.

There were contests for lifesaving teams, races for canoes, fancy dress events, exhibitions of tumbling, bran-tub dips, and every enterprise that could possibly be turned to money-raising ends. The town turned up to picnic on the beach; the transport authorities ran special trams at prices specially inflated; the gas rings in the Pavilion, where prudent councilors had made provision to prevent the lighting of picnic fires on the beach, were fed with pennies throughout the long day, and Pegleg Marmon, the Pavilion's irascible old caretaker, stumped rapidly round them all, hoping that he could catch some miscreant feeding the slots with the tops of lemonade bottles, flattened to penny size upon the tramrails.

It was Pegleg's specialty in the deduction of crime. It was a great day for youth when Pegleg took out after such a criminal. They would stand and cheer on the fugitive with an unvarying formula that maddened the old man.

"Turn round!" they cried. "Stand up to him! Kick him on the wooden leg and watch for borer dust."

And then fled.

Dopey Sanders was there with his sack over his shoulder, mysteriously laden, his eyes on the ground, searching for discarded cigarette butts. He lit them one from another as soon as he picked them up. He was a doctor, it was whispered, ruined by drug-taking. He was a dipsomaniac, that was certain; how he lived was a mystery. He loved carnivals; sometimes he would come on subsequent days and sift through the littered sand with his fingers, retrieving coins, if he was lucky, and small treasure of lost costume jewelry.

Once, in a depression year, two of the surf bathers, unemployed, took a lesson from his book, bought a large sieve and methodically shoveled the beach sand through it, digging down a foot or two to the consolidated mass beneath. They made good wages for their trouble, to everyone's surprise.

Harry Zane had brought his camera and was taking in business enough to keep his darkroom occupied for weeks to come. Marcus Pfeiffer, earnest and sober, judged the contest for the best sand castles, dithering over his decisions as though they concerned matters of great moment; it was his task of every year. Even Dummy Blake could sell balloons and did; though small customers from outside the district deserted him this time for an opposition armed with a gas bottle; Dummy's balloons had never flown so satisfactorily high.

The carnival was a great success that year, and people who would normally have been home with the setting of the sun stayed on for the evening hours.

Now were the divisions of both beach and promenade entirely eliminated; neither dignity nor grace commanded an advantage here. The crowd was concentrated now around the busy stalls with their amateur barkers, around the bandstand, where the Military Band played popular selections that kept the feet light upon the pavement.

Big George the Greek, his pockets stuffed with notes, played every gambling game; three barmaids from his pub were with him and called upon his bankroll as often as he dipped into it for himself; they put their arms about his waist and sang and shouted; and George could only beam on them. But in his normal trading he knew the value of a pound; it was said of him that he was the only man in the town who knew how many notes you could stuff into an oil drum; and he loved to haggle over a bargain.

The moon rode high that night, the Esplanade was festooned with lights, and lights picked out the stalls around the Pavilion. The white lines of surf reflected the rays; the breakers seemed to move shoreward upon a sea of nothing, to disappear in their entirety when their verges crumbled.

The girls in their short dresses walked arm in arm, two by two. Tomorrow and yesterday we would know all the girls upon the beach; tonight their ranks were reinforced by strangers. Two especially captured all our eyes. No one knew them; soon everyone had a story about them: they were a mother and daughter, in spite of the evidence of our eyes; they had arrived in a gaudy new car, unescorted; if your pockets were filled with money your company would be welcome.

With a bunch of friends I passed them on the promenade and felt the compulsion to stare at them, but looked away. And it was true: they could be a mother and a daughter. The mother's head was brassy blonde, the daughter's unbelievably red. They jingled with glittering jewelry, their slipper heels were the highest that ever went tap-tapping along that walk. They had roving eyes and saucy hips, and lips that curled when youngsters looked at them, though one was younger than I.

But nevertheless we looked. They were held briefly in the company of George the Greek, until his barmaids pulled him away, protesting but happy. They perched near every stall where money went from hand to hand — "Like vultures," Buster said. Like parrots, like bright macaws, flaunting their feathers, bold in the confidence of the colors, I thought. They responded to every adult look; they passed from hand to hand.

After a while, Buster and the rest settled for other girls, less glittering, and more approachable, being known to them. And I went home, in my sciolous misogyny, lonelier than from a day spent privately by the sea.

The lights went out, the hubbub quietened, and group by group the last of those at carnival went home. But not the little redhead. A shocked and fearful youth, going early in the morning to wash away the indispositions he had amassed the day before, came upon her body in a little sandy hollow that was formed by hummocks crowned with marram grass, and far above the cleansing action of the tide. Her pretty clothes were torn, her cheeky face disfigured, and there was a trickle of dried blood from the corner of her mouth.

Beyond, at the edge of the sea, across the expanse of trodden sand littered with the debris of the carnival, the Sun-Worshiper stood performing her rhythmic exercises. She had been the morning attraction through all the years since Margie-Bargie disappeared. Some in derision called her "The Goddess"; and Goddess she looked sometimes, when her skinny silhouette was lined in a blaze of rosy gold from the rising of the sun, and the seagulls wheeled above her head.

The youth ran for help; and by and by, when I came inadvertent to the scene, there was a group of shocked onlookers surrounding the blanket-covered body that had been wanton, and now was waste. I went to find out what had brought them there in that unlikely hour of early morning. I caught a glimpse of that impossible red of hair, and heard the talk, and hurried away. The Sun-Worshiper was still at her routine; the waves methodically provided the backdrop for her modern ballet; the world was going on, but not for the little redhead.

They had to wake her blonded mother in the apartment, bright and chintzy, they both had occupied near the town's center. Her daughter's absence had not worried her, but now she broke down, being lonelier, perhaps, than anyone could imagine. The murderer's companion was still with her; the murderer was taken before the morning died, sleeping in his room, apparently believing what memory he had of his crime to be nothing but a horrid miasma from his world of troubled dreams.

It was the first time I ever realized that violent death could be both stupid and sordid, and without any redeeming feature; a passionless crime of passion, a momentary unleashing of a destructive impulse that had no more than the motive of a moment, the whim of some devil of the mind newly wakened in a sleeping brain.

The aftertaste of carnival was bitter in my mouth that year; the wet discarded ribbons, the broken balloons, the paper cartons and the empty bottles were all allied with that pathetic broken body, marked with the defiant flare of red-dyed hair. The storm gathered that night; the rising seas had heralded it the day before; and when it was spent some four days later the sands were fresh and clean.

mY SCHOOLING now was done, my education about to begin; in the search for a purpose and a meaning, no less than the warranty of independent life, I went to my mentor the sea. I became a fisherman, and discovered a new affinity with the waves. And with the elements of my trade barely learned I reached for the asceticism of a life alone on the water.

It was, perhaps, the immediate answer to a monastic inclination; there was time for contemplation in plenty in the long watches, the periods in which the immediate task was simply to travel from place to place; but there was also action and adventure; there were skills to be learned and strengths to be developed.

Mental exercises concerned with navigation or with the pursuit of a quarry became efficient when the ends of living and sometimes the safety of life were dependent

upon them. The importance of attacking the task of the
moment at the time of its presentation was always under-
lined at sea.

In the outside world, outside the cloisters of ocean rollers, the refectory of the wharves, the country's economy
had broken down; but the prospects from the wide windows of my mobile cell were not of bleak disaster nor of
hopeless striving. For a man at sea may own whatever
he can take; he is master of what lies within his capacity,
and if he has an economic problem its answer lies in the
increase of that capacity; it is not a problem to be worked
out in conjunction with others.

I had a goal: someday, I dreamed, I would fish the
wide Antarctic; someday I would be master of that tama-
ble wild. In the meantime I worked hard to increase my
proficiency.

I worked with rope: an elemental thing. In days before
a dawning art and the birth of creativity opened men's
eyes to knowledge, it was with rope that man was enabled for the first time to combine the strengths of many
men into a single strength; it was with rope that he
curbed and harnessed and directed the strength of animals whose lives he converted to his own purpose, and it
was with rope he snared them. It was with rope that he
fastened the elements of his house, and built his water
craft, and provided its motive power. With rope and
cordage he made his weapons and his shelter; with rope
and cordage he emerged from the jungle, the best-armed
creature the world had ever known.

I worked with chain and steel cables, with canvas and

cotton, with line, twine and marline, with mast, spar and derrick, with warps and hawsers, with knots and bends and splices. I learned to harness the strength of the seas; to make the rolling of the ship bring up a tonnage of fish from forty fathoms; to bend the wind to my will, to ride the storm on a sea anchor and break the following seas with a trailed line.

I learned the features of the sea bottom, and sampled them with a buttered lead line, with a fabrication of barbs that snagged the weed, with a hand testing the vibrations of the warp that towed the net. I sought to learn the habits of fish; I followed after them on their swift and unpredictable migrations; I studied the habits of the predators who, like myself, lived upon the mistakes of their quarry. I learned the rhythms of their lives, rhythms of night and day, correlated to and tempered by the rhythms of the tides, marked by the phases of the moon and tempered again by the air pressures, the advancing and receding storms, the influx of rivers, the melting of snow a hundred miles from the sea, the temperatures and the salinity.

I studied my tools: the configuration of the little schooner I had acquired, the rigging of lines, the braid-ing of nets, the shape of otter boards. I made a little trawl, one-twentieth the size of the great massive net I towed with my schooner's power, working it single-handed. I had the model true to scale: the upper and lower wings, the square, the belly, the baitings top and bottom, and the cod-end. I made it with extension warps to fit between the outer edges of the wings and the otter boards, with otter boards the size of butter-paddles, a headrope buoyed with ping-pong balls, a chain hardly strong enough to hold a toy dog.

I towed it with lengths of cord in shallow water where I could watch it, my trousers rolled above my knees, my speed of walking measured to the two and a half knots that was my ship's capacity with a trawl in tow. I cut and trimmed it, introduced new features, adjusted and sewed and braided until I knew why a net flowed. I sat on the beach with my mound of cordage and went over my knots, introducing baitings and creasings in a varying incidence to alter what would be the water-held shape of the artifact, until at last I knew what laws prevailed to make my net efficient.

When the fine weather brought the more timid of the fishermen to sea and the market was flooded, I searched for new grounds; when the storms were wild and fish brought premium prices, I stayed in known areas and worked while daylight lasted. If I was short of funds I did more: I set out lights upon the sea in willful defiance of its man-made laws, and towed my net round them through the night. My lights hung over the dancing water from deck brooms lashed to buoys that were anchored to the sea bottom; in the weather that I used them no authority was likely to find them.

In the pursuance of my dream I learned the command of electricity and the crafts of building; when a cleat was smashed away I cut a new one from the bush; when I smashed a stem-post and half a dozen planks upon a harbor pile I spliced them all myself. I was a plumber and a painter; I wielded needles and fashioned anchors; I threaded bolts, cut brass, set zinc beside my steel to protect it from the electrolytic action set up by the copper fastenings in the bilge water, and came painfully to an understanding of many things.

I studied the stars and the birds and the charts and the winds and the shapes of waves for my navigation; the compass and the sextant were secondary, but demanded understanding.

In my experimentation I came often enough to the bay outside the beach, explored the forest of giant kelp and dragged the barren sand plains. I set crayfish pots around the island — one day of storm I nearly lost my schooner there.

I made companions among the rough and admirable motley that manned the fishing fleet, but it was a companionship of convenience only. They had much to teach me, and in a year or two I could repay in kind, for I would always flirt with theories that cost a little cash to test; they could not, for they had wives and families, or strong and pressing appetites and ambitions. I liked their company, their feuds and their friendships. They formed an independent crowd, but among them I was still alone.

There came a time of warm summer months, when every craft that could float was taking advantage of the clear and fortunate weather to bring fish into a crowded market. It was work for a small return; I put my ship on the slip, got my gear in order, and settled to wait for the more lucrative time of storms. I was restless in my loneliness; when I had done all I could I tied my schooner up at the wharf and came back to the beach.

I was standing alone on the promenade one evening, watching the moon lift like a segment of a great blood orange from the sea. It had been gibbous, and I regarded it sourly; the weather would not change, I thought, until the new moon at least. The sea beneath it shimmered red and gold in its pathway; it was so quiet that the sound of each breaking wave was separate and distinct: a muted, intermittent crashing instead of the gutteral undertones in a continuity.

A girl walked past on the other side of the street and I liked the look of her. She was walking quickly, a component of a small and insignificant comedy, for behind her, trying to look unconcerned, trying at the same time to catch up, a middle-aged man had obviously marked her for a pick-up attempt. She had well-shaped legs, she held herself very well; but her dress was drab, or it looked so in the inadequate light, and she carried her handbag as though it were a parcel.

She glanced my way as she passed; and for a second I wished that I knew her; but I was still ill at ease with girls and getting worse. After a while I heard her footsteps coming back, this time on my side of the road. She seemed to hesitate as she came abreast, but then went on. I turned to watch her, and she took only a few steps and then came back and walked directly up to me, so timing the movement that her pursuer drew alongside at that moment.

"Hello there," she said to me. "For a moment I didn't realize it was you."

The man was passing, gaping; as indeed I must have gaped myself. She didn't leave space for a reply but hastened on.

"You didn't go Saturday night after all," she said. "I did. And quite enjoyed myself."

It was beginning to penetrate, by this time, that this was a ruse to shake off her follower, and I cooperated, though my face was flushed with embarrassment.

"No, I didn't go," I said. "But I heard it was good."

The man had hesitated a little farther on. Now he began to walk again, and passed out of earshot.

"Gee, thanks," she said. "He was just getting ready to speak to me."

"Well, you wouldn't have to answer," said I, more logical than gallant.

She gave me a funny look. "That isn't quite the problem."

She was far from beautiful after all; at least her face was. Her figure was trim and good, except for her hands, which were overlarge, and her rather too-broad feet. She held herself with a perky confidence; her voice was low and throaty, and created ripples of disturbance when I heard it. But her face was ugly: too broad, and the length of it established by jawbones that seemed as though they would run to unusual length, and then were foreshortened abruptly by the intrusion of an overwide chin.

On the right side of her face, just by the point of the jawbone, there was an old and ugly scar. Her forehead was broad and crowned by a head of wavy hair that was comely enough. Her mouth was a shade too fleshy; her upper lip too long. Only her eyes were beautiful; so beautiful indeed that it was not hard to focus attention on them to the exclusion of the rest of her homely face. They were beautiful and framed beautifully, with good lashes and brows, and a good proportion between them. She used no cosmetics save lipstick; and that in a slap-dash fashion as though she had been unable to locate a mirror, and perhaps had substituted the dim reflection from a window or a tiled wall.

"What is the problem then?" I asked; but she disregarded this entirely. She was eyeing me up and down, impish eyes dancing in her otherwise expressionless face.

"What's your name?" she asked, and I told her Joe. I don't know why; it just seemed good enough.

"I'm Jerry," she announced, and I liked it.

"That's nice."

"Are you going to talk to me? You don't have to. I can keep on walking."

"Your friend's waiting for you," I pointed out. He was, too. He had taken a position by the railing a hundred yards away, and I could see his white moon-face looking in our direction.

"That's not what I asked you. If you won't talk to me, maybe he'll do," she said surprisingly.

"I don't talk very much. I like to listen," I admitted.

"Then walk me. Walk me along the beach."

She took my arm and we walked until the promenade ended, she leaning towards me, her shoulder and hip butt-ing against me as we passed the man leaning against the rail.

We went on down the beach, plunging through the soft footing near the wall until we reached the hard sand lately vacated by the tide and firm for walking. She didn't talk much; the proximity she had established, as I thought to deceive her pursuer, intensified rather than relaxed; her overlarge fingers were intimate upon my shirt-sleeved arm. We walked together a good long way, perhaps a mile, while I warmed to a sense of companionship. As far as I was concerned she could outrage all the conventions if she wished; I liked her company.

She asked me what I did.

"I have a schooner. I'm a fisherman."

She stopped walking, her fingers detaining me.

"I knew I'd seen you before. Down at the Customs wharf. Scrubbing a deck. I nearly came down the ladder to visit you."

People were always looking over the edge of the wharf on the alien life of ocean.

"Why didn't you?"

"I should have. I wanted to. There was a man following me."

"Do men always follow you?"

"I don't complain. I like some men better than others."

I was heavily flippant, tasting the first flavor of jealousy, unwarranted and sour.

"Do they catch up with you?"

"Sometimes. If I like."

She asked me about my life; I told her awkwardly at

first, and then the words came in a rush. I discovered that I had longed to talk about it; and there was a compatibility about Jerry that made it easy.

"You love the sea, don't you?"

We had neared the northern end of the beach and were returning.

"Look at it now," I said.

It was a pool of beauty. The moon was higher now, and caught the crests of the lazy combers in a white and gleaming lace.

"This is the best time, the night. Way out there you disturb the albatrosses from their sleep, and they run over the water to find their wings. Tonight their feet would leave tracks of fire; tonight if I were there I'd be so full of it I couldn't even sing. It's magic at night; even to look at it; even to swim in it."

She loosed my arm abruptly and turned her back to me. "Unhook me," she commanded.

I stood like a dummy and she looked back at me over her shoulder.

"My dress," she said patiently. "Unhook it."

My fingers trembled so I could hardly manage it; then the dress went flying over her head as she darted towards the water, dropping other garments as she ran, so that each wanton heap of her clothing lay a few yards closer to the sea than the last. She turned and called to me as she went under the breakers like a seal; and clumsily enough I hurried after her.

The phosphorescence of the summer ocean picked out a rare beauty, for her body had a sylph's proportions molded to a strength of muscle beneath the skin, and the moon sought its highlights, revealing her in glistening movement rather than in outline, accentuating the easy correlation that, I realized, gave such attraction to her walk. Her back was a column of beauty, her buttocks lean and symmetrical, her breasts deep, full and set apart, but still pert. The water plastered her hair close, and the beautiful, beautiful eyes glowed in a face freshened and shining from the quicksilver sea.

For the sea that had encouraged my loneliness, that had demanded indeed the whole of my attention, now displayed in one protracted and beautiful revelation the whole concentration and essence of what I had sacrificed or overlooked in my devotion to it. It was even fitting that I had thought her ugly; it was as though the sea had invested her with beauty, as though the sea had called upon its magic to provide me with this special revelation.

My sex, that had been only intermittently and inquiringly aroused through all the years of my life, was now awakened and clamant; it dominated my eyes and ears, and demanded the full attention of my other senses. I reached for my girl, hunting her far out where the breakers began and the swelling ocean joined the night, and she allowed herself to be caught, but not retained; laughing, wriggling, active; a water sprite, turning against me and away, quick as a fish; so that I knew that if she desired it she could have left me far behind.

We played and shouted in the water until she turned once and, seemingly without any of the calculation I had always found necessary, caught an incipient breaker and rode it to the beach. I took the next, and came running as she rose from her wave in shallow water, and caught her cold and burning body close to me, and kissed a girl in passion for the first time in my life.

We had emerged from the sea a long way from the place at which we had entered it; and now nevertheless ran in the opposite direction, hand in hand, alone in a world of movement between the breakers and the sand, with the water spurting cold against our skins as we raced through the shallows. We ran for half a mile, perhaps, and when on a single impulse we stopped, we turned to each other in an embrace, my chest embodied in her soft full breasts, her hard little belly and thighs straining to mine, and her arms about me.

She drew me down to the sand, and there on the hard wet foreshore I took the generous gift of her and knew the essence of beauty. The sea's music was accompaniment; there was a backdrop of moon and stars and the immaculate white dunes.

We lay like that until a questing wave came up, racing along her legs and chest, chilling my elbows and my legs; and then we rose laughing.

"You're beautiful."

"I'm not. I like you saying it."

"But you are."

The tide was coming in. We started walking back, naked as the night.

"And I was your first girl. I was, wasn't I?"

"Are you glad?"

"No, truly. Was I?"

"The very first."

My shoes were in the water, filled with water and sand. One sock had washed away. My shorts were swinging back and forth in the waves. We followed the absurd double line of clothing back; my shirt and trousers were dry, just above the reach of the incoming water; so was her dress. Her little scraps of underwear were gone, and we didn't care at all. We laughed like zanies, and dressed in what was there. But we walked no farther than the foot of the sandhills, and there I reached for her again, and again we made love, bedded on a nest of our clothing.

She was a priestess of love; she knew the secrets, all the secrets; she involved every part of her body with the duties and the joys of love, from the tips of her toes to her sea-dank hair.

There was not a muscle of her body but was aware of every contact, and quivering its message of response. Her fingers clung and caressed with a delicate intensity that had no parallel in the experience of my imagination or my dreams; her nipples, stiff and live and pliant, clung and caressed like the tips of sensitive fingers. Her lips and her tongue proclaimed her joy and her gladness; the mechanisms of her mouth were a mighty evocation of pleasures immediate and remote; she brought even her eyelashes into play. Her arms and her legs took me in custody; they were firm and gentle servants of her needs.

"Oh, Jerry, Jerry."

"You like the way I make love?"

"Jerry."

1 1 1

"You like it?"

"How did you ever learn?" I asked, and could have bitten my offending tongue away.

"My mother taught me," she said complacently. "Years and years and years ago. She was very beautiful, my mother; she was the most beautiful woman I have ever seen. Me, I look like my father. Ugly."

"Not ugly."

"Well. It's nighttime."

"You're beautiful."

"You know I'm not."

"It couldn't have been years and years ago. How old are you, Jerry?"

"Seventeen. Seventeen last month."

"Me, I'm twenty-two."

"You're just a baby. You're just beginning." She smiled, and then sat up to take my hand and cradle it against her firm and yielding breast, so coldly sculptured in the moonlight, so heated with an inward fire.

"It couldn't have been years and years ago," I said again, and she laughed, low in her throat.

"It was, though," she said. "You'd have to know my mother. She was a flame, a dancing light; she lived for one thing in the world and that was love. She worshiped love, and loving; she used to say that love was in you, that was where it was made, and the more you drew it out the more you had. It didn't matter what you loved, she said; some love came back and you made more, and then the space was always full."

I looked up, conscious of my cheek's movement against her skin.

"You mean physical love, the act of love?" I asked.

"I mean any kind of love," she said. There was sand clinging to her thigh when I looked down, and I brushed it away.

"If my mother hadn't a man to love she would take a doll; or a walking stick and tie a ribbon round its throat, and make a little hat for its head, and hold it against her cheek and make love to it. When I was twelve she used to send me down the street, to find two men and bring them to the house where she was waiting."

"Jerry!" I exclaimed, offended beyond all measure.

"No it's true," she insisted. "And now you don't like me any more."

But her eyes were dancing and she was smiling, and we fell into the practices of lovers once again; but later in the night she talked some more.

Her father was a printer in a small town, a town just big enough to have a daily newspaper. He left the house each night at six o'clock and returned each morning at five. On the weekends he hit the bottle; most of his hours at home he spent snoring in his bed.

As soon as he was safely away at work, Jerry, whose physical development must have been precocious, would dress and go to find male company for her mother, who never left the house in the evenings. The dwelling stood apart from all others in a waste ground enlivened only by the flowers her mother grew in tiny crammed beds, flowers grown only to decorate the house interior.

"And when you brought these fellows back you'd go to bed with one?" I asked.

She nodded.

"Pretty soon. If he wanted me to. Or if I could make him — I'd try to make him. I wanted so much to be like my mother; she was beautiful in everything she did. Her voice was nice too. I bet you've never seen anyone so lovely."

"But at twelve years old?"

"Oh, I'd had a boy before that. Often. My mother didn't know, I guess. Not for a start. She had a regular lover then; he came each night and brought the boy — his wife thought they were walking. I don't know. Anyway, my mother found us together one night when she came in from the bedroom; she caught us right in the act, I guess; she came in the room and she laughed. And it was after that that she began to teach me. And it was when her lover found out that he left her; but she didn't mind that really either."

"And your father never suspected?"

"After I left the house my mother used to sit down and make the lounge room ready. When I came back there'd be a pack of cards on the table, thrown about; but if you looked at them you'd see they'd fit into a hand played. And there'd be papers covered with euchre scores, or five hundred — real games; you could work them out as if we'd played all night. And the ashtrays all filled with butts and only half of them lipsticked; and glasses, and fresh empty bottles — she'd pour beer down the sink, unless the men brought some and wanted a couple of drinks. Even then she'd pour some down the sink when they weren't looking. She'd have me shuffle the cards in the daytime, so they got worn and soiled, little by little. And, oh, lots of other things. She thought of everything, my mother."

We stayed there until the dawn in our nest of clothes among the sand; and beyond the dawn, until the rising sun brought out the Sun-Worshiper to do her exercises at the water's edge. Jerry nodded at the spectacle with understanding.

"She loves her body too, but in a different way," she said. "My mother worshiped hers, and pampered it. She taught me to love mine."

We waited longer, till the sun was high enough to bake us, but then people came to the beach and we left. She caught a tram somewhere; she would not let me come.

I didn't sleep or work; I lay in the sun in a happiness that was clouded with questions. Jerry's could have been accounted a sordid story, but that was the one thing I was not prepared to admit. Still, I think that I was not in love with her; I was in love with loving, and I had fallen harder than most. And, ingenuous and undeveloped tyro that I was, I had sophistication enough to realize that from that chance encounter I had soared above and beyond a fumbling, out-of-balance stage of accidental discovery, and curiosity, and experimentation.

The love of ocean that had kept me chaste these years had brought me in the closing and opening of an eye to this upper level. I had discovered the glory of sex appreciated, and delightedly shared, as one discovers an

island in great waters, with certainty, and instant awareness of the whole event. I had sighted the pain and the
happiness and the beauty all at once; most of the joys of
exploration were to follow, but in the passing of a night
I had come triumphant into new latitudes and now
looked upon the world from a fresh vantage.

I met Jerry by arrangement that night and for several
nights thereafter. My schooner stayed tied to the bollards
on the Customs wharf, her nets slung on the line between
the trawl davits. I made one expedition to the forest for
bark; I had tanbark in plenty to treat my nets and lines,
but when I tanned the sails I used to add a measure of
the green bark of the kahimai tree; it added unpredictable
color to the mixture in the big copper boilers, so that in
addition to being protected against the rot of untreated
canvas, my sails were a riot of high browns and reds, and
when they weathered somewhat there were traces of
cerise and rose among the fawns, the grays and the
browns. It was a conceit of mine that I had discovered
for myself, and I had to travel some distance to locate
kahimai trees.

But that was the only distraction I allowed myself in
the period that I knew Jerry. It was not a long period; it
ended the day following the arrival of the new moon.

Each night we spent upon the sand, engrossed with
ourselves and the sea.

She brought me presents: a red sweater that was too
short, a watch that stopped going the week after I lost
her. Once it was a bunch of flowers; once three white

linen handkerchiefs. I have thought since she might have stolen these things; perhaps she did.

I hid a pair of rugs near our best-loved haunt, so that I would not have to walk to the beach with them at evening, inviting comment. She would not let me meet her elsewhere. She would not let me share her days. She seemed to have no money, or not much; and I had very little. But with the sea and the beach and the night we were rich and had no need of money; we were loose and free and subject only to our momentary desires, like the gulls that played in the daytime turbulence of air above the breakers, or the saffron butterflies that flitted unconcerned among the lupin flowers.

The scent of lupin does not bring her memory back; a certain blending of this scent with the salt sea smell, tinged with the iodine of the sea wrack and tempered by a night moisture is an infallible agent; but it is a rare combination in the places I now frequent.

I worried one night, belatedly, about the possibility of her pregnancy, and was rewarded with a smile so tender it transformed her.

"Well, if I am, it doesn't matter. I won't come asking for a wedding ring."

"You wouldn't marry me?"

"I don't want to marry anyone. But I'd like a baby. I'd like *your* baby, if I had it. I'd teach it loving; I'd teach it from the day it was born."

"Suppose it was a boy?"

She looked up with a smile that was pure mischief.

"You think I couldn't handle that, eh? You think I'm not qualified?"

The new moon came in with a rainstorm, and I didn't think Jerry would come to the beach, but I waited for her in the downpour and she didn't disappoint me. I hailed a taxi and we went to my schooner.

"This is it," she said. "This is the one I nearly came aboard."

"You should have," I told her. "We wasted four days."

Within its fairly narrow confines the schooner offered a little comfort. We had a fire in the galley, a cupboard-like compartment opening off the cabin; and it warmed the whole ship. I had stores there too, and towards morning she cooked a meal, so that we felt domestic. And to tell the truth the schooner never afterward seemed complete.

"We'll come again tomorrow," I said, but she shook her head.

"Tomorrow — that's today — meet me on the beach. In the afternoon. At two o'clock. Be there for sure, no matter what the weather's like."

Two o'clock was only eight hours away.

It was still raining then, but she hurried me along the sandhills to our haven and undressed in the rain with fingers trembling with haste. We had a strange hour of passion, stung with the driving drops, consumed with urgency. Suddenly she jumped to her feet and reached for her things where I had bundled them inside mine and packed them in the partial dryness beneath a bush. Her tanned skin was raised in goose-pimples; her lower lip was quivering, and I thought it was from the cold, but it was not, for she was crying.

"Run, run," she urged. "I haven't long. I have to catch a train."

"Where are you going? When will I see you?"

She shook her head. At the station she kissed me so violently that people stared. She released me just in time to leap to the carriage as it moved away. Not till that moment did I realize that she had no baggage, and I never saw her again. Not till then did I realize that I didn't know her second name; she knew that I was not "Joe," for I had told her; but who she was or where she came from, where she went to and why I have never learned. It was wrong that she should have caught the train; she should have gone back to the ocean. She was at one with the carefree discipline of the wild and obedient water.

8

UNTIL I went to sea I had neither knowledge nor conception of the vast and wonderful landscapes upon which the liquid ocean is based, nor did it occur to me that they are even more surely and extravagantly varied than the familiar hills and valleys filled similarly with the fluid air. And I think that this was the first and greatest surprise that I had of my new companions, that the wisest of them were utterly familiar with this landscape beneath the waves.

They knew its varying composition and its contours, and the way in which the animals they hunted were affected by the physical construction of their world. As a man of the forest knows that deer in the velvet seek the trees, that moose in the winter frequent the frozen lakes, that crows in the springtime follow the line of thaw, so the fishermen were aware.

They knew that sharks, for example, love to cruise beneath the crest of an undersea precipice, to take the traveling herds of lesser fish at the disadvantage they suffer in transit from one pressure to a lighter one. They knew that scaled fish when traveling face, in general, into the current, a life-long movement compensated for by the helpless travel of eggs and fry in the opposite direction. They knew that shell-eating fish range the wide mud plains, that the female crayfish seldom leaves the rock on which she is first established, but that the male is a great traveler (so that crayfish caught in trawls operating over sandy levels are almost inevitably males), and a thousand other minutiae essential to the successful pursuit of their trade.

This knowledge they kept to themselves; not from any motive of making the trade a mystery, but simply because it was regarded as so elementary as to be in the common knowledge. But it would be betrayed from time to time.

For example, old Andrew Linklater, early arrival at the fish wharf, consigns his fish to the market and waits for the later boats to come in. Salty Smith arrives near the last; he has a wonderful freight of good fish which Andrew unashamedly envies; but Salty isn't inclined to divulge where he got them, hoping to keep it to himself for a few days.

"A good freight," says Andrew. "Where were ye?"

"Out on the East Reef."

"Ah, the East Reef. What water had ye?"

"Forty-five fathoms."

"Ah."

When Salty's back is turned Andrew, very delicately, lifts a wisp of weed, like a grass stem, from its entanglement in one of Salty's lines, and examines it carefully. He says nothing, but when Salty returns to his ground next day, thirty miles from the East Reef, Andrew is there before him. His identification of the spot was accurate, and based upon slight but to him substantial evidence.

The fish were the wrong color for an East Reef freight, the scrap of weed did not grow in forty-five fathoms, and there was, among the crated fish, a Jock Stewart on which the pattern (which this fish lights with varying hues to suit its particular background) indicated very strongly a rock formation altogether different from that upon the East Reef. Fishermen in those days cleaned their boats and their gear as thoroughly as it was possible to do. They were unblushing liars, but never resentful when their deceptions were uncovered.

All the main features of the undersea world had their names. There was the East Reef, the South Reef and the North Reef. There was the Baby Farm, where shoals of smaller fish flourished. There was the Hospital, where nearly every captured fish had recent wound scars. The fisherman's theory, and I know no better one, was that on this plain flourished a curative weed, which sick and ailing fish came there to seek. There was the Woman's Chest, a range of hills named not for its own conformation, but for the shape of the hills thirty miles away that were used as a marker here. There was the Cuckoo's Nest and Shinerville, named for Shiner Green and Cuckoo Ryan, two men of the fleet. There was the Tyrone

Rock, which had caused a famous wreck, the Remarkable Rock, and the Rock.

None of these names were on the charts; they applied to undersea features of no interest to anyone at all save the fishermen. There was one large plain where fishing was impracticable because of the prevalence of sea lice, flesh-eating crustaceans resembling their terrestrial relatives the common wood lice found in gardens, but death-white, and about the size of little-finger joints. A young mako shark took my line once, south of here, a line buoyed with an empty five-gallon drum and anchored with a grappling hook. The shark towed them both around the sea for nearly an hour, and then, exhausted, lay upon the bottom. The sea lice, unable to swim, swarmed upon it. When I hauled it up, perhaps another hour later, it was dead. It was more than dead, it was nothing but skin surrounding cartilage; but so packed with the lice that it retained the form of a shark even when I landed it upon the deck. That stretch was called the Barren Ground; it must have been a valley of horror for most of the sea animals.

The fishermen of the port were fanatical individualists, but still armed against the outside world with a tremendous loyalty to their kind.

It was a saying that there was no job the local fleet could not successfully undertake, no problem beyond the capacity of one or another of its members. Included among the personnel who manned the sixty boats were ex-teachers, ex-scientists, builders, engineers, an ex-miner, a jeweler, a draper, several accountants and a man who had once been a doctor. Their nationalities were as various. There were one or two Polynesians, some Portuguese, numbers of Italians, a Finn, a Dane, an Icelander, three Norwegians, a Russian, a Turk, and a mystery who was sometimes thought to be Arab.

The first skipper with whom I sailed was a delightful old shellback named George who had been round the Horn in sail more than once. It was his joy to teach, and the subject at his command was rope and rigging. In the long evenings we worked upon hitches, bends, knots and splices — long splices for hemp and wire, Navy splices, French ball splices, back splices, merchant navy splices, a hundred kinds of knots and splices, each with its particular application, each with its special purpose. I learned the fancy knots of sennet, round and square and half-round and corkscrew, and sword-matting; hangman's nooses and jury-mast knots, manrope knots and rolling hitches and Tom-Fool knots, until the rope would make its own convolutions within my barely directed fingers.

I learned the six masts of a Yankee schooner — the fore, main, mizzen, jigger, spanker and driver — and the surprising switch: on the rare occasions when schooners had seven, they were named after the days of the week: Sunday, Monday, Tuesday . . . I learned the canvas from the deck upward: the main, the maintop, lower and upper, the main-t'gallants, lower and upper, the royals, the skysail and the moonsail, with the stu'ns'ls out from the yards. The rigs: barks and barkentines, brigs, brigantines, hermaphrodite brigs; schooners, ketches and yawls; tops'l schooners and ships. And snows and scows and a plethora of variants.

I had been no more than a week at sea when the occasion arose for us to make an extended trip, necessitating keeping two watches. The *Silver Crest* was powered with a large Scotch Marine boiler and a triple expansion steam engine, and since there were but four of us in the crew it followed that each watch had to consist of a helmsman and an engineer.

George himself was an engineer, but his love was to hold the wheel and set the course; and besides, on the first leg of the voyage we had to negotiate the harbor channel, the bar, and certain shallows and rocks adjacent to the coast. The engineer had long been asleep; it was past midnight when we cast off, and he had come aboard some hours before with a heavy cargo of the local brew. The other deckhand had gone below. I coiled the hawsers and came to the wheelhouse, expecting to be given the wheel while George attended the engine.

"Go down and put a shovel of coal on," he told me; and I went, with some misgivings; for I had penetrated the heat and the clangor of that unventilated inferno which was the engine room no more than two or three times, and then had paid scant notice to the engineer and his task. Moreover, I knew nothing whatever about machinery.

I opened the firedoor, and persisted in the blistering heat until I had thrown a half-dozen shovels of coal into the glow; and then came up again.

George looked at me disapprovingly. "That's no way

to throw coal on," he said. "The steam dropped ten pounds. You want to spread it round a bit, and get the firedoor shut again as fast as you can."

"I'm sorry," I said.

"It's all right. But in a minute or two you better run the slice through the fire."

"What's a slice?"

"That thing like a long poker. Run it along the firebars under the fire once or twice, and then lift it. Break the crust on top of the fire and let the air through."

I went down again.

"You've got to do it quicker than that," he told me when I came up. "You had the firedoor open too long again. Keep watching your steam gauge. You have to keep it high and regular. Did you oil round?"

I confessed I hadn't.

"What do I oil?"

"Anything that's moving."

So down I went. I had some difficulty locating lubrication points on the bearings; for this was not only my first steam engine, but the first engine of any sort whatever that I had had anything to do with.

"You'd better grease the shafts," he said when I appeared. "You'll find a handmop in some black grease. Hold it against the shafts where they go into the packing boxes, and work it round, kind of. And it's about time to put some more coal on. Spread it round this time. Keep it away from the front of the fire but."

For four hours I tended the engine by proxy. When the engineer arrived he was horrified to find all the bearings in certain link gear running white-hot, and rigged a pump to play seawater on them. I hadn't known of their existence. The boiler pressure was keeping up admirably; that was because the water level was well below the danger point. When I heard the stream of Glaswegian invective, I decided then and there to forego my sleep. I spent the watch in the engine room, following every move of the engineer, and then it was my turn again.

I spent twelve hours straight in that engine room, stripped down to trousers and shoes, and emerging briefly into the upper air, where light snow was falling. George, without shifting from his seat in the wheelhouse — located where he could hold or turn the wheel with a foot against the spokes — had trained another engineer.

A few weeks later I had the job to myself. Some time after that I was capable of taking the ship down-channel by myself; setting the fire, throwing off the hawsers and taking the wheel without another soul on board. It was an admirable trait of George's that he could trust expensive gear to his underlings; he never had a moment's worry about it.

My relationship with him was peculiar. I worked on other ships before I acquired my own; at any time I could leave them and throw my gear aboard the trawler. George would welcome me, and sometimes seize the opportunity to take a holiday ashore. I never knew what my pay was. George would come down and give me a handful of notes, sometimes without counting them. In good weeks it was more, in poor weeks less.

The ship was victualed through George's leaving a sum

of money in a tin. Anyone who wanted to add to the stores took money from there and bought them; at the end of the week George would count what was left and bring it up to its original amount, more or less. No accounting was ever made, and no one, as far as I am aware, ever used the money for his private purposes, though each member of the crew would normally buy some delicacy or other that the rest didn't care for. Later, when he acquired a cabin boy, a fair proportion went on chocolate.

That was the security of those years: I could always get a job with George, and it carried meals and accommodation, and money proportionate to what he had. That we cooked the meals sometimes on the lagging of the steam pipes, sometimes on a rickety galley stove made little difference. The meals consisted of fish. On Fridays, when we were paid, we ate meat. George also had an arrangement with a small café; he settled the account if and when we ate there.

Once, on another ship, I went to exploit the unfished waters on the wild western coast of New Zealand. There were seventeen in the expedition, seventeen men on four good ships, each carrying two or three dinghies for dory fishing. The expedition was made possible by reason of the fact that, several years before, a company had purchased an old steel hull, fitted it out with refrigerating machinery, and had it towed to a remote corner of one of the fjords on that coast. The *Stella* had been one of the first lighthouse tenders in New Zealand; it was built of Lowmore iron and was sound, but it had been abandoned for years.

We found her and boarded her. We renewed the crazy pipeline that brought a supply of fresh water from a creek on the rockface not fifty yards away. We cut timber, and fired her ancient boilers with it. We got the refrigerating machinery to operate, and began to fish.

It was an enchanted place. The precipitous mountains rose six and seven thousand feet straight up from the fjord; the sea ran in these deep defiles thirty and forty miles inland among the mountains. In a passage between two of the fjords, between Dusky and Breaksea, opposite a blind defile called Wet Jacket arm, we tied our ship to shrubby trees on the cliff face and on the other side of that slim hull dropped our lines to test the depth. Seven lines ran out; two hundred and ten fathoms, twelve hundred and sixty feet to the bottom of that undersea cliff. And perhaps even that was not the bottom, but a broad ledge. It was too deep for fishing there; that was all we had to establish.

We came in the Christmas season, when the rata trees were ablaze with crimson flowers. The ratas, much prized by us for the strength of the natural bends we cut from their trunks and branches, flourished when their feet were in salt water; the islands and the less precipitous cliffs, then, were banded above water level with this brilliant hue in a depth of perhaps fifty or sixty feet. Growing beneath the ratas was a bush called tete-a-weka; its purple-centered white daisy-like flowers set a tinted band between the crimson ratas and the blue waters. The forest behind was a silent forest; no one had ever come to disturb its solitudes.

There is a rumor still of a lost Maori tribe that inhabits these fastnesses, the remnants of the Kati-Mamoe. But if they live there and are attuned to those mountains they will never be found; a footstep makes no sound upon the damp leaves that carpet that forest floor, and leaves but little sign. There is a plenitude of feathered game, and a wealth of fish.

The charts were hopelessly inadequate. They had not been amended since H.M.S. *Acheron,* in the eighteen-sixties, had made the first survey. We sheltered at night in a harbor called Luncheon Cove; the entrance to it was so narrow that as we crashed through, our rigging caught and broke the branches of trees on both sides of the channel. A stranger approaching that place would have thought that the ships had disappeared into the tree-lined hillside as they negotiated the S-shaped passage; our entire operation, had it been a secret one, could have been completely hidden.

And in that place, a sea level pocket among the craggy peaks, the stars shone as I have never seen them from the earth elsewhere; the night was still and silent, except for the hoarse cries of penguins, swimming guard before the nesting-burrows of their mates, and the barking of seals, and the fish leaping in play.

Waterfalls sprang out from the cliffs, and in the sunshine threw rainbows; though more often the rain mingled with their spray. Permanent snow laced the highest peaks, mated for whiteness with the foam of the crashing surf on the outer ramparts of the district. No other men were there but ourselves, and perhaps the remnants of that lost tribe.

Therefore the birds that lived there had no fear of man; the Maoris among us — there were three of them — showed us how to take them without weapons, concealing each capture from other birds so that they did not lose their trust. We could gather ducks' eggs as from a barnyard. If we waded across a narrow part of any of the sounds the fish came up to investigate; ten-pound moki nubbed against our legs in curiosity. The water was so still and clear that we could follow the commerce of the sea creatures seven fathoms down, and this particularly in a place inaccurately named the Nine Fathom Passage.

There I would lie in a canted dinghy and watch the blue cod about their happy pursuits on the bottom; and be puzzled to see them flash into their crannies in the rocks, and have the mystery explained in a minute or so when the slim and beautiful shape of a cruising shark swam within the compass of my eyesight. In waters shallower still we caught crayfish with a boat hook, needing no skill nor any proper gear where the numbers were so great. We clubbed a seal or two for the table; and once we caught a moose by the antlers as it swam the sound, and lifted it to the boat davits of the *Stella* and butchered it, and put it in the freezer. We lived well, all upon the country, with a little rice cooked for convention.

But the expedition was not a success. Within the fjords the depths did not, in the main, allow for successful fishing. Outside in the open sea they were adequate, even excellent, and the catches proportionately good, but the weather was so severe as to confine us to sheltered waters most of the time.

Nevertheless we caught good fish, keeping only the highest in quality, and freezing it with the resources of the *Stella*. Her holds were almost filled when, after six weeks or a couple of months, the two men we had left to keep watch on the machinery opened the wrong cocks, put pressure in the freezing pipes, and turned the whole chamber into an oven. We did not discover their mistake for more than twelve hours; and all the work of all our men was destroyed; the fish cooked in the cases and quite valueless. At that we gave the whole expedition away, cut our losses and returned to civilization, leaving the *Stella* where she lies today.

Financially, each one of us suffered a disastrous loss. We came back to the tiny town called The Bluff with nothing to show for our efforts. We could not even have consoled ourselves with liquor except that a Maori among us who went by the name of Honey had picked up a sizable lump of ambergris which we sold for a fair price, and Honey and I and a huge redheaded Norwegian spent it on whisky. It was, I felt, a good investment at that stage.

I had many an expedition in good rough company among the islands and the rocks, the storms and the halcyon days; but most of the time I worked alone; never lonely, but alone. For the second time I bought a little schooner, smaller than my first, but a sweet and lovely hull, thirty-two feet in length, double-ended and narrow.

She had a bad reputation, and was lying neglected on the mud of an estuary. She whipped badly in a storm, they said; she was erratic and dangerous. I guessed her over-heavily ballasted, threw out a ton or two of metal and discovered the sweetest-tempered vessel I had known. I traveled into little ports with her; ports where fishermen had not operated, or operated in craft so crazy they were no use except in the best of weather.

I met Alfred in such a port. He was a big, handsome Maori boy, an axman working for a sawmill, strong and full of confidence, a swaggering swashbuckler, unafraid. He'd swim out to me while I put the schooner on its moorings, and give me a hand to get my freight ashore in the small dinghy I owned. Or sometimes he'd gather a bucket full of pipis, and lever them open, working one shell upon the other, half for me and half for himself. Often and often I've basked in the last of the sunshine, compensating for a hungry day with Alfred's pipis and talking about the world outside, which I knew little enough about, and he had never seen.

But Alfred had discovered the key to it. He was practicing to be the best axman who had ever lived; surely he had not far to go. In competition within the district he was unbeatable; his times were comparable to the best in the country, and he was young, and filled with energy and ambition. He was clever too; he had a good intellect; and he had established in his own mind the worth of the theory that prominence in one small field would not be an end in itself, but would provide him with an eminence from which he could survey whatever else offered.

Perhaps the world of motion pictures or the stage might have opened up to him; he was an Apollo, he could sing like a Polynesian angel, his voice had both power and a rare quality. He had inherited too the natural Polynesian gift for oratory. He could make a quick decision, unusual in that rural district. He was inventive and could satisfy his requirements from materials at hand. He had a good personality and an easy address and his expression was always both happy and inquiring.

His attachment to me, as I realized early, was not for myself alone, but for my dinghy. He had the loan of it whenever it was free; he cut a red pine sapling and stepped it for a mast, and hung an old tarpaulin from a yard, and taught himself to sail, though I warned him about the lack of a keel or a centerboard. He little cared that he could travel only with the wind; he'd sail across the many miles of estuary free as a bird, and pull stoutly back with the oars I had cut (with ax and drawknife) from a stand of kahikatea trees.

That estuary provided everything a man could want: fish in the water, and birds and pigs in the forest. There was a seam of coal free for the taking; it underlay the harbor in shallow water, and sometimes at a high tide I'd row the dinghy out and anchor over it, and then swim home. At low tide I'd walk out and fill the stranded dinghy; and at the next high, swim out and row it back.

Alfred helped me, with his muscle and his company.

Came a day in a week of wild and windy weather,

when I was too late to advise Alfred against taking the dinghy. He was accompanied this time by a brother and a friend, the local schoolteacher, and went out to show them the paces of the little boat. He did not tell me his intention, but I saw him flying crazily beyond an island that centered the estuary, in a mist of spray, with wind-lashed torrents of rain pursuing him.

At midnight his mother awakened me with the news that the boys had not come home. Her shawled face glistened with the rain that had soaked her, and in her panic her features had assumed the wild strong set that I identify, rightly or wrongly, with the pre-European Maori. I lived then in a hut near the harborside, and I helped her to raise the alarm.

The men of the district left their beds, and in small parties scoured the shoreline of the estuary, where they could. But in that wild wind, that shrieking night, there was only scant hope of success; most of the searchers stayed no more than an hour or two with their tasks, and came back to wait for light.

With the dawn the storm boiled up to a height. And with the dawn we found the dinghy, empty, floating in the current, its jury-mast snapped, its oars and rowlocks lost, upturned and partially stove. A few hours later we found Alfred's hipboots, neatly together and placed — surely by Alfred's hand — high above the watermark on a distant part of the shore. Somehow he had managed to swim to shore, wearing them, had stowed them safely, and returned to the water to try to save his brother and his friend.

There were thirty miles of coastline in the estuary, thirty rugged miles of rock and cliff and tangled forest, and while the searchers spread out I turned to my own responsibility, went to the launch and put my fishing nets in order, so that I could drag the deeper channels for the bodies. Before I could set out I was joined by eight or ten companions, of whom three were parsons of differing denominations, and all were unused to the water and its ways.

Then, when I was young, I had a contempt and a distaste for this company. With the intemperance of my kind I classified these men as ghouls, avid to taste the sensation of the task ahead, however sad and gloomy it might be. They cluttered up my schooner; in attempting to lend a hand they tangled my nets and my gear. With their questions and comments they intensified the sense of guilt from which I was suffering (for though I had warned Alfred times enough, I had not myself believed in any vulnerability of that splendid body, that indomitable spirit).

But I was wrong, of course. They were driven by their need to give a token help. They represented that vast mass of humanity who, in any tragedy, are capable of nothing more than standing by. They envied me my ability to do something practical. They willingly endured the whipping wind, the biting cold, the infectious despondency. They stood about my deck and waited, and I see now, as I did not then, that they also served.

All day I towed my nets along the channels, sweeping sometimes into adjacent bays, feeling the shortened warps with a constant hand so that I might escape the worst damage from the snags, the anchored tree stumps, the sunken logs that littered the estuary bottom. I ripped my nets to pieces nevertheless on that unchancy ground; I would haul them up and mend them to the best of my ability and set them down again, trying to supervise my unwanted crew, trying to keep them out of the road.

Sometimes they hailed the searchers who walked the shores, watching the outgoing tide. Sometimes they urged me to explore areas too shallow for my gear; and if I trusted one with the tiller for a moment he would, in his anxiety and his ignorance, foul up the tow with some impractical maneuver.

At nightfall we stopped; and next day the press was slighter. I had worked till midnight over my nets, bringing them up to efficiency again, and in the first hour, when I hauled in, the body of the schoolteacher was enmeshed in the trawl. He looked cold and peaceful; we took him to the little landing place where Alfred had often waited with his pipis, and left him there with a somber guard. Most of the population in that place had Maori ancestry, and the wailing of the waiting women was added now to the moan and bluster of the storm winds.

They gave him a funeral on the following day; I was not there. But I could see the little group of returning mourners when I came to the landing place with the body of Alfred's brother. My passengers all had left me then; I was cold and tired, and anxious to leave that place, but I felt that I had the responsibility still of finding Alfred.

Nevertheless I wanted, while I had the chance, to look at the seas that raged outside the harbor so that I might estimate when the practicability of departure would be likely; and without telling anyone of my intention I set my schooner, under power, for the harbor mouth. I had the additional motive that the tide had almost risen to its full height; and towards the top of the flood the seas would, at the junction of estuary and ocean, be slightly less dangerous than at any other time.

The harbor entrance was sheltered by a long rocky cape which extended southward. The river ran between this cape, hugging its edge, and a long sandspit which ran parallel; a sandspit up high, and reaching inward from an ocean beach two or three miles in length. This beach took the full force of ocean, but where it came behind the cape the channel was extremely narrow and the transition here between the wild ocean and the harbor calm was, therefore, abrupt, even immediate. I ran my schooner up on a sandy beach on the sheltered side of the cape, jumped from the prow with the anchor in my arms, wedged it in a safe rock cranny, and climbed the hill to see the ocean.

It was raging, tormented, as wild as I had ever seen it; but, intrigued by the hope that I could soon put to sea and leave that place, I thought I detected a roadway, as it were, leading outward from the harbor mouth, an area in which the huge combers were moderated, sweeping in less precipitous formation towards the beach.

From the height at which I stood I was not sure. I wanted to see it again from water level. I ran down the hill, picked up the anchor from the rock cleft, reboarded the schooner and started the engine. As of habit, I slipped bamboo rods over the engine controls (one for throttle, one for gear lever) so that I could manipulate them from the tiller, and headed down the last two hundred yards of sheltered channel to look at the sea. I was counting on the fact that the tide was still on the flood; when I stopped the engine I would hold in place, without venturing into the maelstrom.

But I was tired, unreasonably shaken by the events of the day — the wailing women, the second corpse, the useless passengers — and I had failed to notice that the tide had changed.

With all those miles of estuary behind such a narrow and confined entrance, the change was immediate, and immediately fully effective. The current, which had been racing inward at five knots, was now, within the space of a few moments, raised to a similar speed in an outward direction. I came to the harbor mouth, throttled down, threw the engine into reverse — and found it too late. I was swept out in the path of the oncoming breakers. Only one action was effective. I put my engine ahead again, and turned with accelerating speed to meet the oncoming wave.

It was a huge wave, as big as any I have seen since; it swept towards me with horrifying power; but at least I knew I could negotiate it. Its ramparts were not so steep but that I knew I could mount them. My speed was sufficient, and I had the utmost faith in my craft. A stone's throw to port the water threw its fury against the toe of the cliff, mounting to the zenith of the sky; behind me the broken combers raced to the steep sandspit, where I would be broken if I went with them. I was in a passage so narrow I could not turn to retreat to the harbor; and if I went astern my speed would not be adequate to stem the outward flow of the tide behind me. I mounted the wave ahead, and from its crest I saw the nature of the ordeal I had yet to face.

For the second wave was as large as the first. But it was more fully developed. It was rearing high, mountain-high, and getting ready to break. And still I had no choice. I had to meet it as it came.

It seemed to take an age for the thirty-two-foot length of my schooner to nose into that concave, moving hill. My bows rose up and up, until in my fancy it seemed that my keel stood vertical against the wave, and I thought that I might pitch-pole, fall back deck-down before the wave, and be carried, twisting and turning, rolling and dashed against the rocky bottom, into the sandspit. My fancy could not have strayed far from fact; my keel must indeed have reared close to upright. And at that moment I threw myself on the deck of the cockpit behind the thwart, straining with back and legs to make myself a part of the boat's construction, and reaching up to hold the tiller steady and central with both my hands.

The wave broke. It flooded the cockpit, put me quite underneath the freezing blow of green water, knocked the breath from my lungs. It shuddered the ship with hammer blows. But even as I felt them, I felt too the ship surmounting the crest of the wave, and going ahead, and finally falling over the crest to slam the surface with the whole length of her keel; and I rose, and looked to the sea ahead.

The following waves were smaller. I could manage them. And then I was free of the sudden shallow by the cliff toe. They were seas great enough that followed; but I could manage them.

With the second look I realized that my foremast was gone. A heavy stay of iron wire had snapped. On the top of the next wave I raced forward and chopped the single lanyard that yet held with the two-foot knife, like a sword, like a cutlass, that was always socketed to my hand, against sharks, against tangles, in the cockpit. I raced back to the tiller. I was free, and at sea.

I steered straight ahead for forty minutes before I could turn north and make my course to another port. In this again I had no other choice. I could not turn and ride those seas into the estuary — I would have no chance, or hardly any, of turning off their crests to make the narrow channel without broaching; I would be carried almost inevitably against the sandspit or the cliff.

I could not continue to face the weather in the manner most conducive to my safety; for that would take me unnecessarily out into the open sea, where land was half a world away. I could not set out an anchor here, nor yet a sea anchor, being too close by far to a lee shore. I decided to keep going with the weather on my starboard bow, at a speed just sufficient to give me headway.

And here, for the first time, I counted the damage. The breaking wave had carried away the mast, contemptuous of its strong and slender resistance. It had swept all my gear from the decks and the housing, except for some necessary fishing gear which had been lashed tightly down. It had broken windows of three-eighths-inch plate glass in the cabin housing, small windows and strong.

I had been pumping by hand; I now operated a cock I had long since installed that, in emergencies like this, sent bilgewater through the cooling system and out over the side. I had fixed filters for this purpose; additionally, my bilge was always kept clean, and the great quantities of water that now flushed it were comparatively pure.

Fore and aft, the cockpits were self-emptying; I walked in water to my knees without overmuch concern; my sole worry was to keep the large air spaces beneath the decks.

My schooner *Alice* was a living thing. Her spirit was compounded of the experience of generations of seamen with the integrity of a tradesman, a boatbuilder who loved his work, who knew his materials, could estimate the stresses to which, in some emergency, they might be put, and enjoyed the possession of a fierce honesty that knew no compromise. Her planks were of kauri, a thousand years in the tree; her ribs of American oak, her deadwoods of Australian candlewood, her naturals of ironwood and broadleaf. Her deck was of Burma teak stripped by the breakers from a merchantman that had carried them round all the world; her fastenings were of copper, the slighter ones roved, and never clenched. The mast remaining was of Norway pine, brought from the Baltic; her chain plates were wrought, not cast.

She was small, but in her being she exemplified integrity; the combined integrities of all the thousand men who, at some stage or other, had been instrumental in her creation. Her general lines had been envisioned nearly a century earlier by the bay-whalers; she was both stout and flexible, light and strong. When I was in trouble I was comforted by her honest strength; I think that no one who has not had his life dependent upon some such lovely craft can understand the living personality with which she was most certainly invested. I have known other boats for which I had a tolerance, or sometimes an affection; for this little schooner I had a love which sometimes, in reflection, still assails me.

And I was much buoyed by my love and confidence at this stage, when I took stock of my situation.

I was on a sea from which I could not approach the land; the temperature was close to freezing and the water temperature only ten degrees above. I had no provisions at all; only the fish that swam beneath me and the means of catching them. My cigarettes were in my pocket, sodden. I took them out and put them in a bracket above the engine head where I sometimes dried such things. My matches were useless. My clothing all was wet, but because of the triple oilskins, sewed like shirts without buttons to catch in lines or nets that I habitually wore, the water against my skin was a little warm. The electrical gear with which I lighted cabin and cockpit had been disconnected and some fittings broken; I could fix it when there was time, but I had no time.

I went ahead until dark; sometimes sighting the land briefly under its mantle of driving scud, but not often.

I was seeing mostly a gray and swiftly changing pattern with, at the times I rode the wave crests, some brief glimpses of the coastline I could barely recognize.

The wild sea was not a true sea. The combers did not come in regimented lines from a consistent direction; they lashed in haphazard force from any point between the eastern and southwestern markers of the horizon's compass card. I would run the risk of pooping a great sea over the quarter; the next would strike me on the beam, throwing the schooner over until her deck housing dipped into the water.

In consequence, when the light was gone, I couldn't steer by the sea, not with any hope of accuracy; nor could I use the compass, for I couldn't even strike a match to see it. I could not leave the tiller for more than a few frantic, scrabbling moments; I had to stand and shiver, and make my course as well as I might, and try to clench the chattering in my teeth until my jaw ached like a broken bone.

But then, ahead, perhaps twenty miles ahead, I picked up the occulting beam of a lighthouse I well knew. I had no way of correlating it, however, with any other light, or with any physical feature of the land; nor was there any sure means of calculating my distance from it or checking on my direction. My task was to come up close upon it, but not too close; it warned of treacherous reefs that ran, I knew, two miles to sea, and in that storm my little craft would have no hope of living.

I could not, therefore, steer straight for the light, but I must hold it upon my port beam, two or three compass points off my heading. By this means I would come ever closer to it; but as I closed it I would begin to circle it. I hoped to halt this movement in time; there was a bay comparatively sheltered northeast of the light, and I determined to find anchorage there for the night.

It took six or seven hours to bring me to a position close to the light, a position in which I was sure I had cleared the reef. In clear weather, from this spot, on an ordinary night, I would have seen the beam of light travel the cliffs behind its tower; in this storm that was impossible. Nor would any very great diminution in the size of the seas announce the anchorage. I had to keep on going into the bay; and I had to be certain to stop before I went too far.

I swung the lead line and took the depths. The best anchorage was, I remembered, in eight fathoms, close to the cliffs. I could not risk it. In twelve fathoms I pulled the engine out of gear and ran to drop anchor. I gave her close on forty fathoms of line; it was a sandy bottom, and the pressure of the waves against the hull were substantial. More, in this bay a great river ran out, a river that leaped a hundred miles down from mile-high heights; it had tremendous power, and its current in the bay held me nearly broadside to the seas.

But it was the best shelter I could find. When at last I made the bankline fast, shut off my engine and pumped the bilge dry, I could think of nothing but the need to sleep.

In such circumstances it was my habit to sleep upon the piled-up coils of bankline under the forepeak. The movement was worst here, and the rope coils far from comfortable, but on the other hand, throughout the night, the groaning of the strained bankline would lullaby my slumber. If the anchor should drag the groaning would stop; and in my previous experience that was sufficient to make me wake immediately and take the necessary measures.

This night I was too tired. It must have been noon when I awoke (for I had no means of telling the time), and my schooner stood far out to sea. The bankline stretched straight up and down at the stem; the anchor hanging forty fathoms beneath was intact, but swinging who knew how many fathoms above the ocean floor. And the storm still raged.

I estimated, or perhaps "guessed" would be a better word, the direction in which I had drifted, and made a wild stab at the distance I had gone to sea. As much by instinct as by reasoning I laid a course for the coast. It never came into view that day; about midnight I raised another familiar light; and in the early morning of my third day came in on my motor — and the last of my gasoline — to harbor.

The lighthouse tender *Tutanekai,* a ship which operated in the wildest seas on earth, had been sheltering in this harbor, and with the storm diminishing was putting to sea as I rode the combers down the harbor bar. The crew came to the rails and cheered, raising their hats and laughing. I knew then that my suspected loss had been reported; their sighting me had relieved them of a duty, and they were genuinely pleased, too, to see a fisherman safe.

I went ashore and slept for twenty-four hours. The girl who looked after me was soon to be my wife; she had lived out the storm too, with the false intelligence that I and my ship had been lost.

I wondered, then, about my leaving that safe harbor, unprepared, unknowing. I wondered whether perhaps my subconscious mind had prepared the sailing orders. I examined my motives, and could come to no fast decision. I had come from the deaths and the wailing to the life and the promise. I had been cleansed and strengthened, I thought, in the ordeal. It was a voyage such as a man must make now and then, must face and carry through. I think perhaps it was the last voyage of my adolescence, the one in which I sealed my contract with the sea.

THE FIRST time that I crossed the larger oceans I went off to the war. It plucked me out of the newspaper world, where I had moved by devious paths after events — the loss of my ship in a colorless episode at which I was not even present; the loss of financial backing — had wrecked my dream of fishing the limitless Antarctic.

I listened to the announcement of war with a heavy heart, but with a mind fully alive to the fact that though my desire had always been for peace, I myself was already personally involved.

Before the event, whenever I had thought about fighting I had hoped my campaigns would be on the seas, for there I would feel at home; there I would understand the field and could hold communion with my surroundings. But when the moment came, I decided not to fight my war there; for I saw myself only in command, as I had exercised a command for years; and I knew myself too undisciplined to rise easily from the ranks. On land and sea, I thought, the day of the lone operator had vanished with suits of armor and caparisoned chargers; only in the air did the fighting man remain, to a degree, executive. I was wrong in this assumption, but I could not know my error.

So I joined the Air Force instead, and learned to be a captain of aircraft. At least in that capacity I was dependent primarily upon my own resources, and the desirability of this was a lesson that the sea had taught me. I knew the satisfactions of a personal effort, and I was romantic enough to want to star in my own right; to ride, as it were, under my own banner, and strive towards a personal as well as a national victory. Though I deplored war, I was not blind to the exhilarations of combat.

And thanks to my first love, the ocean, I found the new element not alien at all; almost from the beginning I was in tune with its rhythms and alert to the necessity of obeying its laws; the clouds and the weather were old companions and the stars beloved signposts.

Even the rules of the road were the same; in a crowded sky I still repeated the jingles in which the Thirty-nine Articles of the seaman were condensed:

> *When two side-lights you see ahead,*
> *Port your helm and show your red.*
> *If on your starboard red appear*
> *It is your duty to keep clear.*
> *But when upon your port is seen*
> *Another's starboard light of green,*

There's nothing then for you to do,
For green to port keeps clear of you.

And so on, the mnemonic verses covering most of the
eventualities that the sea or the air could unexpectedly
throw up.

The compass and the sextant stood to me now, though
I learned to divide the swinging dial into degrees in place
of quarter points; the rudder and the joystick controls
were as natural as a tiller in the hand, and the only funda-
mental that differed was the new concept that greater
speed was consistent with greater safety.

In spite of my efforts I fiddled away half the exciting
years of war in a backwater, flying soberly round Cana-
dian targets to teach the elements of their trade to bomb-
aimers and gunners and radio operators.

I am not, I think, a warlike person. Yet if through ineptitude or ignorance or an unlikely malevolence the
leaders of a nation strike the drums, unfurl the banners
and alter the concepts of the national morality, it is I
with my companions who must answer the call and, as
far as is possible, counter the emergency created by
others.

War, after all, is achieved with pens, with words dis-
persed through microphones and newspapers, with concepts and opinions and attitudes all carefully produced
and weighed and measured. Peace is a product of plum-
meting bombs and drawn steel; it is bought with blood
and sinews, with destruction limited only by the capacity
on the one side to inflict and on the other to suffer. It is
too late to cry *"Pax, pax"* when the armies have been

committed; it is your thinking pacifist who then carries the rifle, throws the grenade, unleashes the torpedo.

Sometimes I think it is too late before that, that the next war is always inevitable, but it is the war beyond that which may be stopped, the war second from now, the war that exists as yet only as a developing hatred that is a weapon in itself and as long as it is suffered to exist will invite some power-seeker, blinded and deafened by his own ambition, to control it, and ride it, and start it down the slope after the Gadarene swine. The power, the control of hatred, will lead to the edge of war; it will lead inevitably to a point at which it may not be halted by the politician crying "Unfair, unfair," but only by the talents of the millions, disciplined to a unified response and perverted to the ends of destruction.

Of such was I: an internationalist by choice, a pacifist by desire, and a fighting man by the accident of my birth date. I was sure of one thing only: since I was forced to fight I would choose my weapons and my position; I would be in the front line with the most effective offensive weapon the world had then developed; I would drive a heavy bomber. And eventually I did. But the years of marking time, of petty discipline on barrack squares, of flying unexciting aircraft on routine errands were hard to take.

There were compensations, of which the greatest was the familiarization with a new element. The cumulus clouds, marching in great ranks of grandeur over the prairie scene, would lift my heart with an excitement that I can feel still; when they appeared I got into the air on some pretext or other if it was possible and chased up to their peaks, spiraling along their sculptured weaving walls, plunging a wing tip into the cotton-whiteness, following the curves as exactly as it was within the power of my machine to do, diving into the great crevasses, sometimes gingerly exploring the heart of the turbulent mass.

Or again, when the lakes were frozen over and deep in powdered snow, we'd chase the elk along; two companions each in his own aircraft, searching lake after lake for the tiny brown figures that we'd find scraping at the snow for the pickings of wild rice beneath. They would be near the trees, where the rice in summer grew high, and when we drove for them, a foot or two above the surface of the snow, they would turn and run.

The art then was to come upon them before they reached the shelter. I'd pick my mark and swoop low. The elk, overtaken, would wheel; and if the timing was precise, the moment neatly taken, I'd pull back on my stick and bowl him over with the slip stream. By that time we'd be close to the trees; sometimes, if the hillside was steep, it took skill to get out of the position.

Cruel? Maybe. The elk were unharmed; the soft snow took their falls. And it was better sport than anyone had with guns. The rivalry was close for it took a lot of skill to register even a fifty per cent success; there was a snow-sparkling joy in the winter sweeps, and danger enough for anyone.

Day after day we flew with pupils learning to find winds by mechanical observation of the drift, and to put their bombs on target, or within a desirable range. Sometimes we checked eighteen or twenty winds a day; we pilots grew so practiced that we achieved a high accuracy with the naked eye. Sometimes, if we liked a pupil, we'd correct the misreading he had made with his bombsight, thus allowing him to pass his tests; my conscience never troubled me over these small deceptions of authority, for personality was as important as prowess in any member of a bomber's crew; perhaps more so.

We flew in bad weather, for the supply of bomb-aimers had to be maintained and increased. We flew at night more than in daylight; at least I did, for the night was my joy. And waited for the chance to get to the front line. Waited for the chance to go to war and then have done with it. Waited impatiently, waited apprehensively, waited.

And taught, and learned, and practiced; flew the railway line along, and intersected the birch clumps. Flew between the grain elevators at the whistle-stop nearby. Flew low along snow-covered roads with our landing lights flaring like searching beacons, bringing the traffic below to a standstill. Flew beneath the telegraph lines. Flew until our oil coolers collected heads of wheat. Flew low on the swamps until the dead mosquitoes on the windscreen blocked our vision. Flew in pairs and threes and fours. Flew blind, and sometimes with a skinful of rye.

We lost friends. There was Roger, who shared my room, played dealer's choice till dawn one night, then went out and flew into a mountain. And Bill Malone: he collided with the drogue plane — I never knew the other pilot. Feathers: forgot to check his petrol tank. Simon: pulled up his wheels too soon for take-off, hit the runway and burned. Sammy: splintered the mouthpiece of the blood pressure gadget and died in the hospital of the glass he swallowed. I ferried him there. They've made mouthpieces of plastic since. Jeavons: didn't increase his speed on a steep low turn and went in like a bomb. Went up like a bomb, too. Ray: mistakenly flipped off his port engine switch on take-off. Jacky-Jack — who knows what he did? His kite was scattered over half a mile and they found his booted right foot.

And more. And hundreds more. Sweet lovely youngsters serious about scraping the down from their chins, shy with girls, kids who had parked their bicycles at the recruiting stall. I lived their youth; I was younger for knowing them. Not many men are forced by circumstances back to the boundaries of adolescence. I was, and the experience was sometimes breath-taking.

They had fears, of which the chief one was that they might prove inadequate under pressure. They were modest in their triumphs and glorious in their achievements. They never read the newspapers with the speeches and the empty threats of politicians they would be called upon to back; they carried books of well-loved poems, and waited for the letters from home:

"Rita is a big girl now — you wouldn't know her. She has joined the church, and last Sunday Dad and I took her to her first Communion. I wish you could have seen her. She wore . . ."

And they had hopes and dreams, and swore to take

the peaceful world in their time, and mold it into something fine and indestructible.

I flew at last upon the battle missions, seated in a throbbing pit of power. On a cold March night we flew on Nuremberg; I with a heavy heart, for since my childhood I had been in love with the image of the city, its story-book profile, its toymakers and its Meistersingers, its fountains and its forests. There was a certain passage in *The Cloister and the Hearth;* there were the works of Albrecht Dürer. I was charged with a share in the destruction of an image that I loved, and I was therefore all the more determined to deliver my cargo to a central mark.

It was a cargo of fire. Nestled in the belly of the Lancaster was a single canister with four thousand pounds of amatol, with the explosive force of four hundred tons of trinitrotoluene. There were one thousand three hundred and fifty four-pound thermite bombs, and two hundred and forty six-pounders; a small load necessarily, because of the ten tons of petrol needed for the voyage.

There was, in addition, half a ton of silver paper in tiny strips that, released into the airstream, were designed to fox the radar-controlled guns and searchlights of the enemy; there were comparable weights of lubricating oil and engine coolant and machine gun ammunition and oxygen for the crew and nitrogen to feed to the petrol tanks against the threat of incendiary bullets; and smaller quantities of all sorts of other essentials designed to keep the great weapon efficient in the air.

There were three thermos flasks, with six cups of coffee in all to divide between seven of us; there were five small drug tablets to keep seven men awake; there was an issue of exactly elevenpence worth of chocolate; for we worked for parsimonious employers. There were flares and life rafts and fishing lines and a deck of cards; hydraulic fluid and smoke canisters and axes to clear potential wreckage. There was a wealth of radios and radar sets, secret equipment all fitted with explosives so that they could be destroyed at a touch.

And ahead of us lay the city of toymakers, slated for destruction because a political perversion had festered there.

We lumbered into the Lincolnshire air so heavily laden that, although we had more power at our disposal than one of His Majesty's destroyers at sea, we could hardly claw the height to clear the towers of Lincoln Cathedral, eight hundred feet higher than the runway and a full twelve miles ahead of it. We struggled out over the North Sea for half an hour, carefully gaining a foot or two at a time, and turned in a wide and careful arc that brought us back, an hour after we had left, to wing over our own airfield two or three thousand feet up. We crossed the Channel no more than a mile high; we staggered at painfully low speeds past the treacherous valley of the Ruhr, and at the end of six hours came to the target . . . four hundred heavy aircraft, twenty-eight hundred men, a staggering concentration of destructive forces.

To tell the truth, I loved the long night journey, the stars and the emptiness. On such expeditions I used to hold a position on the outer flank of where I reckoned the argosy to be, and could have imagined my command to be alone. Sometimes there was the glimpse of a dark shape against the upthrust fence of a searchlight barrage; sometimes dark wings blotted out a section of the stars above. But the moving cylinder of occupied air was four miles wide and half a mile deep and more than ten miles long, and for all that our senses told us, we flew alone.

There was a radio silence, but at one stage our ears were filled with the music of "Lili Marlene," from Radio Antwerp, I think; an enemy station anyway, for to our taste they broadcast better programs. My radio operator, when his other duties permitted, used to search the dial for any station playing "Lili Marlene"; it was his current passion, and when he located that particular tune he fed it into all our earphones.

I could always object and have him shut it off; I seldom did, unless my need for the communication channel was urgent. It kept him happy and reduced the tensions. So did the forbidden cigarettes. The "wakey-wakey" pills with which we were so inadequately provided were hoarded for the much more important function of lengthening leave in London.

Four minutes, the four hundred took to pass a given point. At the target area they closed ranks, crowding into half a mile of sky. Four minutes, from the time the first candelabra flare lighted the target area three miles below until the last dark wings swept away and headed back, by a devious route, to England and a narrow bed. Four minutes; but in those leaping seconds was lit a bazaar of brilliance such as the toymakers huddled below could never have conceived in the most extravagant of their imaginings.

For, divorced from the implications of blood and debris, a bomber raid viewed from the vantage of Mars and the pilot is a brilliant and flashing and beautiful event. High, high above the dust level, high above the falling walls, the leaping flame, the boiling smoke, the world in violent eruption, there is a realm of light and color.

The great pillars of searchlights, blue-white, roam back and forth, across and through the scene, or fasten on a luckless aircraft. Up their misted centers crawl the ruby spider-eyes of tracer flak, seeming to lift within the light slowly, slowly, until a tentative instant (when they are seen in relation to the plane rather than the ground they come from) jets them into a leaping orbit that ends in a flash, a yellow-centered, red-ringed blast of whiteness that adjusts its color according to its distance from the eyes. The candelabra flares below burn out, and are replaced. On the ground beneath, brilliant among the flashes and the flames, the target indicator, livid green and screaming red, marks the target center in what seems to be square miles of burning city. Four hundred photo-flashes, a few at a time, add their temporary white moons to this extravaganza, and up above, on the level on which we fly, are other lights.

Aircraft collide, and are consumed in flame: blasting sheets of ignited petrol, shooting diversions of the signal

flares they carried. Collisions are the worst hazard, perhaps; the unlighted planes here concentrate from their
four-mile spread down to a few hundred yards. In his
cunning, the enemy shoots up "scarecrows" — imitations
of aircraft burning, of pathfinder aircraft, loaded with
signal flares and colored smoke, yellow and purple. Flam-
ing onions leap up from the ground: chains of yellow
lights that describe neat sculptured parabolas in their
flight, winking out in starry flashes as their self-destroying
mechanisms come into play, or taking the target aircraft
with them in gay flames.

The flak comes up in chains; four explosions together,
or five. I give up the effort I always consciously make of
trying to shield my eyes from the brilliance, and call to
my navigator, working calmly at his figures behind his
black curtain.

"Come and see this, Allan. Come and take a look."

But he is too busy.

One two three four five — the flak bursts lead away.
Here is another chain, coming towards us — one two
three four. The fifth must have hit us. But the fifth never
comes.

I have counted so far twelve scarecrows; there must
have been others. I have been unable to count the exploding aircraft, the aircraft on fire; there are too many.
I lead up to the target. The bomb-aimer's voice comes in,
taking a brief command, giving me orders.

"Steady, steady . . . lef-f-ft . . . steady."

The enemy has broken the rules. His fighters are flying
in his own flak. I see the chains of machine gun tracer,

ruby red, like dotted lines, tracing graphs from everywhere to everywhere. There is one on my tail.

"You see him, Joe? I can't depress my guns any more."

That's Ken, my mid-upper gunner, calling to the tail. Surely he will give me evasive action, so I can counter the threat. Till then, I must obey my bomb-aimer.

"Steady, steady."

If I turn towards the fighter behind — but I do not know where he is, and may turn to his advantage. It must be towards him, to tighten his turning circle. Ken is my rearward eye; Ken and Joe. I must await their orders.

"I see him."

That was Joe. He has left his microphone open; good boy. Now I can hear his four machine guns, a unison of strength.

We fly in a rain of strips of silver paper. They pick up the lights: the yellow and red lights of fire, the purple and green and red and yellow of signal lights, the intensity of searchlights. We fly in a rain of jewel slivers, like the crystal stalactites that chemically minded schoolboys grow in tanks, but a thousand times more intensely brilliant. We fly in a rain of light.

The machine gun blast is too long; Joe is too excited. Ken is shouting at him; but the roar of Joe's guns dulls the urgency of Ken's voice. I still have no evasive action orders; the bomb-aimer's voice is like a classroom command: "Steady, steady." I am proud of him. He was one of my pupils, back in Canada.

Charley shouts from the astro-hatch: "Dive starboard,

skipper. One coming right down on us." I kick hard right rudder, hoping I am not advantaging the fighter; a canister of amatol misses the fuselage by inches, and Ken shouts delighted comment. Joe's guns are reduced to two: the fool, the fool. He still hangs on his triggers. He will lose them all and leave us defenseless in our most vulnerable quarter.

The tracer from the fighter behind is passing my windows now, close to the perspex; he must be close. The machine gun noise in the earphones is halved again: only one gun is left in the rear turret. Then it stops.

"Joe got him," Ken shouts. "Just one big flash. He flashed out like a bomb."

And below, the bombs flash out like exploding aircraft.

"A JU one-eighty-eight," Ken amplifies.

Gordon, at the bombsight, says, "Steady. Bomb gone. A lovely shot."

"Why the hell didn't I get evasive action?" I complain, and Ken says:

"Didn't want to spoil Gordon's aim."

The body of a man dressed in a flying suit not issued in our force whips past the windows, a trailed parachute horizontal behind him, and as yet unopened. Whips past, I say; at that moment he seemed to drift slow as thistledown, so that I could see and retain a perfect image: the body lying limp, the hands at the sides, so clear in the yellow-green light of some nearby explosion that I could see the seams of his gloves, the teeth of a forearm zipper. He might have been alive or dead, his parachute might or might not open — what matter? He was dropping down into four square miles of vicious fire, such a conflagration as mankind never before had initiated, such a fury that his chance of life was small indeed.

"You see that, Ken?" I ask. Do I have to assure myself that it was not a hallucination?

"Christ, he was close," says Ken. And, after a while, "Poor bugger."

More than a hundred planes on fire in those few minutes, in those few miles of sky we sweep across. A fantasy of leaping light on the ground beneath — and as though it were not enough, the crafty enemy has lit an imitation fire a mile or two away, prepared long months before, and calculated to draw to the wrong target those of our aircraft with crews unaccustomed to raiding.

The imitation is a good one: a huge conflagration on the ground with constant explosions, with simulated target indicator and a continuity of flashing photo-floods for nonexistent cameras, with imitation crashes and disasters in the sky above, with searchlights and tracer flak of different calibers, different weights and brilliances, with candelabra flares and signal lights. But the imitation of the target indicator is not exact; the red has a tinge of cerise that is unreal, the green is slightly a blue-green; the imitation can be detected.

Nevertheless, it draws off some of the attacking forces. Over the microphones the raidmaster warns about it: "Jumbo to Skymaster, Jumbo to Skymaster, aim for the center of the smoke concentration; aim to the right of the center marker, the center of the smoke concentration. Jumbo to Skymaster . . ." The voice goes on, unexcited.

Skymaster is the attacking force, for this night only.

But the enemy has radio-controlled guns on the raid-master; his aircraft is shot down, as he knew it must be, and he destroyed. A second voice fills the gap in the air-waves:

"Jumbo Two to Skymaster, the center of the smoke concentration, two o'clock from the center marker."

Opening his microphone is his death warrant; he accepts that without a quiver in his voice. Who is he? Some kid or other. Not of age, perhaps. All he has to do to save his life is to find that his set is out of order for the next twenty seconds; the raid can do without him. But he carries on:

"Jumbo Two to Skymaster, aim . . ."

And above us all the stars burn, swinging in the zenith, showing lights a dozen times more brilliant than the light which penetrates down to the dustbound earth — not here, not in the raid area. Only the lights of fires penetrate the smoke immediately below us; only the lights of struck matches show in the caverns where the toymakers hide.

Four minutes; and the sky is empty but for the angry searchlights uselessly sweeping the horizons behind us; four minutes and ninety seconds and we turn for home.

The first cold gray light of the northern dawn discloses the seals on the sandbanks of the Schelde, all unconcerned with the signs and symbols of human warfare and happy in their communal life. I wonder about them as I always do. It seems that whenever there are seals on the Schelde bars there are none to be seen in the Wash; I wonder whether they are the same seals with two resorts, or whether two communities of seals, one living in Holland, one in England, have legislated an arrangement to use the same feeding grounds turn and turn about, so that only one tribe is home at one time; or whether my observation is just not sufficiently acute.

We cross the Channel, and I see the lines of surf far below, and am somehow comforted of the sorrow that laces exhilaration through and through.

We dropped the bombs and brought back the peace; a peace that was instantly assailed by a hundred thousand politicians spouting hatred, creating privilege, and making points that would bring them, as they hoped, to a hundred thousand petty positions of temporal and temporary power.

"I have no liking for the man of war," an artist told me. "I could not take a life."

Well, I was different; and I think it was the sea that made me different. I took the lives of communities: in Hamburg, the night of the greatest fire; in Kiel, the morning we sank the *Admiral Scheer;* in Potsdam and Paderborn and Plauen, in Essen and Gelsenkirchen. But I could not sit, as did this disapproving artist through the war, drawing the cartoons and caricatures that summoned up the reserves of hatred necessary for its continuance. I could not blame him, for by his standards he was immaculate; but I could not do it. My arts, like my wartime efforts, looked towards peace and hailed the happy sun.

In the middle of April that year, with the promise of

1 6 4

spring fulfilled in Europe, we flew on Heligoland. It was a mission of spite and spleen; the war was all but over, and I think that no one, ever, will be joyous in taking credit for what we did that day.

In the expedition there were nine hundred and eighty-three heavy bombers, there were two hundred and sixty-four fighters to cover them, and a hundred and more aircraft of Pathfinder Force directing the operation; a mighty armada, perhaps the greatest the world has ever seen, dedicated to the obliteration of a spot of land in the North Sea three-quarters of a mile wide and a mile long, and rendered previously harmless by reason of the collapse of its country's forces.

When my bombdoors opened, twelve thousand-pounders and four five-hundred-pounder bombs of amatol dropped true on the target center. In every major craft of the striking force was a similar cargo; the amalgamation of destructive power was such that it could not be approached by the atom bomb to come, and even then in preparation. The first of these was the equivalent of a mere twenty thousand tons of trinitrotoluene; the blast from Bomber Command on the little island equaled one million four hundred thousand tons, using the ready reckoning that amatol is two hundred times as effective as TNT. The attack was deadly and complete; the fighters were not called upon; the bombers carried out their mission with every aid imaginable, and without interference or indeed much hazard.

When I pulled the lever that closed the bombdoors I had the feeling that my wartime task was done, and, not for the first time nor as it happened for the last, I disobeyed strict orders. I pulled back the throttles and let the Lancaster drop into a steep driving dive that brought me near to the surface of the sea, far to the south. Then I turned round and, from a distance I estimated safe enough, rode back not far above sea level to watch the progress of the raid — this time a protracted one.

And from that vantage point, I saw two things. I saw that from somewhere in the area of destruction, from among the craters, the leaping fire and the convulsed earth, impervious to the exploding world and true to their vows of service, some of the enemy, with one undamaged gun, were fighting back. Somewhere in that island of unimaginable terror, among irresistible forces set wild to their destruction, among the unendurable sounds, and the heat, and the earth in spasm, men like myself followed their star, though they knew the effort hopeless. Men like myself offset the damage and carried the ammunition, stood calm to the sights and fired the ordnance. They did it without hope of reward, not even the reward of a hero's reputation. They did it without hope of an effectual result. They did it because they were men.

The other thing I saw concerned the red cliffs of the island, and the green seas. The red cliffs crumbled; great boulders ran off into the water; the land was riven and broken and shaken; from where I looked it seemed like sugar crumbling in the lump and trickling to its intended dissolution.

But the great lines of surf, sweeping in to the cliffs and there conforming to the pattern of conflict established when the moon was born, rolled on in thrust and retreat, as though this greatest demonstration of the power of man was a thing of little moment. True, the surf and the nearer ocean were creamed with the scars of bombs strayed from their targets; true, the impetus to the cliff-licking water was aided and overridden by the mighty explosions beyond the line of surf, so that individual waves leaped high to meet the crumbling red rocks, and for a time, here and there, the lines of breakers were crisscrossed by force-waves from these explosions; but the main routine of ocean was unchanged.

The waves followed in their courses, each ninth wave — was it the ninth wave? — bigger than the others; and even while the rocks were still falling began to put the new scheme of things into a maritime order. I swung the wheel and stabbed my left foot forward when I saw that, and headed back to England.

The sea was normal; the land would take a little longer. I thought of the beach where I was born, and of the new life emerging from the close of war. It would be a good place, I thought, to rear a family; a good place for a child to grow.

10

ɴORTHWEST Island is a small, two-hundred-acre cay in the Capricorn group, an archipelago at the southern extremity of the Great Barrier Reef which flanks the northern half of the eastern seaboard of the Australian continent. Each year, from October to January, the nesting season of the white-capped noddies, its bird population rises to a figure estimated variously at from thirty thousand to several millions. The accuracy of such estimates is not important; a more graphic indication of the crowd density is given if a man stands on the beach and extends his arms. The birds will confidently use them for a roost, they are so crowded.

The noddies build nests of leaves cemented together on the brittle branches of the heimerliodendrum trees that cover the island with a low scrub, and each nest shelters in due course a single egg. Throughout the period absorbed in building the nest, producing and hatching the egg, and nourishing the fledgling, each parent at every movement trusts to its agility for its life.

For if its wings should brush against one of the ripened seed pods of the heimerliodendrum, a gummy exudation resembling birdlime fastens the pod to its feathers and its wings to its body. The bird in panic begins a frantic beating, spreading the influence of the lime and probably collecting more pods, but inevitably bringing itself to the ground. Here it becomes enmeshed with seed pods and their glue, and shortly, with leaves and sticks and dirt, until its muscles cannot respond with any quick or effective action. It flops and drags itself along the ground until it is no longer capable of any movement whatever. And here, self-interred in the debris of the coral cay, it dies, and becomes one with the earth, adding its little mass to the fertility of the island sand, and offering its decay to the nourishment of new heimerliodendrum life.

Compared with that of the noddy, the incidence of the human upon the smaller land masses of the Pacific is numerically insignificant; yet the islands ensnare their own human victims with an efficiency equal to that of their indigenous upas tree, the heimerliodendrum. The processes by which they do this are infinitely slower, and pleasant rather than frightening; but they continue inexorably, weighing the victim down to the tropic ground with one retention factor piled on another, and condemning him eventually to a unity with that alien soil.

As with the birds, the process is selective. Many people are unaffected by the snares, and many return year after year on annual migrations and go away unscathed.

The islands of the Pacific generally classified as uninhabited and sometimes uninhabitable have long exercised a tremendous power over the imaginative mind. Indeed, they have been so frequently lauded as paradisiacal retreats that a tally of the numbers yet remaining must evoke amazement, or even lower their reputations. But it would be a mistake to assume that, because these islands are generally uninhabited, either they are unknown or they are incapable of supporting life at a high level of satisfaction.

Where they lie in areas supporting a native population, most of them fulfill functions of seasonally providing an auxiliary food supply, or emergency food depots for the seamen, who venture incredibly far in the frail island canoes, or against the failure of garden crops in adjacent habitation centers. Still other islands are left uninhabited because they stand alone, and if they were populated, an island fleet, vulnerable to a surprise wind, would have no place to run in an emergency. For no island economy is wholly dependent upon the land which it obviously occupies; an association of lands is necessary to give strength.

And again, many islands have supported small populations for brief periods; on many and many a one the vegetation conceals the bones of its lone inhabitant, wedded in his lifetime and now committed in death to isolation and the beauty of nature.

The factors which have led men to these islands and there, often enough, immured them, consist of the mental

states induced by a climate close to perfection, by surroundings of great beauty, by an absence of subsistence
problems, and by a host of lesser attractions. They are
lavish with the lassitudes that beckon when a man con-
siders divorcing himself from ambition or gives way to
asocial impulses. The sea is so perfect for swimming, for
fishing and for sailing that cares and worries seem to dis-
solve in its proximity; the land is frequently Paradise itself. Food is at hand, so readily available that survival is
never a problem. Only the barest essentials of clothing
and shelter are necessary, and even those only when the
mind clings to society's conventions.

In general, the uninhabited islands of the tropical Pacific fall into two classifications. There are the coral
islands, mostly flat, featureless, and without surface water, but verdant with trees if the area is sufficient for
arboreal life to thrive. And there are the high islands,
mostly of volcanic origin, peaked with fantastic spires,
and breath-takingly beautiful. There are mountain streams
in the high islands, and a more varied foliage.

High island or low will provide every essential of life
to man except the one without which he cannot thrive,
the indispensable factor of conflict. Or perhaps it would
be more truthful to say that the only conflict which man
encounters here is the conflict within himself. And perhaps this explains why the enticing challenge is so rarely
accepted; for of all encounters, the inward conflict is the
most taxing, and in a world where a concurrent conflict
with circumstances does not exist to relieve the tension
it can rise, and frequently it does, to an insupportable

intensity. Live alone on an island if you hear the call; but never for long. Yet emotions not engendered by conflict will flourish here.

My first love among islands was the one called Dunk, a high outpost behind that same Barrier Reef that shelters Northwest Island and its nesting noddies. On Dunk's construction coral formations have added to a high granite agglomeration until the total island, as it stands today, is fourteen miles in circumference.

It has, in its history, been briefly populated. A small group of Australian aborigines once made a seasonal retreat of this haven; but apparently had not been long in the habit of residence when they were joined and finally supplanted by E. J. Banfield, an invalid author who, after regaining his strength and health, spent many happy years before he died upon his island, leaving to posterity four books which described his life. After that there were several residents, and several rather unsuccessful attempts to provide accommodation for tourists. During the Second World War a small unit maintained a radar station there and built an airstrip which was not subsequently used. None of these developments spoiled its intrinsic attractions.

From the end of one rainy season, in March or April, until the start of the next, in December or January, the climate comes as close to perfection as man could wish. On the coolest nights the temperature reads no less than seventy degrees Fahrenheit. The sea breezes, from all directions, keep the tropical air comparatively cool in the daytime, so that on only a few of the hottest afternoons does the thermometer record more than ninety. There is little deterioration in the rainy season except for daily showers and a high humidity.

There are two thousand islands on that coast with similar conditions, yet most are uninhabited. There are thousands more elsewhere in the Pacific, and no less agreeable. And in spite of my rationalizations, I often wonder why it is that the recurrent dream of man to live alone with beauty is so seldom realized. Almost anywhere in this ocean man could be competent to translate dream to reality, and until comparatively recent times, such islands were his for the taking. Perhaps the dream is not enough; it must be made practical by the man of action, and it is rare for the two to inhabit a single skin.

I could not, I think, devote my life to the island idyl; yet after the stresses of war I found regeneration and strength in a series of month-long periods spent on such tropic shores in utter relaxation.

Dunk is a lovely island, named by Captain Cook on his third voyage for an earlier First Lord of the Admiralty, George M. Dunk, Earl of Halifax. The First Lord at the time of the voyage was the third Earl of Sandwich, whose family seat was Hinchinbrook, in England. As the legend goes, Cook, in the hope perhaps of future favors, named the three loveliest lands he discovered after the First Lords. They were Dunk, Hinchinbrook (a nearby but much larger island) and the Sandwich group now called Hawaii.

Cook never set foot upon this island; but if, in fact, its loveliness influenced its naming, a landing could only have confirmed his first judgment. And his vision must have been supported by his nose; for these are scented lands, and their fragrance is carried far to sea. It is an elusive scent, compounded of many elements.

There is the fresh loveliness of hoia, a flower-spangled creeper entwined among the tree branches. The native ginger grows in all the glades and is prodigal with its rich and sophisticated favors. At least five of the island's orchid varieties (which grow in unbelievable profusion) are scented. Heavy calophyllum trees, their roots in the seawater, their massive trunks and grotesque branches supporting whole gardens of epiphytes, have the fragrance of the English meadowsweet. The pandanus (which by its growth signals the presence of underground water) has a seasonal odor as, more delicately, do the sighing she-oaks that scatter their flexible needles on every sandspit.

The whole island is scented, and variations of the total offering come from every glade and every rockface. I think that of all scents the tropical ones are the most attractive; I do not agree with those who find them "heavy," and among them I can match the scents of mignonette, and London Rocket, and night-scented stocks, and tobacco.

Not all of the island's attractions were there in Cook's time. The coconut, which now is common, had never grown there. It was introduced by order of the Queensland Government in the eighteen-eighties to provide emergency food for shipwrecked mariners. The palms thrived, as did their descendants, and enriched the landscape. Less happy results came from the introduction of goats to some of the major islands, made at the same time and for the same reason.

But each of the adventurers who came here made his introductions. The passion fruit is native to the islands; its cousin the grenadilla thrives as well. The citrus fruits, pomelos and shaddocks, oranges and lemons, kumquats and mandarins have heavy crops. The papaw is here in several varieties, and the banana. The monstera, the soursop, the custard apple, the five-finger and the guava need no attention. The rosella, the only hibiscus used for food, will grow, and the New Guinea bean.

The umbrella tree covers the island and attracts, with its lavish gifts of nectar, chattering flocks of small birds. The betel nut palms grow in all the darker, more sheltered valleys. Pineapples grow, both large and sweet. Each human occupation of the island has brought new useful trees; and the potential is not yet in sight. The climate is ideal for more products than serve the rich man's normal table, and the offerings of the land are excelled in quantity and quality only by those of the adjacent sea.

The most potent attraction is, however, the reputed glory of the nearby Barrier Reef, a twelve-hundred-mile stretch of savage beetling underwater cliff which parallels and protects the dream-lovely shore of the mainland. In spite of a spate of publicity, this reef is hard to see. For surface visibility it is essential to visit it at a low spring tide, such as happens on only two or three days in a month. The visit must coincide with the glassy calmness of a day with no wind. Reef waters are not so strongly responsive to the lunar influences as most other seas, and as a rule, only one tide a day is a good one. Optimum conditions exist, therefore, on no more than four or five days during the year; but when they are present the coral formations are revealed to be of a fantastic beauty.

The smaller enclaves of coral garden on the fringing reef of Dunk and its neighbors hold beauty enough, and can be seen on any day. Every brilliant color under the sun lights the fish, the shells, the weeds and the coral itself, spread lavishly in such patterns and combinations as the world has not elsewhere developed. The colors are sometimes of such intensity that they seem, like fireworks, to be generated by some incendiary element within; they are matched in my experience only by certain minerals under the "black light" of the prospector.

It is recorded that Cook's men fed upon some of the giant clams they encountered, but few who have followed them to the Reef have tried to emulate them. Clams weighing up to five hundred pounds have been collected; and it has proved impossible to collect observed specimens that have appeared much larger. In some Queensland homes the baby is bathed in a clamshell. Not in many; for though there are shells adequate to accommodate even the largest members of the family, their weight makes them difficult to empty.

There is a legend which tells of the danger the lonely pearl diver runs when walking among the clams. It is said that if he should put his foot in the opened shell he is caught and held, and no power on earth can free him.

It is, unfortunately for romance, no more than a legend. The clam opens its shell to a limited extent only, so that in the first place it would take some clever maneuvering to insert a foot, even though the divers of the reef wear, not leaded boots, but tennis shoes. Then there is the temperament of the clam, which opens its shell for purposes of refreshment and replenishment, is at some pains to keep intruders out, and is so alert to a close approach that the shadow of a keel at the surface above is sufficient to activate its closing mechanism. Clams have been killed — a simple operation — so that films could be taken of a diver with a foot entrapped; but no authentic record exists of any other means of getting past the animal's guard in order to insert an object so bulky.

The other shells of the Reef and the island are myriad, and their myriad beauties indescribable. There are bailers, bright gleaming apricot in color, and big enough, at their best, to hold a dozen and a half good oranges. Cowries come in two hundred varieties, including the pure white porcelain of the egg cowrie, bigger than a fist, and possessed of such wondrous beauty that it is used as a religious symbol or a badge of aristocracy throughout the seas in which it is found. There is the delicate paper nautilus, which is the shell-case of a small octopus. There is the false helmet, from which true cameos are cut. There are spider shells and cone shells and olives and ear shells and murices and precious wentletraps.

There are crabs of an inconceivable variety, from the ghost crabs which race in the moonlight over the beach's open stretches, and the hermits which seize upon every empty shell for a home, to the big mangrove crabs, with claws bigger than a man's hand. There are bright sea snakes, and octopuses colored like Joseph's coat. There is the sea hare, a slug which fills the water with an amethyst cloud whenever it is disturbed. You can find bêche-de-mer in every pool, and sea urchins, and the brittle stars you cannot capture whole, and a brilliant blue starfish a foot across.

The color extravaganza of the land is almost as riotous. The butterflies are at every bush, the Ulysses swallow-tails concentrating in dozens on the red flowers which most enhance their brilliant blue lacquer. There are always flowers, and nearly all the flowers are scented. The yellow flowers of the wild hibiscus turn apricot where they fall on salty sand, and sometimes an argosy of them sails upon the waters of a sheltered bay, with butterflies fluttering above.

Even the beauty has some dangers. Sometimes a stone-fish lies and waits in a coral pool, looking like weathered rock. At the slightest touch he will eject venom from the thirteen strong sharp spines upon his back; and because of his motionless habit, it is easy to stand on him. The poison is so virulent as sometimes to cause immediate madness from the pain, and death usually follows. Fortunately the stonefish is rare. But even some of the sea shells contain a poison and are armed with the means for injecting it. Beautiful as they are, small enough to be held in the hand, they can cause a quick agony and death. Some of the sea snakes, clad in beauty, hold death in ready fangs; the shark cruises here; and, rarely, the seagoing crocodile.

Ashore, in the shaded woods, among the sun-bathed rocks, the deadly brown snake glides. But none of the animals poison-armed will seek you out to do you harm; they will defend themselves only, and an observant man has nothing whatever to fear.

The innumerable fish that swim among the coral formations are equally as brilliant as their surroundings; and so plentiful that in many circumstances it is their absence, rather than their presence, which becomes remarkable. The huge anemones, for instance, always have a pair or two of anemone fish swimming without fear and without hazard among the poisonous fronds, and taking refuge in them when danger threatens; though fish of all other varieties are paralyzed by the anemone's touch, and eaten by it. Such little beauty-fish as the demoiselles, blue and gold, always adorn the clumps of soft coral.

The bird-life of the island is a lifetime's study: the curlews, slinking softly in daylight by the weeds back from the shore, the sea eagles, of whom a pair commands every mile or two of coast, the cave of swallows, the banded nightjar with its monotonous call, the heron, fishing the shallow reef, the megapode, whose nest is as big as a poor man's cottage, the hummingbird, clapping its tiny wings in sheltered garden spots.

It seemed to me on my first discovery that a man could find permanent happiness there, and for some time I had dreams of finding another such island where I could live after a pattern I evolved myself. A year or two later I went to stay with a man called Johnny; he had found such an island and gained title to it; and of all men he had the temperament to enjoy it.

He was an artist, primarily; he painted canvases that absorbed him; that reflected, rather, his abiding interest in his world; and the world he chose was the world of the island. He was in addition a man of great resource and many abilities; within the paradise on which he lived he built, by his own efforts, a house of sun-dried brick, substantial, cool and pleasant. From this house he ruled his domain, a place of beautiful forests, ringed by cliffs intersected by seven fine ocean beaches. He had a launch with which he could maintain an infrequent communication with society. He cultivated a garden that provided him with everything necessary to life. The fish crowded the seas about him; the turtles came up on his beaches each rainy season to lay their eggs. The golden orchids grew so thickly that in places you had to thrust your way through waist-high clumps.

He had lived there for many years, catering by his own efforts to all his needs. He had built good furniture, largely from the stems of the giant bamboo. His island, indeed, was as well provided with essentials for life as the island of those notable exploiters, the Swiss Family Robinson.

Yet it seemed sometimes that the amiable subsistence that the island provided did not satisfy Johnny. His garden produced beyond his needs, yet he worked it ever more extensively. Though he could find his way with ease through the forest to visit loved locations, he constructed pathways far more elaborate than was necessary. He knew the contours of the little bay that served him as harbor very well; yet he buoyed it and marked a channel in days of back-breaking labor, sometimes underwater. He added an art gallery to his house, a long, noble room something after the Spanish style, in which certainly his paintings showed to advantage. He married to complete his life; his wife showed eagerness to share his joys and ability to cope with his problems.

And after a few more years I found, one day, that his estate was up for sale.

It was, I think, the absence of conflict with circumstances that drove Adam and Eve from their Eden; it was logical that they sought the alliance with the Serpent, logical and right that they never rediscovered Paradise.

11

THERE ARE two sides of a man, two components of which one is antagonistic to the other; and one of the many indications of this is that an industry like whaling can be established and survive. In every man familiar with the sea there is an affection for the huge and placid mammals, the greatest animal creations the world has ever seen, massive individuals, friendly in spite of their disputed dominion over the oceans, incapable, it seems, of harboring enmity. Every man familiar with the sea has loved them, and that love was never more apparent than in the same men who, with harpoon and lance, harried and pursued them to their deaths in the hope of gain.

When I was a child I felt the attraction of the whales, though then they were represented only by a flurry on the distant horizon, where some cruising cetacean fought with its ocean adversaries the killers perhaps, shoveling the water up to the sky with its flukes; or in a more playful moment frolicked and leaped with a most unlikely verve in the sparkling sunshine.

After I went to sea, I began to take notice of the whale's interest in man, his rival, and his stubborn refusal to treat him as an enemy. While I served aboard the little wallowing monstrosity of an undersized steam trawler on which I first went to sea there was a period of weeks on every day of which, as we cleared the harbor, we were met by a large snub-nosed whale, of indeterminate variety but identifiable by reason of a highly individualistic, irregular, sulphur-colored patch he carried high over his port rib-case.

This friendly fellow used to accompany us all the way down the coast to the fishing grounds we were then working, and having arrived, would flick a demonstrative tail as we launched the trawl, and then disappear. We would not see him on the homeward journey. He seemed to want nothing but our company; yet he did not seek the company of other vessels, and we appreciated the compliment.

In his pilotage he much resembled another whale, "Pelorus Jack," who acquired fame, and for whose protection the New Zealand Government enacted a special law. Pelorus Jack for years convoyed all vessels negotiating the narrow, dangerous, tide-swept French Pass, a marine short cut between the ports of Nelson and Wellington. He was, apparently, a Risso's dolphin, *Grampus griseus,* one of the rarer small whales, a breed distinguished by their asymmetric skulls. In his lifetime he was always on duty in the Pass. He is believed to be the only individual among marine animals whose services to man evoked special legislation; but many and many a whale before him was known from ocean to ocean by a particular name, because of personal idiosyncrasies.

In the early part of the last century there were "New Zealand Tom," "Timor Jack" and "Mocha Dick"; the last an animal named for his coffee-colored skin. Perhaps because of this circumstance he had been singled out by whalers again and again; for he had developed a passion hitherto unattributed to the whale — a passion for revenge. When he was finally killed about 1820 his body was covered with scars, his flesh bristled with harpoons, and his head, from some conceit of the whalemen, was declared to be "wonderfully expressive of old age, cunning and rapacity."

It has been said that "Mocha Dick" became "Moggy Dick" and finally "Moby Dick," and was the prototype of the animal that Herman Melville pictured after his voyage twenty years later. Other whales proved to be animated by some such feelings as directed Mocha Dick. The ship *Ann Alexander,* commanded by Captain Deblois, sent out a boat after a whale that, on being harpooned, cracked the boat to splinters and then turned on the ship itself, making it a complete wreck within an hour. Four months later the whale was harpooned by the *Rebecca Sims;* it was identified by two harpoons stuck in its flesh.

The whales of my experience have all been friendly. Once our trawler passed a school of blackfish, little whales perhaps twenty feet long, traveling in threes like an army, in a column a quarter of a mile long. The leader, sighting us, whipped round out of its course, and like an ecstatic pup discovering its master after an absence, rubbed its back enthusiastically under our keel. For a quarter of an hour the little ship protested as the following files dived down to exploit the back-scratching qualities of its bottom, bumping and rubbing with appreciative ardor, and then went on their way.

Once too, alone in a schooner, I passed a school of cowfish, smaller cetaceans allied to the porpoises, but twelve feet long, a salty gray in color, and having a falcate dorsal fin in place of the more usual rounded one. They were female cowfish, each accompanied by a baby perhaps two or three feet in length. And each cow was teaching her calf those delightful acrobatics with which cowfish, porpoises and grampus herald a change in the weather.

One mother leaped high, performed a somersault and a half, and landed solidly on her side; and immediately her baby followed suit. She repeated the act without varying it, again and again and again. Another of the herd simply sunfished like a horse that knows no vice, rearing quietly, doggedly towards the sky and falling forward — perhaps she had given birth to an awkward child. Another was doing simple back flips, and still another performed an evolution which, as an aviator, I could later identify as "a roll off the top."

There were eight cows in all and eight calves, and each pair displayed an entirely different evolution over and over again, and all in time. It is difficult to convey now the delight I had from these acrobats. I was critical enough to notice, though, that the babies were fully as graceful as their mothers, and that they were not breathing so hard.

The larger whales were not so common in our waters; but once, when I was alone in my schooner, I came out of a landlocked harbor and saw a huge whale quiescent at a little distance. There seemed something strange about it, so I moved in close to investigate. As I neared her I could see that she was lying partly on her side and feeding her calf.

I had never any reason to be afraid of whales, and so continued to approach in order to observe this the better. I closed within about thirty yards when suddenly I realized how enormous was the bulk of this whale. (I have since read, and found it easy to believe, that the tongue of the blue whale is roughly the size of an entire elephant, about two tons. This one was, I think, a large right whale, and its mass was huge, its length three times that of my schooner.) The calf was on the side nearest me, and without disturbing it in the least, the mother turned in the water to give it the protection of her body. And when I saw that great bulk move to the consciousness of my presence, I pushed the tiller over and opened the throttle and got away from that vicinity.

I am again at a loss in trying to recapture and transmit the influence of that small experience; I had the distinct feeling that the whale was conscious of my curiosity but did not resent it; further, that she was proud of her offspring, but that she could not expose it even to dangers of which she herself was contemptuous. If I am guilty here of the pathetic fallacy I do not retract; men in all the ages who have watched the leviathans in play or in panic have attributed to them feelings and passions similar to our own.

Once, in the early morning off the New Zealand coast, I set my dan-lines and waited for the sun to rise. It was spring, and there was a hint of fog clinging to the heaving surface, like the Arctic sea-smoke that is found in latitudes nearer the poles. As though it knew that I had time on my hands, as though it felt I might be appreciative, a young sea lion bobbed up near my schooner with a sixteen-pound ling, that looked half as long as itself, caught crosswise in its jaws. The ling, I think, had little life left in it, yet it was not dead; it struggled vainly once or twice while its captor seemed to tread water, head and shoulders held high, fore flippers on the surface, its quarry lined up with its whiskers.

Having set the stage and captured attention, this ham comedian went into his routine, first swimming sedately in a slow circle for a couple of revolutions, then, with a toss of his neatly muscled neck, sending the ling flying high in the air, end over end. While it ascended, reached the apogee of its parabolic path and headed downward once again, the sea lion put a flipper to his whiskers (I could almost have imagined an accompanying yawn) and continued to stare fixedly at me. At the last possible moment it raised its head and fielded the fish with an exquisite accuracy. Then it swam in circles once again.

It repeated this trick sufficiently often to convince me of its skill; and then produced its variations. For example, it would give the toss a directional bias, and race madly through the almost undisturbed water to catch the ling a full five fathoms away. Or it would miss altogether, make three or four simulated attacks on the weakly flapping fish, disappear into the depths, and come racing up, bursting out of the water with the ling in its jaws precisely as at first.

For twenty minutes it regaled me with its performance; I could have sworn it was a circus seal escaped, using a fish in lieu of a ball. I almost expected it to produce a trumpet from some undersea table of props.

Again, on another morning, I thought I was going to see the performance repeated, this time by a leopard seal. It appeared with the fish in its mouth, seemed to try for my attention, but then possibly judged my attitude too unappreciative, for it swam off.

Seals infrequently appeared when we raised the great nets of fish to the trawler's side and, mischievous and quick, stole tidbits, venturing right into the net, but apparently aware of its threat, for they were never caught.

I had an affection for the seals, and more particularly for the sea lions. I had made an acquaintance with them long before, when I was a boy about ten or twelve and played upon the beach. Their claim to it was older than mine. Indeed, the first creatures of high intelligence to use the beach were the sea lions. In the days before man arrived to establish himself as their most significant enemy in the southern oceans, the beach was their play-ground.

Its contribution to their food supply was small, but there were rich feeding-grounds within a few sea miles; and in those days, indeed, when the more desirable rookeries were crammed with their fellows, the beach must have been important in their economy.

Of the first men to see them here, nothing, or almost nothing, is known. They were supplanted, eight centuries ago, by the Maoris, with the loose-knit, sea-based empire that covered the whole Pacific. But these were men who did not menace the communal life of the sea lion.

Throughout the whole of Polynesia, from Hawaii in the north to the most southern outpost of New Zealand, from Easter Island to the island outposts of Melanesia, the Polynesian domains, covering a hundred and seventy thousand square miles of land in eleven million square miles of ocean, showed an amazing poverty of indigenous and land-based fauna.

In the entire region, the warm-blooded animals not of air or ocean were represented only by two or three varieties of rat. The Maoris carried with them, to be bred for food, domestic dogs and rats, and to some places, pigs; but circumstances made them gardeners and fishermen. Their venery was almost entirely confined to the hunting of birds and the slaughter of their own kind. Even reptiles were scarce in their domains.

It followed that they became most cunning and re-sourceful hunters, for they had no easy game. They developed an understanding of their quarry and a selec-

tivity that made them conservationists rather than exploiters. When the Maori hunter took a bird, he did so
in circumstances that did not frighten its fellows. Throughout the whole of Polynesia, until the coming of the white
man and sometimes after, the birds retained a friendly
and trusting attitude towards man, their enemy.

The mighty flocks of duck, for example, that populated the swamps and lagoons were safe from the men
they could see walking upon the shores. The Maori
attacked from underneath the water, drawing his air
through a hollow reed held in his mouth. A swimming
duck was drawn under by his legs and quickly drowned,
while his neighbors remained unconscious of his fate and
vulnerable to the enemy's next foray.

I have often watched the Maori call the weka, a flight-
less bird much like the domestic fowl. The hunter sits
immobile, with a blade of grass between his lips on which
to produce the sound of busy weka chicks. And before
long the curious birds come to investigate. When one is
within reach of his hands it is seized and smothered; a
second comes without fear to the same fate, and perhaps
a third. The hunter is satisfied. There is no panic among
the remaining birds, and when he leaves his concealment
they do not scatter, for they have learned no fear.

There is not much doubt but that the Maori used a
similar tactic against the vulnerable seal, which is swiftly
and easily killed by a sharp blow upon the skull where it
is joined by the bridge of the nose. Seal and Maori lived
together, and most of the time in friendliness; for the
Maori would not kill more than he could eat.

The seals upon the beach — fur-seals, or sea lions, but more properly sea bears, the dominant race of the southern oceans — were further protected by the hinterland, which offered no very desirable facilities for gardeners or fishermen. In the fishing seasons Maoris occupied more sheltered bays; when they neglected the sea for their gardens their habit in this district was to move far inland, somewhere near an eel-creek, and land convenient to their hoes.

The Maori did not disturb the seal in his resorts, but when the European with his vasty hungers came to the land conditions changed; and the seals accepted the new order after a time, and dealt intelligently with it. All the pelagic mammals, indeed, modified their ways of life, but only after a slaughter so intensive that it is a wonder that the races survived at all. For the Europeans too were cunning, their hunting ability was sharpened by a greed which knew no personal bounds, and their catches were limited only by the capacity of their broad-beamed vessels to hold the skins.

They brought women to the hunt, naked Tasmanian women, who swam to advance on the rookeries from the sea. The bull seals, guardians of the herd, each in his own eyrie on the rock and surrounded each with his harem of complacent cows, were conscious of the femininity of the invaders. They sensed no danger; they were amused, indeed, at the antics of the dark women from the sea.

The women, sometimes bribed with insignificant rewards, and sometimes driven by the threat and remembrance of unbelievable cruelties, flopped on their bellies like the seals themselves, leaping on all fours over the seal-smoothed rocks, winding among the cows to approach the lords of the harems with a mock humility and the implied offering of their bodies.

When all were in position, each took the little club she carried doubled back against her forearm, and struck her chosen bull on the nose to his death. And then began the slaughter of the cows and the young calves; of everything that moved within the rookery. The women now were joined by the sailors, who had waited in the dories in the sea near at hand; naked and splashed with blood and excrement they worked like flailing demons to gather their harvest of hides and flesh, and few escaped them. And then began the long and weary task of skinning the carcasses and dressing the skins.

Small wonder that great fortunes were based upon the skins of seals. And smaller wonder still that the seals abandoned such of their resorts as were close to the habitations of men.

The abandonment must have been by some edict of the government of sea bears; for members of the race are friendly to individual humans. And the concerted movements of the seal tribes cannot, for a number of reasons, be ascribed to the promptings of instinct alone.

For example, it is mandatory that a seal must navigate. Currents change, seasons are not consistent; yet the seal can so arrange his voyaging that year after year he meets companions on a particular day on a particular rock that is itself a speck in an ocean of unimaginably wide extent. The invariables which he must use are the heavenly bodies. He is aided, in shallower seas only, by recognizable landmarks above and below the water. We cannot estimate the percentage who fail to arrive at the trysting places; we only know it must be small.

And if, in any year, some breeding-grounds are abandoned and the use of others developed, it seems impossible that the situation is arrived at except by edict; by forethought and planning, at least, which is communicated to the tribe. But, as with the human race, there are always rebels; and one such rebel came back to the playgrounds of his ancestors one year when I was small.

We children knew him first, of course. We found him sleeping stertorously on the beach, and we kept a respectable distance. We watched and watched, and finally the others drifted off, for it was more than time for the evening meal. But I knew a compulsion to stay and wait, and watch in something like awe this creature of the sea who had no obvious fear of people.

When the sun went down at last he turned his massive head around, devoted a second or two to an inspection of the small boy watching him and shivering in the evening chill, then tucked his cumbersome hind flippers underneath him and in a series of springing movements made rapidly for the ocean. To my amazement he ran as fast as a dog once he came to the hard-packed sand near the water's edge.

Perhaps he was hungry, and eager for his fish. He looked a humorous fellow with a great love of life, and I decided immediately he was a friend.

As the first breaker struck him he straightened out,

and with his awkward land-legs now put to a more proper use he thrust through the water like a torpedo. After he had negotiated every second or third breaker he seemed to pause to appreciate the accomplishment, though it must have been child's play to him. He lifted his head and shook the water from his whiskers in a gesture so much like a typical one of old Fatty Bargeman who kept the grocer's shop that I crowed and laughed my delight. Behind the farthest breaker he looked round once more, then sped with the grace and ease of a mountain trout towards the island.

I thought to see him no more; but next day he waddled out from the sea. He came in a series of convulsive leaps rather than a waddle, as though the movement initiated about the center of his backbone, and his inadequate legs had no function other than to accept the landing shocks. With his tiny tail clamped tight like that of a dachshund in disgrace, and looking uncommonly like a dachshund with his expression of intelligent determination, he headed straight for the soft sand at the foot of the dunes, and I moved away in some trepidation.

But his only purpose was "a little sleep, a little slumber, a little folding of the hands to sleep," for he cared not at all for the threat of poverty, and his wealth at that moment was the thin spring sunshine that dried and illumined his hair, golden-brown against the dazzle of the sand.

And soon I moved back close again, and lay on my belly as he did, between him and the sea, so that I could watch his great round eyes and count the bristles of his moustache. If a cat needed bristles, as I had been told, in order to know whether it could negotiate a narrow space, why did a great sea bear need them at all? Surely there were no narrow spaces in his life. But when, that night, I asked my mother, she said, "Perhaps he just looks good in them."

The sea bear became a feature of the beach; people became proud of him and christened him "Joey." And he became entwined with my life. My mother's blood came pure from the Shetlands; her traditions were all of the north; and in my reading I was well acquainted with the seal-folk of the haunted islands of the Pentland Firth, and the Blue Men who lived between the Shant and the island of Lewis, and Finn, and Angus, and the King of the Green Isle. Perhaps I knew more of the wintry north and felt closer to it then than I do now; there was a wonderland at nights wherein my mother took me on her knee and sang to me, old songs like "Robin Grey" that still have power to enclose me.

So I tried to make friends with the beach creature; and to an extent I suppose I did. But he was feckless and faithless; he could be lured away with a fish from the fishmonger; and later, when he had acquired the taste, with a bar of chocolate or a bottle of lemonade.

Joey became especially fond of lemonade; he preferred the large bottles. They had to be presented to him opened; he took them in his mouth and tossed his head back and let the prickly, gas-filled liquid gurgle down his throat. He became the most pampered sea bear that ever lived.

But lemonade and chocolate would make him sick,

and when Joey was sick it was a good time to leave the locality. He suffered occasionally, and fearsomely, from badness of breath; he breathed seldom, not more than once in two or three minutes; but when he did his breath would carry.

Some of us who were frequently upon the beach became familiar with Joey; especially on those cold days when a wind was blowing yet it was bright, so that we wanted to enjoy the sunshine on our skins. We would lean up against his great golden sides, and Joey would grunt in comfort, expelling a gusty draught of air tainted with fish odors and worse, that soon, however, was dispelled in the breeze.

He must have weighed a little more than half a ton; he was a considerable length and possessed a good bulk. There were those who claimed that he was recovering from an illness, or that an accident had destroyed his powers of navigation; but boys on the beach never believed that. He liked our company, and that was the whole secret.

It was inevitable that he would one day explore farther, perhaps following some one of us up the concrete steps to the road. He was certainly not impressed or awed by the habitations of man that he discovered, yet aspects of our life must have been pleasing.

Some evenings he would romp into the little sweet-shop where we stood about for an hour or two before bedtime. The shop carried a stock of fruit too, stacked in the cases in which it had left the orchards. The cases had their tops removed, and stood propped at a good display angle against the front of the counter. Joey, in an impish mood one night, swung on his front flippers and sent a dozen cases flying with his hindquarters. With the floor covered with rolling apples and oranges and tomatoes and plums and apricots, he suddenly leaped forward, flopping on his belly on top of them, and slithering and sliding right out the door on to the footpath.

The incident had several results. For one, the shop-keeper thereafter shut his doors when Joey appeared; for another, Joey went out looking for new adventures. The discovery that he had a sense of humor led in the end, I suppose, to his undoing; but the end was a long way ahead.

He had another sense too, which frightened our elders. He knew quite clearly which of the humans about him were female, and would demonstrate his knowledge with antics which (we felt) were decidedly rude. He got the habit of sleeping indoors in one of the few big blocks of apartments then just beginning to be built. In that he displayed a further idiosyncrasy: he would climb the stairs up two or three stories and eventually choose a sleeping place. If a door had been inadvertently left open, that sleeping place could conceivably be a lounge or sofa; and inevitably the lounge or sofa was thereafter bereft of most of its usefulness.

But wherever he slept, if it were not on the beach, it was somewhere in the vicinity of a sleeping girl. He never made a closer approach than that; but Joey loved the opposite sex, and since females of his own kind were not available, he sought the solace of proximity to females of the human kind.

He had a curiosity which led him into queer places too. He managed to push his way into a small phone booth one night, and there somehow contrived to have the inward-opening door close on him; the booth was wrecked by the time he got free.

One night a lover and his lass, absorbed in matters of moment in some darkened haven of the lupin-covered sandhills, had left their car, an ancient model, on the nearby road, and Joey was at hand. Some of us, unsympathetic to lovers, obtained a fish for the purpose of inducing Joey to occupy the back seat of the jalopy. Joey complied; perhaps he had often wondered about the interiors of cars, and anyway he was always amenable to suggestion. He was rewarded with his fish; and finding the seat to his liking, settled down for a few moments of comfort.

We waited a good while, as I remember, for the return of the lovers. When they came, starry-eyed, they climbed into the front seat without a backward glance, and set off down the road. They stopped before the driver had time to change his gears; Joey, delighted to find himself in motion without a conscious effort, had heaved himself up from the attitude of slumber and was gazing with rapture at the road ahead, his great intelligent face beaming, his whiskers tickling the driver's ear. There were satisfactory screams and protests, and the lovers piled out of the car, leaving it in the middle of the road.

Joey wanted more; he had no intention of leaving.

Threats and protests did not worry him. He held his position. We watched and made unhelpful suggestions until the interest palled, and finally left upon our own occasions.

Joey, however, from this experience as I believe, developed an immediate interest in transport which, for a time, he was hard put to satisfy. But shortly he discovered the electric trams; and established, moreover, that at the end of the track, only a few hundred yards from the beach, these vehicles, provided handily with steps he could negotiate and permanently opened doors, had to wait a minute or two while crews switched trolley poles and driving handles and altered the destination plates. He rode happily into town, not once, but day after day for weeks.

Three miles away, the trams approached the harbor wharves, and Joey discovered for himself that he could ride the public transport to a new and desirable fishing spot; altogether an impressive display of applied intelligence for a creature from the wildest of the world's wild oceans.

Tram crews hated him. When they observed him waiting at the terminus they made their changeovers in record time; they learned to have a fish at hand to take care of emergencies; they resorted to all sorts of wiles to circumvent him. But Joey was always patient; if he should miss a tram he knew that another would come along in ten minutes.

The municipality, the owner of the tram system, had nothing to complain of. They owed Joey a considerable debt; for months they had been running special services to the beach, which even on dull days had been crowded with families of children eager to observe the phenomenon of the sea bear.

But Joey's ability and willingness to enter into the life of the community was not sufficient to fit him for the role of public idol. Adulation and flattery went to his head. Gentle and mild-mannered though he was, a super-pinniped, he would have had to be superhuman not to have failed in the responsibilities of popularity.

The hordes of children, emboldened progressively by each other's successes, went too far; there came a day when Joey demonstrated an increasing displeasure by biting a small lad who, in the company of his father, had been interrupting Joey's efforts to sleep with importunities and attentions. The elders of the community held a conference, and a captured Joey was dispatched to a northern zoo. There, they reasoned, he could enjoy the company of crowds and be relieved of the necessity of catching his food. Indeed he could live like a lord.

But Joey lived only a week, and all of us, his friends, believed and still believe that he died of a broken heart. We were close to being broken-hearted ourselves. We had learned to respect Joey as well as like him; we knew when to leave him alone.

We knew that he loved music; that he took a strange delight in the Sunday morning atmosphere charged with church bells; his little ears, that had heard nothing of the like at sea or near the wild rookery where he had been born, could well have been trained to respond to cultivated tastes. He loved the Swanee whistles which at that time were all the rage among us, and he would sway back and forth upon his great front flippers, sometimes grunting with delight.

It must have been two or three years later when Sammy arrived. He was larger than Joey had been, his coat was yellower than gold, but he displayed the same propensities. He became sexually excited in the presence of girls. He learned to ride in the public transport — not without prompting from those of us who remembered Joey. Sammy would try to stop the trams by lying across the tracks; and it took him a good while to learn about the enforced delay at the terminus.

He did not enter into the life of the community with the same verve. Perhaps he was introduced to it too quickly. It was taught him, whereas the habits Joey had evolved were based upon discoveries of his own.

Nevertheless, Sammy was loved. He was a great happy oaf; he learned to join in simpler games; but like the dachshunds he resembled he made rules of his own. He too became a victim of civilization. He was run over by a heavy truck one night as he lay in the road. He could not learn the human rules of community life.

The year after Sammy died, a small female seal came up on the beach and was made much of for three days. Then she disappeared. Several months later she returned, with a youngster. They stayed on the beach one afternoon and one evening. And that night I went down late with a stick, and beat them until they took to the water.

I was sick with what I was doing, but I knew that it

was right. I hated to do it. And perhaps the two of them, mother and child, were there by accident, but I did not take the risk. Nor did I ever tell anyone what I had done; there was no need.

12

THE PACIFIC OCEAN, larger by the size of a second Africa than all the land surfaces of the world, drains an area which is less than a quarter of that which drains to the Atlantic, a body of water which is half the size of the Pacific and less than half its volume. Two centuries ago the coasts upon which it surges were those of hinterlands lightly or not at all inhabited, save upon a sector of its northeast boundary. Human enjoyment and exploitation of its bounty is recent, and as yet far from thorough. Its waterways still are lonely, the traffic thin and undeveloped.

Even geologically the area is mysterious. The absence of granite, a condition obtaining nowhere else in the crust of the earth, is unexplained except by the likely enough hazard that from this point was riven the material that went to the nucleus of earth's satellite, the moon. And perhaps if this be true, the circumstance was, from a human viewpoint, fitting; for nowhere else on earth has the loving study of the heavenly bodies been so essential to survival. Nowhere else has a way of life been predicated upon a communal knowledge of astronomy. The moon and the stars, the sun and the planets were the only invariables in this great area; they were the loved familiars of the many scattered groups of people who came here to find their chances of survival bounded by their ability to navigate.

The history of the Pacific is normally said to begin with the voyage of Magellan, who, to the glory of the then weak but far-sighted adolescent Charles of Spain, sailed westward to the Moluccas in command of the first ship destined to circumnavigate the globe. But Magellan, as a Portuguese, had ten years earlier sailed with Diogo Lopes de Sequeira for the Spice Islands, rounding the Cape of Good Hope, and a little later, with D'Abreu, reached Amboina; he was already acquainted with the Pacific. When he had negotiated the straits between Tierra del Fuego and the American mainland he had not discovered an ocean, but only a new route. Long before his time, Marco Polo had briefly sailed Pacific waters.

Eighteen centuries ago Lucian, the rhetorician whose lecture circuit encompassed Asia Minor, Macedonia, Greece, Italy and Gaul, wrote of certain animals that "use their belly as a pouch." Lucian had no personal knowledge of the marsupials of Australia and Melanesia. In the light of his attitude to the seas beyond the Pillars of Hercules, it is, I should think, out of the question that he could have been referring to any of the few pouched animals in Central or South America. But on his many voyages in tiny ships he must have made close friendships with some of the sailors with whom he loved to travel. And from one or several heard garbled tales of the phenomenon.

This is slight evidence to suggest that before Lucian's day some tiny ship, Egyptian perhaps, had penetrated the great waters south and east, setting out from the Red Sea or the Persian Gulf to navigate the Indian Ocean. But that Lucian's reference is some evidence is a persistent thought. It is insubstantially backed by certain stories and beliefs that have come down from those ancient times — beliefs reflected by Shakespeare, for instance, when he wrote of "the anthropophagi, and the men whose heads do grow beneath their shoulders." A thousand sights might suggest so wild a fantasy; but none more forcibly than that of a doe kangaroo whose well-developed youngster, concealed as to his body, looks out fearlessly and improbably from his thickly furred vantage in her belly.

However insubstantial such evidence might seem, it is certain that the history we assign to the Pacific is nothing more than the history of voyages recorded by Europeans in that area. In general they are voyages promoted or authorized by royalty; so that the motive for making the record becomes apparent. We have little current knowledge of unauthorized voyages, or of those that were authorized but unsuccessful. But it is certain that some were made; that adventurers went out and some returned, and from their related experiences rumors and reports were born to spur the others.

Our knowledge of Pacific history dates only from the time when ship's masters entered up their logs; our concept of the circumstances of its exploration is limited to those explorers who were literate, and we have little knowledge of other probings.

Yet they happened. On the island of Kiriwina is a district called Lekweweia, a hilltop where native gardens produce an amazing variety of lush vegetable crops from the poor, coral-based ground. In back of the gardens the tropical forest has taken over, but if you hack your way through the creeper-festooned saplings you will come, at some difficulty, upon the ruins of a group of buildings. They are four in number and their walls are molded of a mortar of sand and burnt lime, a method of construction you will not find today in Melanesia.

The buildings are regular trapezoids about sixty feet in length and fifteen to eighteen feet wide, and there seems to be an affinity between their angles and the position of the Pleiades in the constellation Taurus. While the Trobrianders have no knowledge today of the men who built the mortar buildings, the seasonal appearances of the Pleiades at dawn or in the evening are still as important to them as Virgil says they were to the Roman farmers of his day. The variable Trobriand year and all the annual celebrations of the islanders are calculated from these appearances.

There are other ruins of the same material at Duwulaosi, half a mile away, and still another upon the neighboring island of Kitava. There are also one or two small enclosures elsewhere. Little study of these ruins is possible, for Allied governments, during the second World War, having nothing else to destroy here, used them for convenient artillery practice targets; and government officers, bored in their comparative isolation, have conducted extensive and destructive investigations on their own behalf, without the mental equipment necessary to draw conclusions from what they might have found.

But some remnants yet offer evidence that men of other nations occupied the island along with the Trobrianders, and possibly preceded them.

Strong clay pots found in underground caverns, and differing materially from the cooking pots which the Trobrianders (being based upon islands without clay) imported traditionally from the nearby Amphletts, confirm the existence of alien men upon the island; in all probability the same as those who knew building practices allied to early European ones.

Only two or three hundred miles away, in Milne Bay, in New Guinea, my old friend Cecil Abel, born in that area (the son of Charles Abel, a fabulous figure in the history of the London Mission Society) found an ancient and complicated irrigation system, many centuries abandoned. The fields it served were marked with boundary stones carrying inscriptions he described as "Egyptian." Near the head of the whole system a sunburst carved on a rock, unallied to any Melanesian carving, proclaimed the identity, the religious beliefs, or the ideals of some forgotten race.

Once in the mountains at Chimbu, in Central New

Guinea, the aircraft in which I traveled was forced to a landing by enclosing fogs; and while we stayed in that place, the pilot and I, I acquired an ancient grain mortar carved of stone. It had lain half-buried for many centuries, during which the occasional passage of naked human feet had worn one side of the ironstone. But the hollow for holding the grain was intact, and so were protuberances carved in a regular series for the purpose of rotating the mortar with the hand that was not occupied with the pestle. No grain had been grown in the district within memory; no crops required crushing.

The altitude of the place was so great that there was some doubt about whether our twin-engined aircraft would become airborne; we therefore emptied the gas tanks except for four gallons a side, which was sufficient to take us to a nearby field at a lower level. We unloaded the cargo and the native passengers, and took off at minimum weight. The mortar was sacrificed. Some weeks later a native, knowing of my regret in leaving it behind, appeared with it in Lae a couple of hundred miles away, and gave it to me, though he did not even know my language.

To me the mortar is yet another indication that at some time men of a higher culture than those now remaining traversed the Pacific to make their settlement in the New Guinea mountains. Its design is far in advance of that of the simple querns with which the aborigines of Australia prepare grain for consumption. As far as I know, no other native grain-crushing methods exist at a nearer distance; though the principle of the mortar and pestle is known, and applied in small hand-carried artifacts with which the elderly, whose teeth have vanished and whose gums have grown tender, crack the hard nuts of betel and pound them to a paste.

Such discoveries testify to intrusions of the Pacific by small communities, communities that subsequently suffered obliteration by either conquest or absorption into the larger indigenous communities. These movements were probably unallied to the several great population transfers that can be traced in this huge area.

When man first came to the Pacific his wealth and his sustenance lay in the water. There were no useful animals on land, very few fruits or vegetables that he could turn to his account, and the barest minimum of useful earths and minerals. There were timbers and cordage for the exploitation of the sea, and that was all. He was not drawn there by any rich natural offerings.

It is unlikely that he was lured by legend, for he traveled to the eastward — this much is sure — while the dreamers, the seekers of Elysium, travel always to the West, following the sun, the moon and the stars. In the Pacific the "Haven of the Blest," when it exists, lies always in the west; or in the northwest, whence the people came.

If his motive was adventure, he came without women; and if he did not return, his race was therefore destroyed. The first who came to stay must have brought their women; they were either returned adventurers, enamored of the lands they had seen, or refugees from intolerable conditions in their own homelands; and in all probability a mixture of both. It is not long since the first of them came. The peculiar problems of the region prevented any penetration before neolithic times (except, and this theoretically, to the continent of Australia); indeed, radio-carbon tests have not shown any artifact which can be dated before the year 2000 B.C. But the great migrations of primitive times all came before the age of metals; as soon as man was even lightly equipped to explore the area he accepted the challenge.

At least three movements spread, from Japan, from the South China Coast, and from the East India tangle of land and water, over the lonely ocean to isolated havens where, without interference, the small groups developed along a pattern conditioned by their similar environments. To exist they had to be adventurous, intelligent and resourceful; and they existed. Their adversaries were their fellows, the denizens of ocean, and the storms of air. There were no beasts of prey; they were remarkably free from disease, the climate was more favorable than in any other place on earth, and they walked in scenes of beauty.

Nevertheless, living was hazardous. On many and many an island there was, in the beginning, nothing at all for them to eat, and they survived on the plentiful offerings of the sea. They had birds and their eggs, and shellfish; but few fruits. Some of the new islands were volcanic and, as the earth rolls, of comparatively recent origin. Others had been lately formed of coral, and held no water.

They brought, therefore, the animals they considered

useful: the dog, the pig, an edible rat, the domestic fowl; and with these augmented their security. They ranged the Pacific for useful plants, and cultivated these to such an extent that near many of their villages no tree existed that did not have a function in their economy.

It is a common illusion that the coconut is distributed by ocean currents; it floats, and retains its fertility in the water for a period. Yet on dozens of new-formed islands the coconut does not flourish. I have seen islands with a considerable vegetation, and on their shores a litter of nuts cast up by the tide, yet none growing. The mangroves have taken root and begun their work of reclamation from the sea, and often a small forest of pisonias or hymerliodendrums is making a humus in the sand. But in my experience, when islands are so far developed as to carry coconuts and bananas, these have been planted by natives against the mischance of being stranded there in some future day, or so they may use the new land as a depot from which to exploit a fishing ground. In such islands you will find taro patches as well, or transplanted bushes of tapioca, long before there is a chance of human habitation.

This acclimatization work of humans seems to me a much more probable explanation of the establishment of the coconut on every likely island eastward from its Indian home than the vagaries of ocean currents. Its incidence in Central America can also be attributed to the primitive voyagers; for there is little doubt that they brought the sweet potato from that place and established it in every point within the area of the Pacific.

They assisted likewise the spread of the breadfruit, and of the paper hibiscus for their necessary textiles. They transplanted vines which produced a mastic for boat-building, and shrubs whose only quality was a beautiful scent; for in those equable climates their aesthetic senses had been well developed. They became conservationists; showing an intelligent selectivity in their hunting of birds, and excellent gardeners despite the poor soils at their disposal.

They came to execute wonderful work in wood, and in some instances their pottery was excellent; though often their clay had to be brought great distances in canoes. Their woven work and sennet was of a high standard, as one might expect of a maritime people. Their transport was the canoe, and they had no need to develop the wheel; they were acquainted with the use and function of rollers. They dug no mines, except in deposits of workable stone, of jade and serpentine; the only other treasure that the earth held for them was fresh water; and once they had established the coconut they had no desperate need for constant supplies of that. They became highly ingenious in the development of means for collecting it from unlikely sources.

Between Lae and Salamaua, in New Guinea's Huon Gulf, there is a village called Bwussi, where the neat clean houses, lifted on piles high above the bright white sand, nestle back against the fringing trees at the edge of the beach. The housewife here, of habit, prepares her vegetables in the surf, and boils them in sea water; the family bathes in it; the edge of the quiet and placid bay is always loud with human life. I inquired about fresh water, and was shown a place where a bank of moist clay was overshadowed by ferns and trees. It was a tiny bank, perhaps a foot wide; and freshly pressed into the clay was a green leaf. Its glossy surface collected moisture; and it was so placed that from its curled tip brilliant drops cast themselves down to be collected by a bamboo which led into a galvanized iron bucket. The whole village subsisted on this supply, which, for as long as the people had lived there apparently, had been ensured each morning by the skilful positioning of a new green leaf. Patience was their great asset; it enabled them to make use of a supply that would have been overlooked by Europeans, who consider themselves more practical. And back to the earliest days, the people had had time enough.

With successive migrations, their great enemy became man himself; and, man against man, they developed skills and strategies that sometimes made them more than equal to the more highly civilized Europeans when they arrived. Each wave of the newcomers developed their spiritual beliefs and increased their mental creativity by nothing more than the provision of the stimulus of competition, a competition in which the communal prize was life and living quarters, and the personal reward was a place in the local history. They became storytellers of merit, and established and preserved traditions.

The movements into their territory were of two kinds. In the first, some hardy buccaneers arrived without their women, and made settlement by conquest or were driven back to plan later campaigns. The record of conquest remains in the diversity of gods they worshiped; for conquered women clung to the tenets of their own people and taught them to their children. An example of this otherwise unrecorded history comes from the Maori warriors who would not touch the cooking-pots or sit by the cooking-fires; their wives and children lost no caste by this, for they represented long-forgotten ancestors seized in some after-battle rape. But the men followed the practice established by the ancient conquerors; only such a domination could have established this pattern.

Later, when the tenure of the conquered lands was firm, the invaders sent for reinforcements; and these arrived with their own women. The pattern of colonization was shrewd and intelligent. The new arrivals were primarily navigators and seamen; their country was the ocean, and whatever island they chose for a base was above all a strongpoint from which they could exploit the waters under their command.

In their voyages they were limited by the seasons, which control the trade winds. South of the equator the southeast monsoon is dominant for six months of the year; during the other six it is supplanted by variable winds, mainly from the northwest, the direction which gives its name to this monsoon. These correspond to the northeast and southwest monsoons of the northern hemisphere.

But the seamen were inhibited in their wanderings by the limitations of their craft, which could not sail well into the wind. In place of the keel they had an outrigger, and the mast carrying the sail had to be so stepped that this outrigger stood to leeward, the bow and stern being interchangeable. Tacking, therefore, was not feasible; most voyages were made with the wind abaft of abeam, and a favorable wind was essential.

With their accurate knowledge of the seasons and the weather, with ample time to plan their movements, this was not a seriously inhibiting factor, as anyone must realize after consideration of the enormous stretches of ocean they explored in days when Europeans were still too timid to coast their vessels down the shores of Africa, in days that preceded the voyages of the Norwegians across the upper Atlantic, so that the Pacific was thoroughly explored before Columbus was born. In the Southern Hemisphere, canoe voyages to the south were made just before the beginning of the southeast monsoon, voyages to the north just before its end, if an early return was desired.

Such voyages were not made every day. In most communities, regular trading voyages were made at these seasons; the great voyages of discovery and resettlement were planned sometimes for years ahead. Man did not cover these tremendous distances by chance; he forged boldly out, knowing that his return was scheduled by the incontrovertible laws of the weather patterns, and he was amply provisioned for both stages of his journey.

But in the day-to-day economy of the islands it was essential at times to ride the prevailing wind, say to the fishing grounds which served the island community. Such voyages demanded a return powered by muscle. More frequently the crews would paddle the empty vessels to the grounds in the teeth of the wind, and sail triumphantly home with their freights.

But Tawhiri-Matea, the God of the Winds, could find it in his heart to be angry, and he was not always predictable. If he raised the storm it might be necessary to abandon the idea of returning home, and instead make for some haven to wait for favorable weather.

The tribes, therefore, as they spread out over the ocean and came to a new group of habitable islands, selected as a rule the more central ones for their headquarters. In a group of three islands, the middle one would probably be selected for permanent habitation, even if the most northerly or the most southerly was the most fertile. In this way were created the emergency havens of the outliers.

Where gardens were essential to village life, their preparation and culture occupied nearly all the season of the less strong monsoon; and fishing was limited to the season in which dependable winds prevailed. Then the system was sometimes modified, so that in the Southern Hemisphere, for example, only small islands to the west and north of the group were left uninhabited. They were not, however, without tribal ownership, nor were they left in their original states.

The absentee owners planted them with the essentials for life. They set sprouting coconuts on the ground, they planted taro and bananas and sweet potatoes in such forest glades as might be suitable, and sometimes fruits. They saw to it that there was a supply of pandanus, of which the aerial roots provided them with ropes and twine for canoe repairs, and the leaves could be sewn into sails. They planted a certain forest vine which, when pounded, made a quick-drying mastic to mend the hulls and caulk the seams. And later, if they found their island in possession of alien people when they visited it upon their annual tours of inspection, they sprang to their weapons in defense of this property.

This is one reason why Europeans have sometimes reported unprovoked attacks by "savages." In the early days of European penetration, many a small ship's crew availed itself of the fruits of such an island and was assailed by the defending spears of its owners. The natives in such cases acted in good faith and with the same motives as any patriot who ever went to the defense of his homeland. The crops they planted had to be left intact for an emergency. In my belief, wherever the first contact with long-isolated tribes has produced any reaction other than a friendly inquiry, some such reason has always been at the bottom of the conflict.

Still others of the islands were set apart so that a dependable crop of some foodstuff or other might accumulate. Islands particularly favored by egg-laying turtles are a case in point. It is essential for certain beaches to be left inviolate until the height of the season, when a special expedition goes to capitalize on the turtles, their eggs, and their predators — the marauding fish which also preestimate the harvest. Where these islands are outliers — as frequently they are, for the turtle is by no means unaware of their comparative inaccessibility — a double function for the island is assured.

A similar crop may be harvested from an underwater reef attached to the island and specially productive of shellfish, or from surf beneath which the huge green snails of ocean thrive, or from sheltered beds of grasslike weed where seasonally the dugongs flock to graze. Still another island frequented by birds might offer an annual crop of eggs. It is impossible to estimate how many un-inhabited islands are essential, or were essential, to some native economy.

Not long ago, on one of the outliers attached to the Lusancays, west of the Trobriand group, a white trader based upon the Trobriands discovered a reef whereon the trochus, valuable for its shell, thrived in quantity. This particular outlier is a small sandy shoal, not more than three hundred yards broad, an idyllic spot where I have swum and sunned to a comfortable repletion. Its name is Kunupuaka; the chart erroneously calls it Gwadarab; and it lies about twenty miles north and west of Kawa, the only high island and one of the three inhabited islands of the Lusancay group.

Kawa, one of the most isolated communities in the Coral Sea, controls several outliers, from Kunuku fifteen miles to its west, through Kanapo, Kuduladi, Konoko-nuvana, Nukuana and Gabwina to this furthest outpost. All of them represent, for the Kawa community of not more than two hundred souls, refuges from the consistent winds of the southeast monsoon. In other seasons the in-habited islands of the Trobriand group, to whose King

Metakata the Lusancay people pay lip service, form a refuge.

The Trobriand trader brought fishermen from the large Trobriand island of Kaileuna to exploit the shell. Normally they would not have ventured so far; but he towed their canoes to the island and ordered them to help themselves to the excellent food growing there. In their modern greed for money the Kaileuna men so far forgot their ancient morality as to accede. They fished until they had nothing more to eat, at which time he brought them back, and bought their shell.

Within a month, four canoes from Kawa, dependent upon the reserve at Kunupuaka, came to that island and were unable to return. One young man had his wife alone in the canoe with him, another his wife and four children. The two remaining canoes were crewed by four and six men respectively. They had anticipated the turtle-fishing, and had expected to wait a week or two for the season to begin. They were unable to do this and would have been on short commons except that they were rescued by another trader, who was making his first visit to the district in two years. They were, therefore, lucky.

The trader took them to the Trobriands, where they appealed to the Australian administration against the despoiling of their island; but the local representative, a youth of twenty-three years, on making inquiries found that there was no permanent habitation on the island.

"The island belongs to the Queen," he said in his judgment. "Therefore anyone is permitted to use its vegetables and fruits."

I was not present at this dispensation of justice, but I spoke to the disinherited later, and their brown eyes were blank with puzzlement. They accepted the judgment, though, and that was not strange, for they had known for sixty years that a new era was on its way. But at this moment the old ways had had their foundations cut away, and the new ones were not yet established.

Kunupuaka looks today as it has looked for centuries, unchanged, except that in the quiet water near the reef the wreck of a Liberator bomber, not much damaged, has stood a couple of decades to mark the coming of war to these lands. But in the eyes of Kawa it is a different place. The solace and assurance of its presence have gone. It no longer counters the hazards of canoe-voyaging in the southeast season; new customs and new laws have erased its significance.

13

Four years after the end of the Pacific war I was visiting New Guinea for the second time on behalf of a group of Australian newspapers. My principals had given me a free hand to report on whatever excited my interest. The only restriction was a date set for my return; and I had exceeded this limit when I heard that it might be possible for me to join an expedition bound up the main stream of the mysterious and mighty Sepik River. Such an opportunity was not likely to come my way again. It was seven years since a patrol boat had tackled the upper reaches of the Sepik, which were little known; and that expedition, conducted under the necessities of war, had done little to meet the tribesmen who lived in that country without any knowledge whatever of the world outside.

That world, in the intervening years, had changed its

collective attitude. It had demanded that the country be opened up, that contact be made with the people, that they be introduced to the startling proposition that men could live at peace with neighbors and trade with them, and be accounted members of the human race.

Our expedition was successful to the degree that we made peaceful contact with two tribes who had never seen Europeans or dreamed of their existence. We renewed what had been a brief wartime alliance with a third, and made the first peaceful overtures to a fourth, with whom previous encounters had always been warlike, ending in deaths. We brought representatives of all four back to civilization in order to teach them a language that would facilitate future communication, to show them some social advantages in future contact, and to train them to encourage their people to establish and maintain at least a slender acquaintance with others.

For our convenience we named these tribes for the tributaries that ran into the main current near their concealed villages, so they became the April River people, the May Rivers, and the Yellow Rivers, though they carry other names today. The fourth tribe was the Wagamush, whose name had been known. Our journey had secondary effects among other tribes: the Swargup people, for example, who had known the Japanese but not the Australians. Still others who had long remained upon the limits of previous European influence could verify, because of the expedition's existence, the Administration's beneficient intention to spread its authority.

Wherever we went we bought weapons of war, as

many as were offered, and paid for them in cloth and fishhooks, and machetes which well might be used for weapons, but not in the traditional fighting of these canoe people.

From other aspects the expedition might have been counted a failure, though Horry Niall, the experienced Australian officer in charge, was well satisfied with the results we achieved. But he had previously seen, from the cockpit of a cruising light aircraft, a village composed of houses built and laid out in good rectangles, which is not the native fashion; and he suspected that these might be occupied by the remnants of General Haruda's Japanese Army, of which a large number might have been deemed to have disappeared into the still trackless forests of these New Guinea mountainsides. We proposed to reach this village if we could; but we never did; the falling river might have trapped us had we tried.

Then there was a recovery of buried treasure. At a point on which a patrol center had been briefly established at the beginning of war a cache of silver coins had been made. When we reached the spot we found that the river had changed its course and bitten deeply into the area; the trees that had been used as markers had been swept away.

There was the body of an Australian officer to be recovered, if we could manage it, from Wagamush territory. We found no trace. There was an expatriate to return to his people, so that he might bring them to us in friendship. This we accomplished, but with unforeseen results.

The expedition consisted of five white men including me, eight New Guinea police boys, all picked men and fine types, a few boatboys, houseboys and interpreters — though these last could interpret very little — and Meera, a native lad no more than nine or ten years old.

Meera's function was to appear on deck through as many of the daylight hours as was practicable; to be seen by hidden eyes, and to indicate by his presence that we were a party coming in peace. For this purpose women, theoretically, would have been better; in the cramped condition of the expedition such an inclusion would have been impossible. In the mornings when I awoke in my hammock I had to stretch a foot downward and gently kick among the brown bodies sleeping beneath until I could find a place to put it.

We traveled for days upon the calm surface of the river. The water was thick with mud; and perhaps because of this opaque quality it reflected all the colors of the forest and the sky. I have never seen such sunsets as came each evening to delight us, and to offset somewhat the irritation of the swarming mosquitoes; the sky was ablaze, and the blaze lit the river; and the afterglow in the east was rich and quiet.

Day and night the surface was studded with the floating flowers of the yellow hibiscus, like palm-sized buttercups, spinning and nodding in the current, each weighted by its calyx and given some independent motion by the breezes in the yellow silk of its sails. The surface was studded more importantly for our pilots with huge trees, a dangerous flotsam; and with the floating islands I have not seen anywhere else in the world. The sugar cane with which these islands were inevitably grassed was usually broken and flood-swept; sometimes it harbored snakes, or a sleeping crocodile. Some of the islands that passed us were as large as half an acre; the old hands on the river tell me that islands of a three-acre spread have negotiated the channels. They are formed by the river undercutting the matted stands of wild sugar which establish themselves on all the newer banks of this water-course; and they can be a considerable hazard to navigation. Each night as we lay at anchor there was a danger that one would tangle with the chain. We kept a constant anchor watch; and indeed we had several struggles with tree trunks that swept us from our anchorages.

The Sepik comes at such speed from the mountains that it is forever cutting new courses, and as quickly builds up sandbars. The bars are covered soon with sugar, thick and matted, sending its arrows on stalks twelve to fifteen feet high. Almost everywhere this rapid process of reclamation was matched, on the other bank, by the inroads the river made into primeval forest. It was in its annual flood at the time of our expedition; several times in a day we would watch a forest giant fall, slowly, impeded by the mass of vines which joined it to its still-standing fellows.

In early days, explorers on the lower reaches frequently reported headless bodies floating on the Sepik current. We saw none. On one stretch, though, we saw four war canoes, an expedition with a complement of forty men. They sheered away from us and were lost in the channels that threaded the sugar. But one of our number reported that the wrapped bundles in the slim hulls were, in fact, human heads — fresh heads, he judged, because of the blood on them.

Each evening the black fruit bats, prehistoric in their shapes and in their silences, invested the flaring colors of the sunset, the fading rosy glow of the river, with an ominous life. Each night the sounds of movement, the cries of a distant animal tragedy, seemed to emphasize man's insignificance in this terrain. The dark would come, intensified where we lay in the shelter of the forest, and with the dark an awareness, allied to fear, allied to self-preservation. It was easy to believe in spirits of no beneficence.

In the morning, when the sun dispelled the river mists, the oppressive thoughts of the night retreated, but did not disappear. The golden miles of sugar no less than the dark upstanding forest were a camouflage for a world beyond our understanding, a world that hid away from us. Yet when some aspect of this world came to our attention, and revealed itself to be innocent, even charming or attractive, the respite was a temporary one, the encouraged confidence transient, the will to resist the unknown unaffected.

For example, in a little bay we saw a woman alone with her child in a canoe. The child was a baby, no older than a year or so, wearing only a bright flowered necklace and jetty earrings. Her head was shaved except for a central line of curls; she was the pride of her mother's eye. In her hands she held a tiny carved canoe paddle, no longer than eighteen inches; and with this she kept time with her mother's strokes. The woman smiled at us as they sailed past; her daughter was wild-eyed with fright. Their canoe carried a freight of innocence and love; beyond them the river was empty.

At Wagamush, several channels merged, and the waterway became so confused that in the fog of early morning we cruised for several hours, trying to find the main stream. We kept a sharp lookout here, for people. Somewhere beyond the river was a village; it was concealed, but we searched the treetops, hoping to find a concentration of breadfruits. Sometimes we caught glimpses of scouts peering at us from the branches. We anchored, and set out gifts for the people on a sandbank at a little distance. The sound of tauls began; trumpets carved from wood, replacing the conchs used by people who lived nearer the sea. The drums joined them. Tauls and drums kept up a constant noise; from their volume we judged that there was a considerable population hidden in the vicinity, and this tallied with the reports of earlier voyagers.

At night we played bridge upon the foredeck. From a vantage above, two police boys, well armed, kept a bright spotlight circulating through the night. Circling our table two houseboys operated spray-guns, to discourage the unbelievable armies of mosquitoes that emerged from the sugar. But all we saw in the shafts of the searchlights were the red eyes of crocodiles, dozens upon dozens of them. We could not shoot, for the Wagamush were well accustomed to the sound of modern weapons, and above all we wanted to stress the peaceful nature of our expedition.

In the morning the gifts were gone from the sandbar and we immediately replaced them. Such natives as we carried who claimed to have had past contact with the Wagamush were set to calling invitations. We could not tell whether they were understood.

On the second afternoon an old, old man was sent out from the bank in a decrepit canoe to collect the gifts from the sandbar. He was trembling with fright. He had been chosen, obviously, as no longer possessing a tribal value, as had the canoe in which he traveled. We called to him, offering more gifts of the same nature — red cloth, fishing lines, razor blades, knives and hooks — from the rails of the ship; but he ignored this, and scurried away with his prizes. Immediately we sent police boys in a canoe to set out more. As soon as they were aboard again other Wagamush men came to the collection; and finally we lured some to the rail.

When they came there we gave each man a gift; and then with gestures persuaded each to sell us, in addition, his spears and daggers, his bows and arrows.

From this moment the canoes came out in strength from hidden resorts along the bank, a hustling fleet of them. There were no women in any of the craft, and every man had a variety of weapons. The canoe paddles, pointed or double-forked, were in themselves weapons; the paddlers were so adept in the slim dugouts that they danced in them — for myself I am unable to maintain a steady stance. Each canoe carried a small fire, built upon a foot-square hearth of clay or sometimes on large shards of pottery, and on the fire the elements of a meal; breadfruit, and fish, and slain birds and opossums.

We tried hard to establish communication with the Wagamush; concentrating upon a request to be shown their village. In this we avoided any reference to women, but we were anxious to see the women, because it would be an earnest that they accepted the peaceableness of our intentions.

After another day they agreed to show us where they lived.

Our expedition consisted of a large vessel about sixty-five feet in length, a smaller launch about forty, and a canoe we used for brief expeditions ashore. From the direction in which they proposed to take us it was obvious that the larger vessel would be useless; we left it therefore in charge of its skipper and a companion and five of the police boys. We had traveled only a few miles, however, in the smaller boat when we came to swamps it could no longer negotiate, and beyond the swamps, in full sight, a group of three large houses standing in the water. They were surrounded by floating constructions we afterwards identified as pigpens; roofed for protection, we thought, against crocodiles.

But there were no people surrounding the huts, no dogs, no hens, no pigs. The Wagamush still did not trust us. Either they had brought us to a group of unoccupied hunting lodges, or they had removed the women and the children, the pigs and the dogs during the previous night.

The houses were further protected against approach by river by a floating log boom.

Horry Niall and I decided to investigate. We left Ralph Ormsby, a New Guinea magistrate, in the launch with the police boys, and transferred to two of the Wagamush canoes. When we came to the floating log boom I accepted the invitation of the natives to disembark; another floating log led from the boom to the platform of the nearest house. Horry, more experienced, sat tight, and the crew of his canoe, with some difficulty, transferred their craft to the other side of the boom and paddled him up to the house.

Trying to walk on the floating log, I slipped, and immediately was caught by the elbows by the man walking behind me. He supported me in such a way that I would have been unable to get at the revolver I was carrying in a pocket of my shorts. Moreover, when I looked back I could see that the three police boys in the launch had raised their automatic weapons and taken aim, not knowing the cause of this seizure. At that moment I realized that both Horry and I were in some danger. We were completely surrounded by several hundred natives accounted savage, and unable to return without their help or co-operation. Nevertheless, the very fact of our having put ourselves trustfully into their power was our strongest asset; and personally I decided that there was no point in giving expression to any fears I held.

On the platform of the house, Horry and I further divided forces. First I stayed on the platform while he minutely inspected the interior, and then he came out while I went in. Only in this way could we maintain a communication with Ralph and the police boys; he watched me through the door opening in his turn.

The interior of the hut was roomy and large. It was apparently a sleeping place for up to a dozen families; though sleeping arrangements were, at first, a little difficult to identify. A family's bed consisted primarily of a large woven tube of fabric similar to coarse muslin, with openweave spaces; obviously a protection against mosquitoes. Within this twelve-foot long tube were certain utensils of bamboo; and there were signs that favored animals had also shared its protection. Uprights ensured that the fabric would not rest upon the skins of the sleepers. I had not seen such sleeping bags in the huts of any other tribes.

There was some good pottery; some of which I would like to have bought; but at the time I did not think of it. It was heavier than the Melanesian pottery of the sea-coasts, but of good shape; and shards of broken pottery had been preserved for various functions. The floors of the hut were of limbom palmwood; the walls were woven reeds from the sugar. We saw what we could, and left.

But this promising start of contact seemed now to have come to a dead end. We continued upriver the following day without having met anyone but warriors, and without persuading any to accompany us. Some of these warriors were young enough, perhaps twelve or fourteen years old. More than half of these youngsters wore the skins of flying foxes at their loins. On the river this is reckoned to be a homicide badge: these lads had taken the heads of enemies. Many of their elders, however, wore nothing save breastplates of pig tusks, and sometimes a curious flowerlike emblem, made of four money-cowrie shells, on the tips of their noses. Apart from those who wore flying fox skins, none wore any covering for their genitals; but many had decorated their penises with fabrications of bamboo, of gourds, of lizardskin or of weaving.

Before we left we indicated, as well as we could, our intention of returning.

Similarly we met the people at the May River and the April; people who had never before seen others not of their race. We had passed the April and moved into a region in which the mountains began to converge on both sides of the narrowing river, when our expatriate began to draw attention to himself.

He was a poor unfortunate named Wamloo. The other natives with us called him "Leg-no-good" or "Leg-he-broke," as took their fancy. In the trading with the Waga-mush he had become the possessor of a taul, a long wooden trumpet ornamented with the carving of a sun-burst — strangely enough, for it was not a common sym-bol in that area. He had paid for it, undoubtedly, with government fishhooks; but in the need to establish com-munication and good will, and in the wild extensive out-burst of trading which had followed the first contact, Horry had allow the crew to keep what items they most desired.

When the country began to assume the loved contours of the hills of his home, Wamloo squatted cross-legged on the deck all day, blowing sadly into the trumpet, monotonously and to no effect. The deep vibrations of sound fled weirdly from the ship, rude and meaningless, and echoed back emptily from the surrounding hills. If any people heard them they were too frightened to emerge from the shelter of the heavy forest. And it is possible that if they could have recognized the notes they might have been even more frightened, for the Wagamush were no friends of the upriver tribes. In any case, Wamloo began the exercise fifty miles and more from his people's lands.

Mounting excitement held him to the useless activity. He blew the trumpet through all the morning, the afternoon and the evening; and he would have continued to blow it through the night except that Horry sent a police boy to take it away.

"Got to get some sleep tonight," Horry said. He posted the guards and climbed in under a mosquito net on the afterdeck.

But Wamloo didn't sleep. He sat on his haunches through the night. He was excited, and it was probably the first excitement in his life that was not tinged with fear. He was almost happy, and happiness too must have been a rare emotion for him. I questioned him about his early life without much result; but later, when I met his people, it was possible to arrive at a reconstruction of it.

He had been a small boy, very small, when his significant sickness struck him down. He lay ill for many days, until the sickness and the lying in the hut seemed to have always been the pattern of his life. Just day following night, and the lying on the planks of the hut floor, long planks, convex in section, split from the trunks of the limbom palms. In the morning and at night his sister brought him food.

The happiest thing about those days was when he could watch his sister preparing the sago which was the mainstay of every meal. She would pour the creamy yellow flour into a folded palm sheath and add water from the clay pot on the fire, stirring it with her hand until the mixture thickened and its color clarified. Then she could measure it with her hands into banana-leaf plates, setting each little parcel aside to cool until it became a cake to be eaten with the grilled fish and the birds.

He was naked, and lay uncovered in the hut thatched roughly with palm fronds, but his sister was clothed. All the women were clothed and all alike. Each wore a strip of dyed fibers beaten from the flower of the sago palm. The strip was an inch wide, and was fastened round a string tied round the waist. It was pulled tight between the thighs, to reappear behind in a round rosette that clung to the buttocks and looked like a rabbit's tail, bobbing about as its wearer walked.

The women wore clothes as a sign of their weakness, but none of the men wore coverings. They had ornaments, and a bracelet about the upper arm to carry a bone dagger. They emphasized their sexual equipment by adorning it with a gourd or a bamboo section or some dexterously woven ornamentation. Men and women wore their hair short, in a style unlike that of their neighbors upstream or down.

Wamloo's sister washed him from time to time, carrying him to the river in her arms. Washing was a ritual of the tribe, particularly of the women. When Wamloo was a little better he went with the men to wash; always in company, for if there was company the crocodiles did not, as a rule, attack.

Wamloo's illness did not primarily attack his legs; but the long months of lying immobile, with no exercise and inadequate nutrition, wasted his muscles. When he began to move about again he dragged a withered leg. It took him a year of comparative health before he developed an efficient method of walking. He had at each step to bend his left knee almost to the ground in order to manipulate his right leg and his fingers to gain a few miserable inches.

But he did learn, and he learned without a crutch or a stick. No one thought to make him one. Had he not learned to rise on his good foot, it too might have withered, and he would have had to drag himself along on his knuckles and his bottom in the manner of an elder cripple of the tribe. It frequently had happened within this society that illness left the legs withered, simply because they had not been called upon for use. Yet no one thought to make instruments for his easier walking, although his tribe was an inventive one, proud of certain innovations. Their bows, for example, shot arrows longer than themselves; longer by far than the medieval English clothyard shafts (which in their time were reckoned the longest arrows in the world) and tipped with bone from human forearms. The bows were equipped with two strings, the second lashed tightly almost in place, so that if the working string broke it would not put the bowman out of action for more than three or four seconds.

Sometimes enemies raided the tribe, and then one of its members would lose his head. Usually it was some old woman who had ventured out from the village too close to dark, for the raids were never in force. They were carried out by youngsters of neighboring tribes under the social necessity of blooding themselves. Retaliations occurred only sporadically, for the tribe was a weak one.

They had plenty of sago and breadfruit and game and fish. They had betel nut for chewing, and tobacco that they smoked in gourd pipes six to ten feet in length. But they were not good hunters. The men were more interested in decorating their arrows and canoe paddles than in hunting. Their artistic work was very good, and their passion for it kept them hungry.

Wamloo was approaching adolescence when the white men came. The leader was a Major Raleigh Monash Farlow, who established a police post at the Yellow River by Catalina flying boat, a hundred and sixty miles inland from the Jap-held river bastion of Yesan. He had police boys and cargo boys with him, and the majority had been picked because they were familiar with the Sepik.

Quite as important as the defense of the tiny post he established was the task of ensuring the loyalty of the natives if the Japs or the war should come closer to them. The routine measure at the time was to take representatives of the tribes back to Port Moresby, where they would be impressed by the Allied lines and the extent of war preparations. Additionally it was thought, rather optimistically, that this procedure would offset the influence of the religious fervor known as Cargo Cult, and inhibit the Japanese from using this movement to gain local co-operation.

Captain Milligan, in charge of the natives at this Yellow River post, picked six from the three nearest villages. In Wamloo's village he saw the youngster making his awkward way about. He gave his leg as thorough an examination as was possible for an informed layman and could see nothing intrinsically wrong with it, except that it was just skin and bone. It was a possibility, he thought, that doctors at Port Moresby might be able to set it right; and acting on this humanitarian view he made Wamloo one of these six representatives.

So with no idea where he was going or why, unable even to speak the language of the people with whom he went, Wamloo embarked in the Catalina, "the canoe that flies." In Port Moresby his case was regarded as hopeless, and he would have been sent back to the Yellow in another Catalina except that Sorkiau, the other representative from his village, contracted a fever, and Wamloo was retained to keep him company.

The four men from the other villages were sent back, no doubt vastly impressed by Allied efforts; but as they had not been picked from among the elders of their people, they could not have been expected to carry much influence. Such as they possessed might have been expected to persuade their fellows not to lend assistance to the Japanese in circumstances in which they might be found out. As far as anyone knows, however, the Yellow

River people gave the enemy no assistance during the war.

Wamloo and Sorkiau disliked each other wholeheartedly, and their enforced association intensified these sentiments.

About this time the Japanese sent a captured Mission launch, the *Gabriel,* up the river, and the post at the Yellow River opened fire on it and sank it, in the Sepik's only naval engagement. Almost immediately after this success, the Australians abandoned the post, clearing out in an overland trek and burying supplies and money. Of these we uncovered the rusted fragments of hundreds of small tins that had contained wax matches; all else had gone.

No more Catalinas were sent to the Sepik, where a landing was always hazardous because of the tree trunks which normally break the surface of the swift current. It wasn't considered necessary to make a special trip to re-establish the two lost Yellow River people. Sorkiau got a job cleaning up round the police barracks. Wamloo was merely kept in rations. He was slow-witted, almost half-witted, and his education didn't progress much. His leg hampered his thinking as much as it did his other activities. A childhood spent in the solitude of a village hut could not have developed mental activity. He considered always that he was a luckless victim of witchcraft, that nobody could do much for him, and that he couldn't do anything for himself. He was slow and morose, and no one took any notice of him.

But at least he was clothed and sheltered. And after

the war he came a big step nearer home when someone sent him to the Lower Sepik, where he might have a chance to join any expedition going up the river.

He settled in the minor administration center of Angorum. And though he was the most unprepossessing of humans, he found romance. He married a girl from Ratu village and they had a couple of children. He was still living without any work and without any effort.

When Horry Niall planned his expedition he made a place in it for Wamloo, hoping to use him is an interpreter, though with no great optimism. Wamloo accepted with alacrity. He stipulated that he wanted to return; he had no use for a life on the Yellow River. In spite of this, he packed all his belongings: a little cloth, some knives, a few shafts of steel; and brought them with him. No one noticed the manner of his farewell to his wife.

Now on the last morning of the upriver journey he took up the taul again, and, trembling with excitement, began to produce low mournful notes like those of a distant foghorn. From time to time he put the instrument down and sent a weak, reedy call into the unresponsive bush. In midmorning the ships passed three huts standing near the water's edge.

Landing, we found no people in the huts, and none of their possessions. But the ashes from the fires were warm; they had been live on the previous evening. Just as we were turning away a yellow dog ran into the clearing and stopped short in amazement at our appearance. We sent a police party to find the people.

When they returned in the dark of that night they had

with them a brother of Wamloo and some of the elders of his tribe. Wamloo wept for a little while, because there was nothing good in the news they brought. Two of his brothers had died in an epidemic — a mass killing which had been attributed to witchcraft. The people up-river, the Wagu tribe, had in the past week killed a man of his community. But they were overjoyed to find that he had been well, that he wasn't dead, that the war was over, and that they might expect to see white men again from time to time.

By morning Wamloo's expression was happy, happier than anyone had ever seen it. He announced to Horry that he was going home for the day, but that he would return and bring some of his younger relations to work for the white men at Angorum and Wewak. Also his people would come to trade and to accept the presents that the government had for them. And finally and above all, he himself would bring a pig as a present.

We made, that day, an unsuccessful attempt to probe farther up the river. The water levels were receding, and at this point the volume of the river was not great. We abandoned the idea of reaching the village where we suspected the Japanese might be living, and returned to await developments.

The other people from the forest now gathered round the boats and followed our every movement. They were thin, reedy votaries of a primitive beauty, quite unrelated in appearance and capacity for expression — for noise, anyway — to the tribes downriver. The babies all seemed to be suffering from malnutrition; their limbs were like tiny sticks.

One old man came down to see the ships that night and died in the early morning, before the day had lighted them. Considerately, relatives adjusted a bark rope round his chest to keep his soul within his body, so that technically he remained alive. In that way they postponed any necessity for sorrow or weeping. Throughout the day they spoke to the unheeding man; children sat upon his knees and curled their fingers in his hair. His enormous tobacco pipe was set near his hand. The revelry which attended their meeting with us went on without check; afterwards, when we had left, they would remove the bark and mourn the dead.

We persuaded six of the young men to join our expedition. To this day I do not know whether they thought they would be away longer than a few hours. The police boys stripped their ornaments away, shaved their bodies and heads, scrubbed them clean and showed them how to dress in a strip of cloth. They enjoyed the experience so much they wanted to be scrubbed again, though the instruments used were the deck scrubbers.

But Wamloo did not appear. We delayed departure and sent messengers, but there was no sign of him. He had gone back to his home. It was a home in which he had never known much happiness, nor any comfort; but it was his. For it he gave up the new life he had made with a wife and family; for it he resigned all the advances in living to which seven years had accustomed him.

He could look forward to no very great happiness. The

staple diet of sago would fill his belly without adding strength to his limbs. The sores he contracted would be treated with an application of red clay. His skin would be covered, in a little while, with the crocodile-scales of the ugly disease called grillae. His European possessions would rot away.

His contact with people not his own had given him a wife and family and seven years of a clean skin and a full belly, seven years of living in safety from his enemies, of freedom from fear and oppression, of freedom of thought and belief.

But my conviction was that civilization would not see him again, for it was not difficult to pick the prize for which Wamloo bartered all the benefits of modern society. There was only one thing waiting for him at the Yellow River that he hadn't been able to find among white men and sophisticated natives. That was the friendship of his fellows. He went back to the Stone Age with its discomforts and its dangers to find friendship. And probably, if he has survived, he is happy at last.

The voyage downriver was a succession of small triumphs. At every place we had traded with natives we met them again, in amity and with a glow of recognition. We persuaded goodly numbers to join our party; or they persuaded themselves, seeing with their own eyes that our numbers had been augmented and that the newcomers seemed well enough.

Two had later misgivings and left us at night, swimming the river with its hosts of guardian crocodiles to traverse country peopled with their traditional enemies.

But the remainder learned our words and were hungry for more knowledge. And when we came at last to the Wagamush country, a chief made a speech we could not know the meaning of, and a dozen lads jumped aboard and stripped themselves of their belongings, and came with us. And in the final gesture of trust the women came in their canoes to watch them go and bid them farewell. The Wagamush had trusted their women in our company, and it was the end of an old enmity.

I T WAS an adventure of the mind that lured me, some years later, to the Trobriand Islands: outcrops of coral inhabited by a gentle, handsome and intelligent race whose customs have only a scant relationship to those of the people who live in the countries surrounding their kingdom. They sing more often, they laugh and play with greater zest, their loyalty to their own social structure is unquestioned. Their customs are based upon a scale of values almost diametrically opposed to those of the great majority of mankind; yet the society thus constructed is in no way inimical to others. There are few places on earth where life seems as pleasant.

For example, the marriages, which normally are monogamous and persist happily throughout the lives of the partners, are not based upon sex, but upon food. The cooking pot is the symbol of marriage. A young girl may indulge in sexual activity with the partner of her choice whenever she wills; should she eat with him she has advertised her serious intentions and is compromised. The marriage dates from that first meal together. In later years if a husband should wish a divorce, it is sufficient for him to break the family cooking pots; sufficient for his wife to abandon them and to assume the costume of an unmarried woman. But divorce is not common.

The yam and not the scepter is the symbol of the king; his royalty demands each year the accumulation of a vast store of these vegetables, and if he makes a gift of one it is a pledge of his respect and friendship. If, by any chance, his subjects in one of the islands of his kingdom should have a crop failure, it is his responsibility to make the seed good.

The social structure is further based upon a complicated aristocracy which is both matrilinear and patriarchal; the religion is monotheistic, the arts are highly advanced, and in the sciences astronomy has reached the point where it is responsible for the pattern of the year, an unwieldy year, consisting sometimes of eleven months, sometimes of thirteen. The men are by nature voyagers and traders for half the year, gardeners of outstanding excellence for the rest.

The "blackbirders" of the Pacific's evil days found them poor material; they sickened and died when taken from their beloved lands. Today, recruited for service on the mainland of New Guinea, they are treasured for their ability to understand the principles of bookkeeping; their intelligence is in general too high to be wasted on mine and plantation labor. This is so, at least, in the general dearth of labor suitable for clerical training.

The Trobriand Islands were sighted briefly by the Frenchman Bruni D'Entrecasteaux in 1793, and named by him after the captain of one of his ships. They lie in the central portion of the Coral Sea, in a sector so shallow that, were the water to recede a couple of fathoms, the islands' area would be increased twenty-fold and more.

They are coral formations, hollow with limestone caves, undermined, almost floating, it seems; of a composition so porous that no water stands in their hinterlands. There are no freshwater streams or creeks, and the islanders must slake their thirst with the cold clear limewater of the caverns or, in the more common habit, with the rhythmic drainage that feeds into the sea on a receding tide.

To the north of the islands is the great length of New Britain, out of sight but, unfortunately for the Trobrianders, so close that Kiriwina, their main island, was used during the Second World War as a base for fighter aircraft to contain the Japanese bomber fleets based at Rabaul. To the east, and a long way off, is the volcanic island of Woodlark. To the west, beyond a small chain of islands called the Lusancays, is the great bulk of the mainland of New Guinea; and the D'Entrecasteaux Islands, sixty miles away, rear their huge peaks over the southern horizons of the Trobriands on every sunny day.

The ancient Kingdom of Boyowa consisted of these Trobriand Islands — Kiriwina, Vakuta, Kitava, Kaileuna, Tuma and some others — the Lusancays, which they called Simsimula and today are known as the Sim Sims, and out to the southeast, the Marshall Bennets. The Boyowan people traded with their neighbors: with the Amphletts, in the south, for pottery; with Woodlark for stone for the manufacture of axes; with the D'Entrecasteaux for leaves of sago and nipa palm for roofing; with Goodenough for the special pandanus leaves which made the best canoe sails; and with all the islands of the Coral Sea in a strict sequence in the great ceremonial trading venture called the Kula, a rigorous voyage series which has puzzled most investigators. But they never entered into closer tribal relations with any of these people.

There was some intermarriage. In all those lands a Kiriwina wife was reckoned to be a great prize. She did not work much, but she laughed and she made herself good-looking; she dressed in bright clothes and decked herself always with fresh flowers, she scented herself and knew little games to play, and her sexual knowledge was detailed. She was not obedient, but neither was she hard to live with. Her fey demands kept a husband busy, but she saw to it that he was rewarded.

The few strangers who sought to join the community were welcomed to the Trobriand villages. Women from outlying islands were the wives of the men of Tuma, who moved much among spirits who frightened their own women. And sometimes an outsider decided that the tempo of life in Kiriwina suited him better than his own home, and he was not repulsed.

But the Trobrianders recognized great differences between their own culture and that which these strangers had relinquished. And they had and have a fanatical love of their own homeland.

The most recognizable difference concerned the social structure itself. The Trobriand aristocracy was a highly developed system of five grades of nobles leading upward to a king; while their neighbors practiced variations of that primitive communism which is one of the earliest forms of social structure.

And the Trobrianders, while surrounded by cannibals, abhorred the eating of man. Indeed, they were not warlike, though able to give a good account of themselves when called upon. Head-hunting, which dictated, or at least strongly influenced the entire way of life of most of Melanesia, played no part in their activities. And in their stories they proclaim themselves proud of these facts, arguing that savagery is simply the reverse of that coin of which the obverse is fear, and claiming that they themselves were not afraid.

The Trobrianders, unlike their neighbors, never repulsed the stranger within their gates. And perhaps it is because of this hospitality that they differ in appearance from all the other people in the Coral Sea; though additionally they are heirs of an exotic ancestry. For the sexual freedom of the youngsters was instrumental in adding the genes of a myriad strangers to the racial inheritance. North, south, east and west a million people frowned upon sexual latitude with a much more than Puritan dislike. In this one center sexual activity was the prerogative of the individual and did not concern others.

Until the coming of the European, the influx of strangers was small. The coral base of the waterless island offered no very great inducement to conquest. There was no treasure. Even the native jewelry, common to all the Coral sea, came there in trade: the red oyster shells from the Louisiade Archipelago, the serpentine stone from Woodlark, the cone-shells for armlets from the barren outliers of the Lusancays. They had pearls, but did not regard them as valuable.

And then the white man discovered gold in Woodlark; and discovered, too, that in that island and indeed elsewhere through the Coral Sea the native women rejected him when they could. He tired of the unwilling sexual partners obtained by rape and conquest, and the sullen, dour and aging women otherwise contemptuously made available to him, and turned to the Trobriands, where the girls were happy and obliging. They were obliging too in the Polynesian sectors; but those were far away. Then he discovered the Trobriand pearls.

But long before the influx of the white man, which indeed did not begin before the last four years of the nineteenth century, the natives had a Caucasian cast of countenance, overlaid, in general, with Melanesian features. Some of them had fair hair, some red. On some heads the hair waved, black and glossy; on a very few it was crinkled, on a few more it was straight. Features in general were more like the European than, say, the Polynesian. And red hair was highly regarded; it was traditional for the king to wear a red wig, so cunningly made that its artificiality was not apparent. Elsewhere in the Pacific the Polynesian has a redhaired intrusion. Maoris in the Urewera country of New Zealand have it, for example; but this coloration is despised in tradition, and is still unwelcome today.

The system of government is outstandingly simple and good. The kings and chiefs abandoned the monogamy of their subjects; in tradition the king has seventeen wives, one from each major village in the Kiriwina domain, except that two come from the village of Liluta, where artistocracy is concentrated in a kind of Boyowan Versailles. Each wife was a girl chosen from the leading family of her village, a girl born to her destiny.

Now inheritance came through none of these wives. The heir was generally the son of the King's eldest sister. The heir to any of the lesser chieftainships was selected by the same rule, and it followed that, since in practically every instance such a sister was one of the king's wives, the king's sons held, as it were, the baronies of the kingdom, and were at one with the ruling house. On the death of the king, the heir, as a matter of course, became the husband of the seventeen relicts. And as each wife died, the leading female representative of her village, which is to say the potential mother of the next chief of that village, took her place.

I stood one day with Metakata the King, waiting while arrangements were made to take a junior wife to the hospital for a serious operation. The old man, a figure of great dignity, found it difficult to restrain his sorrow; his love for the girl was evident, and was matched by the sorrowing of his other wives. There were twelve of them, thirteen in all, for the King no longer marries women from villages that have turned to Christianity.

Surrounding his house, in his capital village of Omarakana, were the thirteen houses of his wives. For each wife there was also a yam-house, where the garden crops were stored. These yam-houses were filled by the brothers of the wives in tribute to the king.

The king himself had a yam-house larger than any other. It reared at least thirty and perhaps forty feet high, a tall boxed column of peeled and carved logs, an adjustable house that fitted itself exactly to the capacity of the annual crop. Each season, the King and his retinue ate from the yam-houses of his wives. The symbolic yam-house he owned himself stood as insurance against famine. If a dry season wiped out the crop in the main island or any of the outliers, the King replaced the seed.

As a result of the clever and efficient administration the people were prosperous, well-fed, well-integrated and well-ruled. In addition they were advanced in the arts, particularly the arts of dancing, poetry, sculpture and design, the latter as expressed in weaving, net-making and the production of jewelry and such clothing as they found it necessary to wear. The history and the laws were contained in a series of legends, with a hereditary story-teller as final arbiter to decide on the traditional form of each.

The chiefs cemented their relations with sub-chiefs by the same system as the king: by a controlled polygamy. Beneath them, beneath the whole structure of aristocracy, was a happy peasantry. Ownership of the pigs, the scanty coconut palms and the even more scanty betel nuts was vested in the aristocracy. Village litigation was reduced to a minimum. But though every man bent his head before the king, noble and commoner alike met on terms of apparent equality. The best dancer led the dance, regardless of his status. The best fisherman commanded the canoe.

There were totems, four of them. They were named for the red parrot, the green parrot, the eagle and the Torres Straits pigeon; and the members of one totem were not permitted to marry except in the others. But as the totem was established by the broad pattern of the lines in the palm of the individual's hand, the rule was of little practical value; and there is some evidence that the strictures were not final. There was probably a good deal of latitude or laxity in the interpretation; for the aristocracy, in any event, were all of the totem of the pigeon.

There were no priests, but the religion they followed is still today a dominant feature of their lives. It is the worship of a god named Topileta, an all-powerful deity who rules the spirits of the dead in Tuma, the most westerly island of the small group (as most students of religion might anticipate). Topileta is there attended by the residents of a small village whose chief is the son of the third wife of the king. They guard the coconuts and the betel nuts of the island, and deliver their fruits to the king, or a token proportion of them. They otherwise lead a normal village life, at ease with the spirits.

"This Topileta," I asked an islander I had come to know quite well. "Is he a big man?"

"Not real big, Taubada. Not big like you. Bigger than me, perhaps."

"Is he very handsome?"

He considered that.

"You wouldn't call him handsome. He's not ugly. He looks, oh, ordinary."

"Is he very clever? Or very strong?"

That amazed him.

"Taubada, he doesn't have to be. He can do anything."

There are few responsibilities associated with the creed. While Topileta is both beloved and respected, the wicked go to Tuma as well as the good; goodness, with its lack of friction, its promotion of friendship, is its own reward. In Tuma the wicked remain wicked, for that is their fate. The crippled remain crippled. For the Trobriander is fond enough of people as they are to wish them unchanged in the afterworld. The only requirement of Tuma is that the spirit claiming admittance should have been an inhabitant of Boyowa. Even one or two Europeans have qualified, according to the natives, who claim familiarity with the identities of the spirits. But there are some lorn individuals who, having died, have not found their way there.

The Trobriands, as you approach them from the sea, are unimpressive, the more so because, in your journey there you have traversed a realm of beauty, where land and ocean mate in an idyll. You have coasted near Goodenough, a circular island no more than eighteen miles in diameter, yet crowned with a diadem of peaks that soar more than a mile and a half into the tropic sky, a jewel of an island, like no other on the face of the earth.

You have threaded the narrow channels between Fergusson and Normanby, two major islands of noble proportions, set about with flowered rocks, inhabited by lively races whose gardens dot the peaks, whose canoes maintain a busy traffic in the bays; lands in which every hour brings you to some new wonder, a waterfall that drops from a height into the sea, a tract of geysers and boiling springs and silica terraces, a field of orchids, or a pool crowded with brilliant fish. You have admired and feared and felt the brooding influence of the quiescent volcano of the island of Dobu, right in your path, its riven flanks rising in an incomparable symmetry. In the passage beside the peak the canoemen fly their fishing kites, hanging their spider-web baits from aerial platforms so that they skip like flying fish atop the waves to the destruction of the giant garfish. You have negotiated the channels between the beehive rocks that are the Amphlett group, clear channels in which the coral gardens, fathoms deep, seem just beneath the surface; and there you have seen the potters put to sea, in the hope of selling you earthen pots that for delicacy and design cannot be matched throughout the whole Pacific.

And then at the end of the day the Trobriands lie ahead, flat, featureless and disappointing. But when you are close enough to see the villages set close to the water, and the beaches straked with the hulls of outriggers, the people come to meet you: lively, laughing, self-confident; more beautiful than any others, dressed in a minimum of bright-colored clothing that seems to have no other function than to attract the eye, bedecked with flowers and shell jewelry. They possess nothing that is purely utilitarian. Every artifact has commanded the attention of some artist, and they are proud in their belongings.

A village in the Trobriands is a delightful place. It is surrounded by high trees, and this in itself is remarkable, for on every square foot elsewhere, except in the rugged areas where some forest still survives, the trees have been sacrificed to make garden land. The gardens occupy all the country, in a rotation of about seven years. Therefore the tropical growth over most of the land is young and undeveloped.

It follows that all the trees at each village are useful, in that they bear crops essential to living. Nearly all are fruit trees: the high-mantled mango, the New Guinea apple, the Jamaica almond, the tree here called iumgwila, hung with gray-skinned pumpkin fruits that taste like stewed apricots, the mokolu and makaninai with rose-scented brilliant red-skinned and white-fleshed fruits crowding the trunk and branches like cocoa beans, or so heavily in flower that the light beneath the trees is a cool cerise. The fingered leaves of the breadfruit are prominent, among a dozen other varieties of trees with edible crops. Within the circle of their surrounding thicket, among the houses, are groves of betel nut and coconut palms. The creepers that seem to have sprung from a careless growth provide dyes for skirts or for cosmetics, or their roots produce a poison to stun fish, or their fibers make rope or twine or mastic. The little plots of ginger or of turmeric are for the ceremonies of magic. The bananas are for food, their leaves for the manufacture of women's underskirts. There are scented shrubs for making love charms, pandanus palms for sails and cord. There seems not one useless plant adjacent.

The houses are small, set low on the ground, aesthetically satisfying in design; and each is accompanied by its yam-house. The dwelling, as a rule, protects the yam-house, standing between it and the encircling trees; and within the inner ring of yam-houses there is a level space for dancing. Between the house and the yam-house are the ashes of the cooking fire, with three or four hearthstones for the support of the round-bottomed pots.

In the more important villages the house of the chief is larger than the others. His yam-house carries certain symbols of coconut fiber and the shells of the white egg cowry which certain anthropologists recognize as sexual symbols but which here, for their perfection, are tokens of aristocracy. The chief's house is situated, as likely as not, at a point higher in altitude than the rest of the village, and in addition to the low porch on which the Trobriander habitually takes his ease, there is a platform built near the eaves where the chief can sit for his evening delectation, his head above that of any other man's.

Within the houses, hard by the door, there is a rack for bottles made from the shells of coconuts; perhaps a dozen; and these contain the household water supply. There are alcoves for sleeping and otherwise there is little furniture.

Of recent years, government officers have tried to bring the Trobrianders into line with the majority of the Coral Sea people by having them perch their houses upon stilts, with an air space under the floor. This has been stoutly resisted by the people, who maintain that spirits, in such an instance, would be able to reach them from under the floors. As a result of this and other tenets they have been reckoned to be riddled with superstition.

Yet I saw for myself that on the island of Kawa, properly one of the Lusancays but inhabited by Trobrianders, the houses are perched upon stilts and always have been. For in Kawa, and in Kawa alone, mud is a problem, it being a volcanic island. The coral rock and light sandy soil of the other islands will not hold water. So in the battle between the overwhelming fear of spirits with which the people are credited, and a distaste for muddy floors, the more practical considerations have an easy win. No Kiriwina man visiting Kawa has any fear that spirits might get at him from underneath his sleeping place, and from this observation I conclude that the fear he professes in his own village is no more than a convention.

It has been recorded of these people that they have no knowledge of what causes the birth of children, and that their women will not bathe at high tide, believing that at this time the bailomas, the spirits in the waves, will impregnate them. This is difficult to believe of people who breed pigs and selected hunting dogs, who ensure the inheritance of chiefs by matrilinear selection, and whose wise women sell contraceptive methods. That the last are effective may be deduced by the fact that while hundreds of the girls bestowed sexual privileges upon many of the Allied troops quartered there in wartime, only two conceived in the whole period, and one of these two was three-quarters European. In the Trobriands women bathe at low tide because only at this time can they fill their water bottles from the little freshets that drain from the limestone sponge which is their island. There is always a practical reason to supplement the story.

There are many marvels to see in the Trobriands, much that is food for thought; but of a host of memories the one most compelling concerns a day on which I walked from a village called Labai to its beach. I was following the route of a story, and my guide was the storyteller.

The trail leads over a tumbled mile of coral rock upon which flourishes a forest of mekeo, a South Sea timber somewhat resembling teak. It traverses the highest part of the island, but at no point does it climb more than three hundred feet above the sea. Nevertheless the hills are so pocked with deep crevasses, with well-like shafts and subsidences opening up a vast subterranean system of limestone caves, and with curious small peaks and precipices, that the negotiation of the track is an exercise requiring the full use of limbs and senses, and constitutes an experience that few people repeat unless they are natives.

The track has been used by barefooted islanders for

thousands of years, so that each handhold and foothold is worn smooth and slippery; yet an inch to either side the dead coral is armed with splinters and edges which cut the skin at a touch, and a misjudged effort almost anywhere along the track could bring a painful injury.

Some of the hazards are hair-raising. In one place a natural bridge less than a foot wide and perhaps twelve feet long spans a drop of sixty feet. In another, a bridge consisting of two peeled and slippery saplings leads over a chasm at the foot of which, thirty feet down, an unseen cataract mutters among the rocks. In what was fortunately a safer place than these I missed my grip and went clattering down. Hearing the noise, our guide turned with an anxious inquiry, and solicitously offered me his stick. It was an incredible gesture, for he had been blind from birth.

Yet never once in the lead of our little party did he hesitate or falter. Even more remarkably, never did he fail to bring to our sighted appreciation the views, the physical features and the peculiar formations along the trail, including some minute rock markings. At one point he lifted a boulder the size of a man's head from a niche, asking us to mark its resemblance to a human face.

And he had carried out this astonishing performance because it was his business in life to do just these things. He had inherited the task along with a high and honored position in the island economy. It was his responsibility, in spite of his blindness, to show us the features of the land; but far more than that it was his joy.

In the Kingdom of Boyowa, Tolosi of Labai is Keeper

of the Archives. He is so identified with the stories of the people that sometimes it is difficult to know when he is speaking as Tolosi and when, though he is still using the first person, he is talking for a long-dead ancestor — one who inevitably, in his lifetime, performed Tolosi's functions.

Neither his blindness nor his position interferes with the proposition that like every other man on the island he must earn his living. Therefore he works in his garden. Traditionally he should be a fisherman — but a fisherman in those dangerous seas must have his eyesight. Yet because of his identification with his ancestors he thinks of himself as a fisherman first and foremost. He makes a little copra, and climbs the palms himself to get the nuts, making the frightening ascent with ease, and at the top, tapping the nuts and listening to find whether they are ripe enough.

When he has smoked the coconut flesh into copra he bargains with the trader personally, and when he has made his purchases, mostly of betel nut or tobacco, he is extravagantly generous with them to his friends. He is the man who is always willing to carry a message, walking, and sometimes running, up to fifteen miles to other villages; and never once lost in the beloved country he has never seen.

Apart from tobacco and betel nut his wants are simple. He wears one scanty garment, the folded sheath of a betel nut fruit-spur. He is housed in a small but sturdy hut of native material. I never saw him without a smile on his face and his words were always happy.

During my stay on the island I collected as many as I could of the legends, and was not long in discovering that Tolosi's was the official version. His stories represent the island's code of ethics, about half the nature lore, some rational explanations for such of the Trobriand beliefs as may be rationally explained and a little pre-European history. He is, in person, the talking Bible of the Trobrianders, their Aesop and their Humboldt, their demagogue and their entertainer. There are, of course, among the forty or fifty villages, other storytellers. There is a man in Gumilibaba who will tell you why, of all the Boyowans, only the Gumilibabans will eat dugong; an old man in Liluta who can tell, to tested perfection, the story of the origin of fire; a man in the big canoe port of Sinaketa who can detail the evolution of the fishing net. And some of these are raconteurs better than Tolosi.

He is a young man, and an audience from a distant village sometimes gives him a touch of stage fright. His blindness prevents him from gauging audience-reaction as accurately as he would like; and there are too many of his elders among his listeners, old men who have heard the same stories again and again throughout their lives. There are a great many old men among his audiences today. The younger men are not so interested: a new world is opening out to them, and to some extent the missionary and the government official have skimmed away the awe and dread of the story.

So Tolosi tells his stories without the conviction of a sighted man. To the native ear his versions are academic, but accurate in detail.

When he told me his first story — a version of the creation legend, he said: "My name is not only Tolosi. Sometimes I am called Kotakwati." I knew what he meant. Tolosi was the man, the gardener; but Kotakwati was the guardian of the story, the custodian of a communal truth.

Tolosi's creation legend, among many other points, describes how, when the world was peopled, his ancestor and the ancestor of Metakata the King came last; and consequently by Trobriand reckoning are the most important of the population. The two stand together, the ruler and the recorder, the man who establishes traditions and the man who preserves them, the wielder and the interpreter of power. It is a thesis that could command a lot of intelligent support in other, more advanced communities.

I was intrigued, too, by the gentle, happy, unassuming Tolosi's personal identification with his ancestors, and his assumption of all their rights.

"Metakata is first in the land. He is above all, and I am second," he said. "If I should catch a shark and take it to Metakata, Metakata would kill a pig for me, and Metakata's pigs are therefore my pigs.

"I could wear the segadula, the royal ornament of sapi-sapi shells. This is not the king's alone, for I could wear it. I could wear by right the garters of egg cowries, the belt of egg cowries about the waist, the armbands of cone-shell — the sacred mwari; but I am a fisherman. What use would a fisherman have for things like these? I do not wear them; this is a choice; and by choice we have never worn them, neither I nor my ancestors.

"I can do the things that belong to Metakata, but I will not. Pride is sufficient. We came from the earth together, out of Tuma, out of Eddis, out of Olualawa the World Between, out of Otumaveaka the land of stone, out of the place of many names. Metakata carries the symbols of power on his person and on his yam-house; but I carry mine in my thoughts, and that is enough."

He told me his stories first at a trader's store, but he was not at ease. He repeated them in the village where he was staying, yet still he failed to repeat them rightly by his own reckoning.

"Come to Labai where I live. That was where creation happened. I can tell the stories better there," he said.

That was why we found ourselves on that crazy track, looking for the beginnings of the Boyowan world, myself and Vanoi and Waibadi, the heirs of the king. Tolosi almost skipped along the track, retelling his stories, penetrating huge caves and pointing out the features of the stalactite-patterned roofs, and finally bringing us to a simple grove of trees that for centuries had been held sacred as humanity's birthplace.

There was a little hesitation before the group entered the grove, for reasons I could not then understand. But later, at the sea's edge, Tolosi made magic. He fashioned, one at a time, three tight little baskets of green leaves, and holding each close against his mouth, he spoke to his ancestors, begging their forgiveness for going to the sacred places unprepared, and explaining that it had been necessary to be considerate of me, the stranger. Each

time he ended this speech he would enclose the basket
carefully and hand it to one of the other natives. He took
the last himself, and all three bathed in the sea, using the
words addressed to the ancestors to cleanse themselves,
as though the basket were a sponge.

It was a simple precaution, designed, obviously, to
keep the sacred places respected. I asked Tolosi whether
I too should wash. He said, "No, Taubada. They are not
your ancestors. It was not the place of your creation."

Once or twice, when I accompanied him over un-
familiar ground, I had to take him by the hand to lead
him, and twice, through my inadvertence, he stubbed
his bare toes on the coral. When I apologized in haste he
laughed gently and squeezed my fingers in assurance that
he was not hurt. His face, with its closed eye sockets, is
the kind of face, and wears the kind of expression, I
always imagined a saint should have.

But the picture I retain of him is that of him sitting
on a canoe on the beach, talking reverently into a basket
of leaves held close in his cupped hands, with the two
heirs to the throne standing deferentially beside him. In
those moments Tolosi was, in his belief and mine, in the
company of his ancestors, and he looked extremely
happy. But then he is always happy. He is a good man
and industrious, and most of all he is happy. Perhaps in
his blindness he sees a great deal more than the rest of
us can imagine.

Tolosi's king, Metakata, has his headquarters in the
village of Omarakana on the large island of Kiriwina. His
dominance extends over the immediate seas to the island

groups of the Trobriands, Vakuta, Kaileuna, Kitava, the Lusancays and the Marshall Bennets; and such is the loyalty of his people that the European intrusion which began in the closing years of the last century has not much disturbed his influence.

In the Trobriands the shark is a royal fish, just as the sturgeon is a royal fish in England, and when caught must be carried to the king. Sharks are, however, considerably less rare in the seas round the Trobriands than the sturgeon on the English coasts; and consequently this perquisite has a considerably greater value in the Trobriands, where the shark is much appreciated, too, as a table dish.

I was walking one day in the company of the two heirs of the king on the beach near a village called Kaibola, and we stopped to rest ourselves, sitting on the outrigger platforms of a couple of canoes drawn up on the coral detritus. We had cigarettes but no matches; and when we discovered this, Vanoi, one of the heirs, broke off a portion of the platform, sharpened it to a chisel point with his knife, and carved a little runnel in another part of the platform. In a few moments, by working the point methodically and without haste in the runnel, he had fire. We lit our cigarettes at it; and then I searched in the canoe hull for a bailer or some other receptacle to carry water to douse the tiny flame.

I found it; but lying beside it was an artifact the use of which I could not determine. It was a hoop of cane, threading a series of the inner shells of coconuts, cut in circular plaques each pierced with a hole in the middle.

The diameter of the hoop was about two feet and the plaques, which moved freely on the cane, were gathered in a bunch at the bottom end. It seemed no more than a gewgaw, a plaything, of no importance; yet it lay among the essentials in the deep narrow hull of the canoe, and seemed to have been put to some use.

Vanoi and Waibadi, my companions, spoke a slow and careful English. They had been educated in the Methodist Mission, though they remained worshipers of their local god, Topileta. Both seemed a little hesitant about telling me the use of the artifact.

"It is a shark-caller," Waibadi finally said. He demonstrated its use. It was to be clasped firmly in the hand, and shaken underwater, in such a manner that the hard plaques of coconut shell made a small submarine clatter like castanets, a noise supplemented by the swish of water through the artifact's construction.

"Does it really bring the sharks?" I asked; though I should have known the answer.

"That shark, he'll come all right," Vanoi said.

I asked, then, if I could accompany a canoe from which the sharks were called, but came immediately against a difficulty which was, to the young men, insuperable. For the use of the hoop was attended by certain unalterable conditions. The man who called the shark to the canoe must be by himself, and out of sight of other craft. His engagement with the shark, by tradition, had to be a purely personal affair in which no help was at hand or available. Nor could I find out by what method he despatched the shark; which in those waters could

well be the length of the canoe in which the fisherman
sat. I gathered it was a trial of strength for the adolescent, the emerging man, who must learn by himself for
he could not be shown by precept. When he landed his
quarry it became the property of the king, and a fitting
centerpiece for the feast that followed his achievement.

Later that year I came upon similar equipment from
the Duke of York Islands, and here the cane hoop was
supplemented by a peculiar carved implement shaped
rather like the twin-bladed screw of an aircraft, about
eight or ten feet long. Attached to its center was a short
length of rope which ended in a noose.

The islander who used the equipment called the shark
to his canoe with the hoop, and then with a fish fastened
to a stick lured the great beast until he entered the
noose spread wide in the water. The fisherman thereupon
pulled the rope tight about the shark's gills, and immediately flung the large wooden "airscrew" clear of the
canoe as the shark flashed into action. By its construction it bucked and dived and skidded as the shark attempted to reach the depths; its flotation power was
great, and the flurry of this fight tired the shark. The
fisherman followed the commotion, and when he judged
the time was ripe he recovered the flanged float, brought
the shark to the canoe by means of the rope, and clubbed
him to death.

It sounds an ingenious and effective way to catch
sharks. But the enormous size and speed of the quarry
must have made it one of the most hazardous feats on
earth. It was complicated by the conscious effort of main-

taining the balance of the outrigger canoe; a delicate skill not easily acquired by an adult tyro, as sudden immersions in the Coral Sea have taught me more than once. The whole exercise is a rigorous test of proficiency in canoe management; the insistence that it be performed in solitude seems to indicate that the islanders esteemed it as a supreme examination in sea skill, with death a likely punishment for failure.

Sitting there on the beach at Kaibola, I thought that the efficacy of the shark-caller derived, perhaps, from the fact that the sound produced imitated the sounds made when a school of fish find swarms of smaller fish at their mercy: the swirling of the waters, and perhaps the snapping of teeth. I though that if I were to become a fisherman once again I would, when opportunity offered, take a submarine tape recording of such a slaughter, and later amplify the sound to bring the predators to my boat; for though he is armed with technologically advanced weapons, the fisherman is still a hunter, the sea is still a primeval place.

But that day, sitting on the canoe platform, I was conscious of my inability to probe further into such a matter. My companions were pleasant lads, intelligent and sympathetic to my desire to find out as much as I could about their lives; but their traditions silenced them.

We were shaded, as I remember, by a huge barringtonia, a giant tree with dark glossy foliage flecked with water lily cups of blossom a foot across and filled with sheaves of long stamens. The sun was dancing on the water and the air was still. Some people from the village nearby came down a steep track across the face of the coral cliffs, and when they saw my company flexed their knees and bent their heads, which was proper in the presence of royalty. But they spoke familiarly just the same, and were answered in the same manner, for the relationship between royalty and the commoner in these islands is not easy to define, and respect is never obsequious, never divorced from friendship, and quite uninjurious to independence.

15

𝕒 MAN IN the village of Okopukopu had a dream; and
in this dream he went, before his allotted time, to
the Land of Spirits, the western island of Tuma, where
beneath the ground the great god Topileta holds court
with the happy ghosts of the dead; and there, in honor
of this man, who is the great choreographer of his place
and time, these spirits danced a new dance. Waking, the
man remembered it; he taught the dance to the people of
his village, and month after month, each day as the sun
dropped towards the west and the workers returned to
their homes, they practiced it, hour after hour into the
darkness; for there were three hours or more between the
opening movements of the dance and its completion.

I heard the distance-muffled drums as soon as I arrived
on these Trobriand Islands in what must have been the
same week as the genesis of this dance. Each day the

music fractured the evening langor of that paradise and invited investigation; and because of my curiosity, and because too (without much actual participation) I have always been strongly responsive to the seductions of the primitive even more than the sophisticated forms of the dance, it was not long before I traced the sounds and rhythms to their source and fell into a habit of joining the audience.

Night after night the orchestra of drums announced the village excitement; the deeper reverberations led and punctuated by the staccato of the tiny finger-drum — the length of a man's hand, the thickness of his wrist — with which the orchestra leader set the time and evoked, in their correct sequence, the ninety-seven stanzas of the special song from a choir massed behind the bank of drummers. The conch shells, blown erratically by boys too small to dance, added their mournful notes. The cockatoos, swift white bodies swooping down upon their roost in a dead tree behind the mangroves, supplied derisive comment.

Day after day, while this continued, I would resist that tropical seduction, the lassitude of afternoon, and walk the four or five winding miles between the village of Tekwaukwa, near which I stayed, and this staunch outpost of the arts. There was a constant traffic along the way, a traffic of villagers bent on missions that seemed to them important: a woman with a clay pot of about ten-gallon capacity balanced on the crown of her head, a man exercising his dogs, another in search of a particular flower to wear in his hair, three children returning from their play, a girl with banana leaves from which she would extract soft fiber for an underskirt.

Each encounter was accompanied by an exchange of information which is the greeting of the islands, a happy thing, which underlines the comforting knowledge of man's preoccupation with his fellows:

"Where you going, Taubada?"

"Taubada" is Motuan for "Big Man," and means a European.

"To Okopukop'."

"Long sing sing?"

"Long sing sing."

"Okay, Taub'. I go long Tekwauk'."

"Okay."

It is a pleasant greeting. It means something a little more personal than "Good day." It will become part of the village news tonight. "The Dim-Dim Taubada went to Okopukop' to watch the dance. The Sydney Taubada."

They are beautiful people, beautiful as flowers are beautiful; and that beauty is enhanced by their desire to enjoy it themselves, to make the most of it, to accentuate it. The men wear nothing but a belt which supports a narrow sheathing of the flower of the betel nut palm, unless they are aristocrats, in which case their status is announced by an additional belt and a garter, both formed of threaded cowrie shells. The women wear a skirt brightly dyed, so fastened at the right hip as to leave a space — from that aspect they are naked from foot to shoulder. If they are married, the skirt stops six inches above the knees; the single girl wears it shorter yet. So scanty is this attire that the whole graceful back is exposed to the separation of the buttocks, and the belly to a fringing hint of body hair.

The women have the proud erect stance, the balanced gait of people who carry their burdens on the crown of the head. The necessity for maintaining the skirt in its precarious position adds another delicacy to their walk which is further conditioned by the circumstance that in that island there is never need for hurry. From all these factors, their wear becomes a constant provocation, as well they know. When they work in the gardens they discard the skirt; then the soft underwear, a mere tuft of banana-leaf fiber, is considered a sufficient gesture to the proprieties.

Iama the prostitute passed me, swaying along the track, wearing the studied expression of disdain she commonly affected. Though she was not in mourning for anyone dead, she had shaved her head, as always, in the manner of mourners, knowing how truly delicate were the proportions of her skull, how surely that dolichocephalic shape concentrated the attention of the male observer upon her exquisite features, her delicacy of skin and the care with which she had applied the cosmetics that enhanced her eyes. She had tucked a flower into the complex of turtle-shell earrings that, with a jewel of red oyster, lengthened each ear lobe; and she wore, as was her birthright, the insignia of aristocracy. Her profession was a voluntary one, of which she was proud. Her success in it testified to her attractions displayed and hidden;

for there were no restrictions there upon sex indulgence by the unmarried.

Hand in delicate hand with her walked Bogerwa'ine, her light brown curly hair trimmed to a soft cap and festooned with small green and yellow flowers, her skirt dyed in soft grays and greens, as was not commonly the case upon that island. Bogerwa'ine had lately divorced herself from her husband by the simple process of moving from his house and cutting the unnecessary length from her skirt; she walked with Iama not only for friendship, but to emphasize the freedom of her new status. She was a tall girl, always laughing.

Behind them came a stranger, nervous in my vicinity. His codpiece proclaimed he came from the island of Kitava, for there the fashionable menfolk, for pride in their apparel, lightly scratch designs into the growing betel nut sheath upon the tree, designs that develop with the maturity of the sheath and are preserved in the codpiece. So proud was he, indeed, that he had fixed the sheath loosely, so loosely that from most angles his genitals were in full view; but he could see no incongruity in the fact. That was the way of his island. He had observed the conventions and was dressed, and in that polite society any criticism would have been unthinkable.

More Kitavins came — a canoe must have crossed the strait not long before. The next was a girl of twelve or thirteen who wore the overlarge earrings peculiar to her island, twenty or thirty in each ear, so that the lobes reached down to brush her shoulders as she swayed. She walked straight to me when she saw me on the track, and stood so close that her little pointed breasts thrust into my shirt while she smiled up at me. I smiled back, and took her by the upper arms to move her aside, refusing her invitation as gently as I could. It was not hard to refuse, for it was founded merely upon her curiosity, and there was no other communication between the two of us.

The track curved round some inlets of the sea. There was a dark place where great limbs of trees overhung a shallow pond, supporting small gardens of orchids, and curtains of lianas from which, incredibly, sprouted festoons of red blossoms, curiously shaped. A patterned snake threaded the outcrops of pale coral beneath the water, and near him fish that were living jewels quivered in the delight and beauty of being alive. Reeds and sunshine lay just ahead, bathed in the hot yellow afternoon.

Near Okopukopu the trail thrust into the groves of trees which always, in these islands, mark the outskirts of a village; and here the predominant variety was one which I have not seen elsewhere. The people call it makininai. It is a tall branching tree which has the habit, like the cacao, of producing flowers and fruits in profusion from the bark of the trunk and branches. The fruits are rose-flavored, white-fleshed, crimson-skinned, about the size of plums. The flowers are a brilliant cerise, and are produced in such quantity as to alter the composition of the light which strikes down through them. At the end of the grove a thicket of betel nut palms gives contrast and marks the proper boundary of the village.

Coming toward me through the grove, haloed with the unearthly light of the pink-stained sunshine, swayed a girl whose appearance was so incongruous that for a few seconds I did not realize that it was also beautiful. Her hair was red, not the dull deep red of lime-bleached hair, but the rare, bright, iron-pigmented hair that is the glory of certain individuals among the northern races. The color of it was carried through to her brows and lashes; she had not come at it by artifice.

Her eyes were blue, clear, light blue; and her skin, though it was lightly tanned, was also freckled. She was dressed in the delightful habit of the islanders; very little of her beauty was concealed. She was tall by the standards of her fellows, but not so tall that she attracted attention for that reason. And she walked like an islander, which is to say with grace and distinction. So European was she in her features that my impulse was to turn my eyes from the exquisite offering of her breasts, never in her life restrained, and firmly muscled.

As she came nearer I saw, with a pang, that her ears had been pierced in childhood and supported an extravagance of tiny rings, so that the lobes were nearly two inches longer than in nature. She had "bitten the kailoi," too, as they say there; she was in love, she had a lover, and advertised that happy fact in the pride with which she displayed the partial loss of eyelashes. For lovers in those climes nibble eyelashes away and swallow them, to take some part of the inamorata to themselves; and a ragged fringe is a matter for great pride. She wore, in a bracelet on her upper arm, a fragrant spray of the kailoi itself, a mint bush that tells, when you wear its flowers, that the attentions of a lover will be welcome. It is so strongly scented that its message penetrates the dark; not all the other scents of the bush will drown it.

There are not many half-castes upon the island for two reasons: the first, that undoubtedly the natives practice contraception, though the means is a secret of the women. The second is that the young girls are ardent and skilled long before pregnancy is possible for them, and most of the roués of other races pick and choose among these free and careless children for their temporary attentions. There was little doubt, though, that this girl was the unrecognized daughter of a certain red-haired trader who had died upon the island some years before, and whose profligacy was something of a byword, even in those parts.

Yet in the genes of her mother too there must have been a conformant strain that combined to produce a type so triumphantly Nordic in appearance. There was nothing about this girl, except what had been achieved by artifice, to suggest her island blood — and those were superficial features only: the slit ear lobes, the nibbled lashes, the feet that had never known constraint and the graceful poise of hands of which the finger bones were incredibly delicate.

Her fellows very frequently had hair that was straight or slightly waved, light brown to black in color, but seldom with the woolly characteristic of the Negro common in nearby island groups. The king wore, as his predecessors had worn, a red wig; a number of his subjects of purely native inheritance had red-tinged hair. It was an esteemed color; yet the only other red-haired natives I have known — certain Maoris from the Urewera country in New Zealand — were looked down upon by their fellows for their differentiation.

I never saw that girl again, but her memory remains vivid: as clear as my memory of that dance upon which I spent days of study. Looking back after the passage of a few years, I realize that the dance was interesting, the girl significant. I have thought about her a great deal, and it seems to me that she well represents the problem of the Pacific migrations and perhaps its key. The tendency for anthropologists and historians has been to propose a single, simple solution to the great mystery of origins; and I think that few if any of these propositions have been tenable. One fact is sure and certain: the human race was not spread about the globe by accident. Great nations did not arise by the circumstance of a chance arrival upon an alien shore, from a migration by happenchance, like that of a lizard upon a floating log.

Wherever man went, he went of his own volition, his mind aware of the forces driving him, his strength and determination influencing his destination. In proof of this he seldom or never traveled alone. He took his dogs or his pigs or his domestic fowl, except only in the case of the Tasmanians, of which extinct race our knowledge is so slight we can make no such assertion. But if the Tasmanians came from elsewhere to the country they finally inhabited, at least the menfolk brought their women.

Consider them first. They are classified, in our imperfect knowledge, as Negrito; the nearest of other humans in that category inhabit the island of New Caledonia, far to the north, and the great continent of Australia lies between. Moreover, the Tasmanians had no boats or any knowledge of boatbuilding, and their fragile rafts, made of three slight bundles of bark, were never put to sea except in sheltered estuaries. The Tasmanians never reached the island outposts that circled their country, and apparently had neither the will nor the means to do so. If they ever possessed the capacity for sea-voyaging they had forgotten it centuries before the white man came to discover and obliterate them — a process which occupied less than three generations.

Certainly they could not have come by sea from New Caledonia, still less from the Andaman Islands, to whose inhabitants some have seen a resemblance in them. Poles, not paddles, were their means of propulsion. They had no sail, and even though the smallest children on a tropic island soon learn the advantage of using a coconut palm frond to harness the wind, this method is impossible upon a long voyage. It calls for a following wind, and there is no season in which continuous winds could propel voyages to Tasmania from either of the other points.

It has been further said that the Dravidian aborigines might have driven these Negritoes to Tasmania from the Australian mainland. Assuming that they could make the voyage across Bass Strait, and from what we know of them they could not, we still have to find any evidence that people of their kind ever set foot in Australia. To this end there is a conjecture based on the similarity of Tasmanian cranial measurements to those of some South Australian tribes, and little else. Some students have seen a similarity in their tools to others found in one site in New South Wales; but paleolithic stone workings all bear some resemblance one to another, which increases as the materials used have a closer relationship.

There remains a possibility that they may have been discarded slaves, transported to that land and there marooned by people of a higher development who were able to build vessels; but this is the worst kind of a guess. The final desperate venture is that they were abandoned here when developing units of their tribe sailed away; that they were here from the beginning. Their incidence has never been examined in relationship to the rest of the world. There is nothing that we can prove from the Tasmanians.

Ethnologists have discovered a relationship between the Australian aborigines, some small groups of people in Malaysia, the Veddas of Ceylon and some aboriginal hill tribes in southern India. At their stage of development, with their known capacity for building and handling small, efficient craft, credence must be given the ready assumption that these people could have migrated by way of the Malaysian complex to Australia. Journeys of four hundred miles at sea are not uncommon among them even today.

They could, and very likely would have brought the dingo, a magnificent and highly developed dog which is not only one of the few placental mammals preceding the European to Australia, but is a probable ancestor of most of the world's best and cleverest breeds. Despite the reputation Europeans have given it, it is remarkable for its intelligence and its courage.

A comparatively recent arrival date for aborigines is deduced from the fact that penetration to the region which is now the southern state of Victoria was made only a little while before the Europeans came. But this in itself is not conclusive, for there is no doubt in the mind of anyone who knows the whole continent that the northern areas offered by far the most attractive living conditions to primitive tribes.

Some slight evidence that there were humans in the country before the aborigines has been uncovered in caves in the sparsely settled northwest, in a wall art dissimilar to aborigine work. But we know that there were intrusions. An image of Shou Lao, the Taoist God of Long Life, made in the T'ang dynasty (A.D. 618-906) was dug up from beneath the entangling roots of a huge banyan at Port Darwin in 1879. The banyan itself, widely found in the north of Australia, is not native, and presumably was introduced from Asia.

There are Melanesian and Malaysian influences among the aborigines of the far north; and because these do not exist in the south, the inference seems to be that the aborigine covered the land before the Melanesian arrived. Yet neither may have been there very long. On the other hand it is possible that the migration went the other way: that the aborigine, who is said by some to represent the ancestors of both the Caucasian and Dravidian races, emerged from the Australian continent to leave his traces in Malaysia, India and Ceylon. Many a castle of logic will be overturned if the Caucasian some day looks to the Great South Land for the birth evidence of his race; yet it is not impossible, for a total view of human development, based on evidence collected in all the world, has not been attempted.

The appearance of the aborigine is said to be similar to that of primitive man — the jaws prognathous, the mouth wide, the nose broad and the eyebrow ridges heavy. Yet it has ever seemed to me, as I have moved among them, that these characteristics are more noticeable far from the coast, and again when the tribe is living in conditions that are still primitive. They are, in fact, most prominent when the babe comes from his mother's milk directly to the consumption of tough meats, hard grains and the Spartan fare of the arid areas. Therefore I have wondered whether the primitive molding of the face might be environmental and not congenital; for the early development of facial muscles, at a stage when the skull is still in process of formation, could indeed produce those bone changes which are so noticeable; and the process could be accentuated over the generations.

In the coastal natives, where the juvenile diet consists more frequently of fish and other, softer foods such as come from the sea, the skulls of natives seem akin to our own. There is also a more settled way of life, and the tribes have more artifacts. The apparently arrested development of the inland people is not related to a more "primitive" skull or to any inability to construct, but derives from the fact that this nomad's greatest wealth, in this country of swift-changing seasons, was the development of his individual independence. With the distances he had to cover it was necessary for him to be able to survive unarmed and unaccountered, and he did so.

He was capable of working textiles, and restricted his use of them to the making of the dilly bags his women carried. He had developed the spear-thrower and the boomerang; he could work stone and wood; he had some knowledge of the arts, a deep interest in spiritual values; and he developed a great love of country. He went naked for preference, and kept his life uncluttered. He had no chiefs and no kings, but he had the self-discipline to ensure a strong adherence to complicated laws. He was a product of his environment.

So, in a less spectacular fashion is the Melanesian who, with his mixture of bloods, including the Negrito, could still have been the original inhabitant of his own islands. That is to say that original settlement of these parts could have been made by people whose blood was already mixed. On the other hand, the analysis of mixture may have been wrong; some of the tribes of the New Guinea highlands may have developed characteristics wrongly classified as Negrito by a local stabilization of mutations caused by inbreeding and isolation. I cannot believe that many races came whole, of pure blood from some source area to their present whereabouts. I believe that the components of almost any given people were drawn from sources which in their totality encompassed the whole earth and every variety of man; and that in each place certain dominant genes gave character to the tribe within the nation, and the nation within its hemisphere.

I think back to the experiences of Count Luigi Maria D'Albertis, who visited New Guinea in 1871. At Kapaor on the Dutch New Guinea coast he spoke of seeing "European" types and "true Arabs" among the natives. He also saw seven large praus from Macassar. At the little islands of Ghesser and Kalvari he found at anchor a schooner from Macassar and two praus. "It appears that they visit this island — which is a commercial emporium in these seas — to obtain slaves, skins of the Bird of Paradise, a small quantity of tripang, mother-of-pearl and tortoise-shell. Some of the traders are Malays and others Arabs," he wrote.

Year after year the praus and dhows came seeking slaves — was there ever a time when they did not? The ships themselves were crewed with slaves; a sick slave was put ashore, traded for another, or for salable commodities. In this way men of a thousand nations could have reached New Guinea and stayed to add their stock to the common inheritance.

It is of little value for the ethnologist to come and classify the tribe "Negrito," or "Papuasian with a Polynesian influx." Such pronouncements say too much and too little. The race of man, wherever you find him, is descended from all mankind; we are all inheritors of pasts so varied that they could be one. The slave and the slaveowner alike left their marks upon the people; even in the hidden valleys the intrusions and the extrusions altered the common stock.

On this supposition the racial types have evolved in the environment in which we find them; in Melanesia these processes have been hastened by the self-imposed isolation. In New Guinea are seven hundred languages; the interplay of trade has traditionally occurred only in channels rigidly controlled by conventions imposed by the suspicious and the vulnerable, and these mainly upon the seacoasts. Without an aristocracy, without, for the most part, hereditary chiefs, personal ambition was not developed to institute changes. And similar conditions prevailed in Micronesia as well.

But in the great body of the Pacific, the homogeneity of the Polynesian race seems to challenge these premises, and it is among the Polynesians that the great mystery of human penetration is most intriguing. From Hawaii to New Zealand, from Easter Island to the bounds of Melanesia they spoke a common language, kept pure in great part by the quasi-religious exercise of repeating the genealogies, the charms and the rituals in exact and sacrosanct formulas.

Despite the great distances which separated the components of this nation, the sixty dialects which developed differed so little, each from any of the others, that understanding was complete and immediate whenever individuals met. Not only do the dialects differ in less degree than do the dialects, say, of the British Isles, but the same types of people can be recognized in much the same proportion in all the major island groups. Yet the long separation has induced the appearance of artistic conventions which differ materially, and promoted the ascension of differing gods in a theogony which has otherwise suffered little change.

The genealogies of ancestors, which were sacred, show correspondence, at least as to the more prominent individuals, in island groups as far apart as the Marquesas and New Zealand; and amazingly, have been upheld as to accuracy by radio-carbon tests — for instance, both the genealogies and radio-carbon put the date of the occupation of Hawaii at a thousand years ago. There was a general expansion at this time, and others earlier, from Hawaiiki, the legendary home of the ancestors. There have been several Hawaiikis, but this one may confidently be reckoned to be Tahiti.

It is supposed to be about 2500 years since the Polynesians came to the Pacific; and the slow colonization of many of the major groups testifies that over a long period, population pressures were insignificant. In general the people retained their homogeneity because the conditions on the various island groups remained the same. There were some exceptions.

On the Chatham Islands, the Moriori people, Polynesians who had migrated from an earlier settlement of New Zealand, have been held to have deteriorated. The timber on the island was unsuited to the building of canoes, and this art was altogether lost, reed rafts taking the place of the larger vessels. The builders could not add significance to their work with the traditional carving; as their construction did not permit of overseas voyaging the raft also eliminated some stimulus for art. This stimulus was further stifled by an early edict of the chief Nunuku-whenua, who limited fighting on the islands to the use of quarterstaves between two opponents, and stipulated the cessation of the fight upon the drawing of first blood.

In these conditions of peace the Moriori, in the space of seven hundred years, did degenerate. Enterprise was still further limited by the abundant food supply, centered in the albatross rookeries and a wealth of fish and shellfish. In 1835, Maoris from New Zealand attacked the Moriois, conquered them, seized their women, and contributed materially to their obliteration half a century later.

The lengthy voyages which testify to the excellent navigation of the Polynesians were by no means as arduous, under normal conditions, as most writers have imagined them. Sir Peter Buck (Te Rangi Hiroa), in his book *The Coming of the Maori,* has shown that the large sixty-foot canoes could carry ample supplies of food and water, as well as plants and animals for acclimatization. Their seven-knot speed would take them from Tahiti to New Zealand, in the season of their choice, in less than two weeks; and probably they normally had an intermediate stop at Rarotonga, in the Cook Islands.

The existence — the exact location — of their destination was well known, and usually had been known for centuries. The earliest fleets were followed by others over long periods. Voyages were made not only to effect population movements but to establish plants and animals that could make living easier.

Thus in Hawaii, the vegetable introductions of the Polynesians included the coconut, breadfruit, Malay apple, taro, sweet potato, yam, banana, arrowroot, sugar cane, gourd, paper mulberry, candlenut, turmeric, ginger, and several plants for providing fibers, dyes and navigational requirements. Not all of these could have been brought on a single voyage; and the probability is that the early settlers sent back for those plants they felt to be essential. They made these importations in spite of the fact that Hawaii, before their arrival, had an exceptionally extensive range of flora. They were not just feckless wanderers who made use of whatever came their way; their whole regimen was planned.

It is generally supposed, or accepted, that the Polynesians came to otherwise unoccupied islands; and in the instance of Hawaii and one or two other places this is undoubtedly true. But in the period after they reached the Pacific, and before they moved to these more outlying groups, it seems inevitable that they conquered or absorbed some earlier arrivals. They are usually assessed as a Caucasian race with some Mongolian intrusions; these latter, however, are slight, and can be accounted for by a problematical stay on some Asian shore before they set out into the broad Pacific.

Therefore any absorptions they made subsequently were, in all probability, of other people with a Caucasian inheritance. For these are the only absorptions that could not have affected their physical homogeneity so remarkable at this present day. In their legends and their habits there is much to suggest that this was, indeed, the case.

In New Zealand legend, which was undoubtedly altered by the great schools of priesthood to fit later knowledge, and is therefore undependable, the first discovery of the country was made by the voyager Kupe. Kupe existed and discovered New Zealand; this much can be established with reasonable accuracy, but persistent stories say the land was inhabited before he came, somewhere about the year 925. Two or three waves of people arrived before the great migration at about the middle of the fourteenth century when — and this is interesting — the canoes brought the sweet potato, the pig, the dog, but not the fowl, whose name "moa" was then applied to the great wingless bird already disappearing from the New Zealand scene.

All these people came from one place, Hawaiiki; only the third migration is well known, for the spoken histories commemorated only the ancestors of the orator. It is not surprising that no mention is made of any indigenes unrelated to the Polynesians; but that they existed is suggested by a great deal of evidence.

For one thing, in New Zealand, and only in New Zealand, the Polynesians developed the fortified stockade to a high pitch of excellence. It follows that they had a cunning and wary enemy from whom they had to be protected. In the legend the enemy was the "patupaiarehe," the fairy folk of the forest — a red-haired people. Story after story relates the theft of women by the patupaiarehe and the seduction of Polynesian men by the red-haired women.

It is in the legend of the Urewera tribe that their forefathers, not long after their arrival in New Zealand by the Matatua canoe, went inland, and in the forest country round Lake Waikaremoana fought with the redheaded inhabitants of the country and finally amalgamated with them. When the European arrived, many of the Urewera people were redheaded; such individuals were called "urukehu," and were looked down upon by Maoris of other tribes.

There are several other indications that such people existed — in their recorded distaste for Maori methods of cooking, for example, and for the painted face. Such national or tribal characteristics could not well have been imagined by the Maoris. But the fear of the patupaiarehe exists in other island groups; in fact, in nearly all groups of the southern hemisphere that are mountainous, with thickly forested hinterlands.

Still another mystery that adds cumulative evidence to the theory of an earlier race is the discovery, in certain of the Polynesian islands but not in others, of megalithic memorials. In the coral islands the traditions of setting up such things would die for want of suitable stone; though it is said that the great trilithon in Tonga was apparently brought there by sea. It must have represented some belief highly significant to its builders. The stone monuments of Easter Island are well known. And there is some value in the coincidental thought that nearly all constructors of megaliths had a Caucasian inheritance.

Little serious archaeological investigation of the Pacific area has been undertaken. While this gap in historical research remains, all is surmise; yet it must be true that no complete history of man is possible until the mysteries of the Pacific are solved and its story correlated with that of the rest of the world.

We can only suspect, from the limited evidence, that

there was a population here before the Polynesians came; and we can make a hazard as to its constituents. We can guess, perhaps, that they were related to the redheaded people who show their influence today in the Trobriands, where there is also some trace of people who contained tribal memory in megaliths. We can guess at a hundred solutions. Only one aspect seems to me sure: there was no single origin of the Polynesian people; their roots, like ours, are in every part of the world.

Some additional evidence comes from an examination of the religions of the Pacific; but here again much is obliterated by the invader, and this time it is the European invader: the missionary and his adversaries, the trader and the government representative.

16

THE ISLAND of Tuma is the most northerly and, what is more to the point, the most westerly of the inhabited lands which form the Trobriand group in the Coral Sea. Materially it is of little account, but it is here that the ancient god Topileta welcomes the spirits newly dead to the world beneath the land, and it is here that they pursue their chosen avocations in the happiness of a life which exactly parallels that which they knew upon the earth.

I sailed here once upon a trading launch, motivated by some curiosity as to the temporal signs by which this god, without churches, priests or altars, without precepts, threats or promises, maintains such a hold upon his island followers that they are yet unwilling to relinquish his image for that of the Christian deity.

The skipper of the *Labelle* answered to the name of

"Horse," with which he had been dowered in the distasteful tradition of unintelligent Europeans reaching for humor. He was a Dobu kite-fisherman, a serious, pipe-smoking young fellow who, in the manner of the sea, had a wife in every port. He was a good cook as well as a skipper, and on one occasion I found him making my bed to save the time of a crew boy. And once, when we anchored too close to a shoal, he put on a pair of pearl-diving goggles, went over the side, picked up the heavy anchor and chain and walked the bottom with it, towing the craft out to deeper water.

In the remainder of the crew, Cockroach and Mwap-weia were Trobrianders, brothers from the family of a Methodist mission convert. Melody and Baldy came from Goodenough Island and Gilpin, another Methodist, from Normanby. The only worshipper of Topileta was Big Eyes; but there was none who held the god in any contempt. When they knew our destination the whole crew came in a body to warn me to behave, in that place, with the utmost decorum; a course to which I had already committed myself.

We approached the island over miles of sea so shallow and so clear that every detail of the coral beneath was plain. Along the verges of shallow undersea valleys whole forests of antler coral, brown and purple, thrust toward the surface. Elsewhere were great banks of brain coral six feet and more across. Tiny fish, perhaps half an inch long, showed clearly as sparks of light of the color and intensity of the brilliant green of malachite, the blue of sapphire, flecking the white-tipped antlers; and there were other varieties, all shapes, all colors in all intensities, to be glimpsed from the deck. There were sandbanks between the coral gardens, and sometimes niggerheads reaching for the ship's keel. Only expert local knowledge could have brought a ship within miles of the island.

Never more than ten or twelve feet above sea level, and with no trees taller than eighty or a hundred feet, the five-mile length of Tuma showed first as a series of small dots on the horizon. When we came nearer, it disclosed itself to be a typical small island, the dots resolving into the heads of coco palms. Interspersed with units of this fringing palisade, mangroves filled some bays, and elsewhere were dense growths of small shrubs, broken at intervals by enormously bulky trees.

There were callophyllums sending long wandering branches over the water, their heavy trunks so overgrown with orchids, staghorns, creepers, ferns, parasites and epiphytes of every kind that each single tree was itself an extensive garden. There were barringtonias, with flowers like large white water lily cups, each holding a thick sheaf of purple stamens; and with squared nuts large as a dog's head, the kernels wrapped in a fiber like that which protects the coconut. And there were giant figs, hung with creepers and vines. The natu tree — I know it by the Trobrianders' name — erected a magnificent tower of greenery to bear its fruits, pulpy and scented, the size of a large apple. There were saida nuts, with meat more delicate than almonds and twice the size. The yellow hibiscus spilled its flowers into the quiet sea, whereon they sailed in rafts of cuplike boats.

Upon this island of Tuma there is a village of which
the inhabitants live like any other natives, by fishing and
gardening. They harvest yams and taro and beans, and
when the gardens have given their year's offering they
plant bananas. They grow pineapples for eating, and red
hibiscus to feed the soul, and sugar cane to make the
children happy, and spider lilies whose thick stems they
use for fish lures. Their clothing comes from the pandanus, the betel nut and the banana, their stimulant from
the betel nut and from lime they burn from the sea shells
on the beach; from the coconut they get food, drink, and
a copra income which is sufficient to buy them kerosene
lamps and steel axes. But their duty and their joy is to
keep the whole island in such condition that Topileta will
commend them.

Most of the coastline is bounded by coral rock barriers,
but opposite the village is a shelving, sandy beach which,
with its accommodation for canoes, is the reason for
building in that place. We stopped here and picked up
Two Bob, a guardian of the god's preserve who would
smooth the way for me; and under his direction set off
for the southern end of the island, a rocky promontory
above which, as we approached, circled a magnificent
pair of sea eagles.

We pulled ashore here in a dinghy and landed on a
little beach not more than five yards long. Here, by request, I waited, while Horse and Big Eyes and Two Bob
went ahead to prepare Topileta for my visit. Later, Horse
told me that Two Bob had approached a hole in the rock
through which the spirits reputedly descended to the

afterworld, and speaking in his normal voice told Topileta that a Dim-Dim (European) was coming to pay his
regards. He asked the god to open the way through the
coral so that I could see clearly. And further, that Topileta should send his fish up to the surface of the sea in
demonstration of his powers.

We left the beach then and pushed our way through
pandanus and scrub until we came to the bare rock that
was the island's southernmost extremity. As we walked,
Big Eyes kept nudging me.

"Look, Taubada," he would say. "No fish."

In the sea about forty yards away was a mushroom-
shaped rock named Modawausi. This too is a significant
place for the worshipers of Topileta. A round crown of
coral ten or fifteen yards in diameter, it stands on a
strangely slender shaft; and Two Bob told me that a little
way under the water the shaft continues to narrow until
it is no thicker than a man's thigh. At the surface it is a
pillar of two feet diameter.

Modawausi is the last earthly resting place of spirits
still traveling to their eternal home. From the rock they
must float in a final effort across the intervening water
and land on the coral where we stood that day, there to
follow a special crack in the stone until they come to the
hole named Ogegela, which opens up on the underworld.

The hole is perhaps nine or ten inches in diameter,
looking downwards at a forty-five degree angle, a per-
fectly ordinary-looking hole of a type very common in
coral formation. I bent over to look down. The boys all
drew in their breath.

"Don't shift any stones," one said. "Don't disturb anything."

I left tobacco and betel nut in a depression in the rock by the mouth of the hole and tried to see what I could. The hole seemed to go down and down. To my puzzled eye it went much lower than the surface of the sea only five yards from it. It was in porous rock, yet I could see no water.

I had been told that sometimes you could see a long way, but that sometimes Topileta closed the hole to exclude the light of the temporal world. This was, apparently, an occasion when he had left it open. It seemed to me there was a slight mystery here, but probably one that could be explained in terms of optical illusion. When I looked up the boys were staring silently out to sea. Cockroach, who with Mwapweia had joined us, was plainly scared, his eyes expanded to the limit. There was an atmosphere of devotion about the place which could be felt, but there was also an overriding tension.

Big Eyes spoke again.

"Look, Taubada. The fish!" He pointed out to sea.

Now on the windy, tossing strip of ocean between us and the rock Modawausi there was quick movement. Pike five feet long were jumping from the water. Pike and kingfish and trevally. Suddenly there were dozens of fish jumping, some of them less than ten yards away, monsters of fish and little ones all together, but none of them in pursuit of the others.

Then alongside Modawausi the red emperor bream came to the surface. They swam side by side, all the fish facing me, not altering their positions in the water, but rising and falling with the restless waves, their fins moving gently. They were in two masses near the rock, and I could only guess at their numbers by the extent of the coloration. Between us and the bream the pike continued to jump. There were many different kinds of fish I could not identify. But the pike did not attack the bream and the bream did not break formation. I had never seen any bream on the surface before except momentarily, when they were in pursuit of smaller fish; and this display left me amazed.

A gentle rain had begun to fall, and we left. The two masses of red emperors were still by the rock and the other fish nearer the shore. The two eagles still circled overhead, and did not stoop to the challenge of this sea bounty. Horse, Big Eyes and Two Bob waited behind.

When they caught up with me they told me that Topileta felt pleased. I did not believe in him, he had said; but I did not disbelieve — which I felt was an accurate enough summation. He would send me a fish to eat, he said.

There had been green bushes with trumpet flowers blooming all about the site, and there had been the consciousness of a metaphysical presence, engendered, no doubt, by the intensity of the emotion registered by those about me.

Within a minute of the launch getting under way, a fourteen-pound trevally hung itself on the lily-leaf lure of the troll at the stern. This was the fish, the boys said, that Topileta had promised me.

Later, when Two Bob had gone, when the evening had come and we lay at anchor, the crew engaged me in discussion.

Cockroach began it.

"Can Jesus Christ send up the fish?" he asked.

"Sure He can," I said stoutly.

"Will you ask Him?"

"No. I don't have to."

"Then you don't believe he can do it. We ask Topileta without any hesitation."

"Then why don't you ask him whenever you go out fishing?"

They looked scared. Finally, when I pursued the subject, they told me of a time when the fleet had fished for two days without success. In desperation they had asked Topileta to hang fish on the hooks.

"He did. But the fish were all so big we lost our lines and our hooks. No more," Cockroach said.

The point was that you did not ask Topileta for things to your own personal advantage; only those which were to Topileta's advantage.

I have no explanation of this demonstration of fish, other than the abiding power of human faith, and I am not sure that I am possessed of such faith, or of the courage or the simplicity to put it casually to test. There was nothing in the incident that could truly be called supernatural, and for the problems it presents there are possibly explanations that have eluded my search.

But if the natives have some method by which they can induce fish to come to the surface, it is surprising that it does not play a part in their fishing methods. An example is the method I have already described by which the Trobrianders call sharks to their canoes, using a rattle of coconut shells strung on a cane, a semi-magical procedure which is successful. But the shark meat is eaten. And there is no harvest of these fish which Topileta sends from the bottom of the sea in demonstration of his powers.

The religion of the Trobrianders has but this single god, with no priests, no devils, and consequently, no threats. The absence of a devil seems to indicate that the form of the religion has not been superseded by conquest, for the devil of one religion is the god of its predecessor. The sacred places of Trobriand belief stud the ground the islanders use in their daily movements, and each current day is indentified, closely, lovingly, with the era of their yesterday and its traditions.

Christian missionaries have found these people difficult to convert, perhaps the most stubborn group in the Pacific. They do not care to exchange the intimate happiness of the sacred places in their own land for those of a barren Eastern shore that is half a world away.

This seems to me a highly developed religion. Elsewhere in Melanesia are places where animistic thoughts have barely developed sufficiently to produce the fetish; and above that there is a wide variety of beliefs, of gods and pantheons. The field for research is narrowing; there are many places where the old gods are forgotten, and others where the people show an almost indecent haste to replace them. . . .

In the Torres Straits Islands, in the closing decade of the nineteenth century, the London Mission Society had little trouble in inducing the entire population to turn to Congregationalism. About 1915 it seemed convenient to exchange this area for another then held by the Church of England, and in a remarkable package deal the transfer was made. The newcomers were rather High Church. This second conversion was made en masse, without any friction whatsoever. Only a year or two back I asked the Bishop of Carpentaria, of whose immense and far-spreading diocese the wooden Quetta Cathedral of these islands is now the headquarters, just how deep was the penetration of their faith.

"It isn't a question to be answered lightly," he said. "To tell the truth, it is one that worries me a great deal. On the surface, their acceptance has been so complete as to be almost disturbing. They attend the church services, they live according to the beliefs that we have given them, and it is almost a temptation to sit back in the assurance that the task has been concluded. It has been too easy. There is no way of testing the strength of their beliefs; and one is left with the uncomfortable suspicion that possibly they might turn as readily as they did before to something new."

The native religions, and sometimes the new-fledged Christian flocks, have shown a frightening tendency to give way before the host of new religions that have sprung up following contact with the white man. Whenever an indigenous people is presented in material form with the achievements of a more highly developed race who come as conquerors, rebellion will center about a new religion which may be good or bad. In such religious fervors lie dangers to the invaders.

In New Guinea they have had Cargo Cult, in Papua, Vailalla Madness; in the Solomons, Marching Rule; in the New Hebrides, the Jon Frum Cult; in the Admiralties, Peliau Madness; in New Zealand of the last century, the Hau Hau cult; all engendered by the mysteries brought to the sleeping land by the conquerors. Such religions are known throughout the world; indeed there are few beliefs which have not been born under similar conditions; and still more will rise from the increased expansion of such things as the motor road, the radio, and the earth-circling satellite. A good many of the Melanesian creeds may not be much older than these, though they have native characteristics. There is so little information upon the nature of Melanesian gods at the time of the first contact with Europeans that much is hazy.

The Australian aborigines, reckoned to be among the most primitive races upon evidence that is far from conclusive, have a religion that is well developed. They worship the Earth-Mother and recognize in their graceful, plaintive stories the prior existence of culture heroes as well limned as any in Valhalla. To an amazing degree they feel the reality of the metaphysical world they have created — the dream-time, which is neither a dream nor a period, or if it is a period is one which has no dimension, so that the past and the present exist together.

There is much in their belief that corresponds with Christian dogma; there is also a relationship to the pre-

Greek female deity which was once worshiped by the known world. Over generations the missions have not much disturbed these tribal beliefs; conversion is often no more than a symbol of the native's desire to please; for they are a gracious and a considerate and a kindly people.

The aborigines walk much in sorrow and are tenacious of old belief; but the carefree, careless Polynesians show little sign of ever having drawn their abundant strength from any single religious source. Religion of a kind was visible in every aspect of their living day; but it took so many forms and was so variable in its content that it seemed but a decoration upon the social life. Priests of one sort or another controlled every activity; schools for the formal training of these priests were revered institutions. Some were little more than guild leaders at that; but the communal function of this part of the religious system was to preserve the laws and the important history.

In addition, there were practices purely fetishistic. And objects credited with divinity could pass their magical powers to others. Alongside a worship of images was a concurrent worship, by the same individuals, of gods without images, in groves without temples; a system of priests who could set up altars wherever they were, and a scattering of certain gods that could only be worshiped in solitude.

The holiness of the genealogies which is such a feature of Polynesian history is only one of a series of aspects that point to a tradition of ancestor-worship. Some chiefs and some priests were elevated to godhood; when this happened, rarely, in their lifetimes, still another classification was created. There was a strong element of magic and witchcraft. There were personal gods, family gods and tribal gods, and a pantheon which in general supervised humanity. There was a belief in ten heavens; the figure was later raised to twelve; at the same time the spirits of the dead descended to an underworld which was not a hell.

There were culture-heroes, of whom one, Maui, was so eminent and so well remembered that it is almost certain he commemorates a historical figure, probably the leader who instituted the earliest of the great migrations, the Moses of his time. There was strong evidence of the worship of the sun and the moon; all Polynesian spirits travel to destinations in the west. Phallic worship had considerable influence. There were water sprites and wood elves; and practically every variation of metaphysical being that was ever conjured up by human mind.

In the pantheon were goddesses; the majority if not all of these were inhabitants of the underworld and were not admitted to the complex of heavens where their male counterparts were installed. This presumably points to an earlier phase, when a tribe of worshipers of female gods was overwhelmed by the conquering ancestors bringing their male gods to the dominant position in an amalgamation.

In a great part of Polynesia, at the time of the European influx, a supreme god had been created, or was in process of creation. This god, where his worship was most highly developed, was unknown to the common people; his existence was a secret shared by the chiefs and the priests — the priests continuing, in their public ministrations, to expound the former beliefs.

In New Zealand, this supreme god was Io, self-created in space and the creator of the gods and the firmament. The discovery of this god was not made by European investigators until after Christianity had made considerable inroads into Polynesian belief; Matorohanga, the chief priestly informant, was himself a Christian convert at the time his manuscript was written. There is consequently very great confusion as to what attributes Io might have possessed in the belief of his worshipers, for there is no doubt but that he has been shaped to fit a later concept of the Christian God.

In Samoa, Tonga and the Society Islands, Tangaroa was the principal god, and in the latter place had been elevated to a state of supremacy possibly more advanced than that of Io. Yet in Hawaii, Tangaroa (Kanaloa) was the least of the principal gods.

The functions and capacities of these major gods — the departmental gods, as Te Rangi Hiroa (Sir Peter Buck) calls them — altered from place to place and from period to period. The astounding homogeneity of the Polynesians, which they had maintained in language, in habits, in ideals, even in physical appearance, here had no application whatever.

An obvious reason for this state of affairs, but a superficial one, lay in the frequent failure of gods to respond to the supplications of their adherents. When Maori went to war with Maori, the tribal god whose adherents were defeated lost caste. If this happened too often his worship was set aside. Familiarity bred contempt: the habit of seeking supernatural assistance for every problem, however small, reduced the capacity of the gods to give satisfaction. The Trobrianders, in their supreme faith, ask nothing from Topileta but a continuance of the conditions they enjoy; and perhaps it was the more insistent ambition of the Maori that contributed to the decadence of his gods. The Maori had a semi-voluntary aristocracy; the Trobriander was set in the strata of society in which he was born.

It seems to me that the remoter gods are those which retain their power the longest; that the longevity of the deity is increased by thanksgiving, and weakened by supplication.

The sanctity of human life itself was not seriously regarded in the Pacific. I am in some doubt as to whether we, with our constant wars, with our development of a permanent elite of warriors and a strong tendency to impose our morals and our creeds upon the rest of the world, have ever paid it more than lip service ourselves; but it is a matter of record that the first missionaries were horrified by the casual slaughter which propitiated the gods or enforced the laws.

The death penalty for breach of the latter was an obvious, and indeed necessary institution. Governments rule by fear, most efficiently by economic fear; but in these fortunate islands no such concept was possible. Naked man, unequipped, could live comfortably the year round in that climate; therefore a cohesion of the populace, necessary to the exercise of power, could not be achieved by the interdependence which, for example, was essential in the cold winters of Europe. Without economic fear the priests created the conditions for mental fear; the chiefs imposed the fear of elimination.

But propitiation of the gods by human sacrifice brought recriminations when the gods failed. The complexity of the spiritual world of Polynesia inflicted a mirrored complication on living, to such an extent that the exposition of the Christian belief was often amazingly successful. Remembering that, a thousand years after the arrival of Christianity in England, the worship of Hou (or Herne the Hunter, or the Horned God by whatever name) was still current, the swift conversion of Polynesians cannot be taken for granted as a normal development.

Among the earliest converts, the most assiduous of the mission workers were very frequently tohungas or witch doctors of one sort or another. Likewise, the sons or heirs of chiefs were prominently among the earliest converts; for it was the mission of such people within the tribe to cherish and add to the storehouse of knowledge belonging to the people.

An instance is that of the great chief Taufa'ahau of Tonga, who later became George Tubou I. The Methodist mission commenced its work in Tonga in 1822 and converted Taufa'ahau in 1831. He fought in the savage civil wars and became king in 1845; and there is little doubt but that the archipelago's wholesale conversion to Methodism was due to his influence and to his conviction that a single, simple and sincere belief would advantage his people. He was a farsighted man who made treaties with France, Germany, Great Britain and the United States, who gave his people parliamentary government, and who introduced a system, unique in the world, by which every male Tongan acquired title to land at his maturity.

The remarkable speed of this conversion might have been equaled and excelled elsewhere in Polynesia with fortunate results, but for the fact that a good many of Christ's representatives were not wholly motivated by the joy of spreading the Word; moreover, many were types of people who should not have been chosen for the responsible task of representing a stable European civilization. A whaler, his ship moored at Lahaina in Hawaii, has recorded his astonishment at the arrogance of a missionary who fined a middle-aged female convert a fullgrown pig for her presumption in laughing with a group of children while she was on her way to a church service.

Moreover, a great many missionaries suffered no qualms in building up large personal fortunes at the expense of their parishioners, on whose hospitality most of them, in the earliest days, depended entirely for their very sustenance. Some of their names are commemorated today in Honolulu, in great buildings and trading institutions, and are carried all over the world in the advertising of their heirs and successors.

For seizing the opportunity to personal profit they cannot be condemned, except inasmuch as they lowered their standards to do so; but their methods were not always of that quality one likes to describe as "Christian." Their morality — and I do not necessarily refer to sexual behavior — was sometimes no more commendable than that of the whalers, traders and slavers of their time. Sometimes a false standard confused their intended converts, for the morality of Polynesians was strict, though unconcerned, in general, with sex.

In June 1797, the mission ship *Duff* approached Tahuata Island in the Marquesas carrying two missionaries, William Crook and James Harris, and, among other things, a deckload of goats. Captain Wilson, commanding *Duff*, has recorded the arrival:

"There appeared around the ship seven beautiful young women, swimming quite naked, except for a few green leaves tied round their middles. They remained swimming and floating round the ship for three hours, crying 'Vahine, Vahine,' which means 'Woman.' "

When finally they were allowed aboard, the goats, which had been starved of green fodder, rushed them to eat their girdles; and when the girls understood that these strange creatures — the first of the kind they had seen — meant them no harm, they thoroughly enjoyed the joke.

"They turned this way and that to avoid the goats, but they were attacked at each side alternately and completely stripped naked," the captain wrote. Thereafter they were given "Tahitian cloth" to clothe themselves; but this "tapa," pounded from the bark of the paper mulberry, fell apart in the water, so that the women carefully removed it before swimming, and continued to arrive naked on board during the several days that the crew were engaged in off-loading cargo for the two intending missionaries.

One of these, James Harris, "behaved as if fear had taken possession of his mind, and in short seemed entirely to have lost his firmness and ardor." Over his extreme reluctance he was persuaded ashore with his companion to assume his missionary duties, and the *Duff* put to sea to avoid bad weather. William Crook went off to explore the island. During his absence some of the women, intrigued by Harris's avoidance of them and his extreme aversion to nudity, came by night to ascertain whether any physical peculiarity or deficiency could exist to explain his behavior. When the *Duff* returned after an absence of ten days, captain and crew saw "a forlorn object" sitting on his sea chest on the beach. Mr. Harris had refused to assume responsibilities upon an island where the women were so shameless and, the weather continuing bad, was hauled back aboard by means of a line sent through the surf.

Though Captain Wilson's narrative of this incident, an extensive and detailed one, was written for his superiors in the London Mission Society, it is obvious that Mr. Harris afforded him and his crew some ribald hilarity, in which they were joined by the Marquesans. It was straight comedy; but it had its sober side; and even at this distance removed in time, one can only marvel at the complete unsuitability of this aspirant to missionary honors. At the same time, it should be noted that his companion, William Crook, a youth then only twenty-two years of age, stayed ashore to establish a sound reputation as a sincere and hard-working man of God.

The story underlines the diverse attitudes, in the beginning, the almost complete incompatibility, of the Christian missionary and the pagan he was trying to influence. The native knew no shame in nudity and found nothing but happiness in sexual license. The missionary conceived it one of his first tasks to alter this attitude. He invented the Mother Hubbard, from which the muu-muu is derived, to cover the glorious voluptuous bodies of the earth's most beautiful women, to lower their standards of cleanliness, and to conceal this noblest work of God. He was singularly successful in banishing nudity or its near equivalent, but he made little impression upon the Polynesian's uninhibited delight in dalliance, which still continues.

Another campaign, prosecuted with equal vigor by missionary and trader, sought to make the people economically dependent upon Europeans by introducing civilized artifacts and habits; indeed, the introduction of clothing was accelerated because of this motivation. The necessity of wearing cloth brought with it the necessity of earning money; the trade in copra and shell began, and the missionaries engaged in it as fully as they could.

No effort whatever was made to find what contribution other than economic the native or his philosophies could make to the combined ethos of future generations of dwellers in the Pacific. People whose creed contained no Prince of Darkness were summarily described as devil-worshipers; ancient customs, sometimes of considerable communal value, were outlawed, and their followers viciously penalized; men and women of aristocratic lineage were pressed to menial service.

In the end, a balance was achieved. The splendid self-confidence of the people — for which self-justification is never a match — forced their acceptance by the intruders upon terms so nearly equal that in large areas of the Pacific color-consciousness has never flourished. It was established in the early days, but it was a sickly plant, though tenacious, and still withers.

I N THE European exploitation of the Pacific the superior technologies with which the invaders were armed have tended to becloud the basic proposition that this movement hardly differed in essentials from all the others preceding it. True, it carried new diseases, new disruptions, at bewildering speed into the remotest corners of this ocean; its effects were accelerated, and its timing coincided with discoveries which were to change elemental human attitudes throughout the world. But the pattern of the movement varied not at all from the patterns of the earlier invasions, as far as we can establish them. Possibly the greatest difference was that this movement alone was described in records that were indestructible because of the quantity of their reproduction.

The first of these European newcomers came without women and mated with those they found. They included the explorers of whom we have record and some others whose deeds and thoughts were also given to the world and are today available. But also there were seekers of gold, of pearls, of whalebone and sealskin and blubber, of ebony and sandalwood, of swallows' nests and bêche-de-mer, of birds of paradise and of human slaves. Such men came in untraceable thousands. Their numbers were augmented by those of men fleeing from the laws of their own communities, of visionaries hopeful of establishing empires and dynasties and havens of brotherly love, of pirates and buccaneers, of scientific investigators and their hirelings, of naval officers with pressed and careless crews, of missionaries avid to save the immortal souls of uncounted and unregenerate heathen.

The missionaries were the first to bring their own women; then, in a pattern that must have varied but little from the pattern of conquest in the beginning, the others followed.

If we can judge the quality of those earlier, unrecorded migrations by that of the one we know, and I think we can, we may attempt a historical evaluation closer to accuracy, perhaps, than we can get otherwise. We can at least judge the tempers of the communities; we can probe the nature of the material of which they are composed.

Some essential differences between this migration and its predecessors must be noted. With the exception of the criminal element, which was present in force, and certain other nonconformist factors among the original European intrusion, these new arrivals were, for the most part, secure in their ability to return whence they came. They comprised the first migration to be better equipped and armed than the indigenes. Humanity in a couple of thousand years had discovered so much that they must have seemed armed with magic.

Because I met, and indeed was well acquainted with, some few of the survivors of the day, and because I know the territory and the natives, I find it easy to envisage, as typical of those early intruders, the port of Samarai in the closing decades of the nineteenth century. The island on which it is located was once an isolated outpost of the London Mission Society, and seems much more suited to that purpose. It has few of the accepted qualifications for a port. You can walk completely round it in forty minutes — the local resident says twenty, but that is the time he would expect an employee to take. Under the tropic sun it is best to spin the journey out a little longer.

The savage, unpredictable tides that rip through the China Straits make the berthage dangerous for shipping — Samarai is probably the only port in the world in which you can find the gold-lip pearl oyster at home, and at its magnificent best, under the wharves; for the gold-lip loves a racing tide.

There is no anchorage worthy of the name; boats at anchor must be forever ready to up killick and make for the other side of the island on a change of wind or tide. There is no hinterland, and the cargoes from the infrequent steamers are all transshipped, sooner or later, to one or other of a constant jostle of little schooners.

But in the early days of Papua it was the only island in the vicinity sufficiently remote from its neighors to offer some apparent safety from marauding head-hunters, and sufficiently close to provide a useful sanctuary. And it bestrode the deep sea route between Australia and the East. The government therefore made a deal with its mission owners, giving them in exchange the vulnerable island of Kwato, a few miles away; a deal for which the mission principal, Charles Abel, was roundly condemned when the details were brought to the attention of his superiors in England, but which, after decades, proved happy enough for them.

The tourist today finds Samarai an island paradise; the inhabitant, selling stamps at the Post Office or souvenirs at the stores, a tight little prison. It has a sufficiency of flat land to provide a sports ground and a club of which the chief amenity is a bar, and there is a boardinghouse high up on the central mountain. But in the early days of European penetration the place was lively enough.

In 1884 a state of law was proclaimed in Papua. Previously the islands had been the haunt of outlaws who here found a far from spiritual sanctuary. They supported themselves with the slave trade, termed "blackbirding" in the Pacific, and by trading with the natives. In September 1885 the first representative of law, Sir Peter Scratchley, Her British Majesty's Special Commissioner for New Guinea, reported:

"These traders are often reckless, unscrupulous, brutal and piratical. They cheat the natives and are apt to appeal to their revolvers. They go where they have no business to. They are a thorn in my side and I do not think the life of any white man should be risked in avenging their deaths."

A couple of months later, he died while on his way to arrest two of these "traders," the French Comte de Guise and a man named Currie. "The *Harrier* is waiting to deport them if I find I can do it," he wrote in his diary. But two days later he was taken ill, and he died in a fortnight; and the traders stayed. They were members of a gang now deemed colorful, but in fact, a pack of criminals devoted only to the satisfaction of their own appetites, and completely careless of the cost.

But shortly, with the discovery of gold on other islands, this vicious nucleus was joined by a small army of other men, more honest, just as tough, and ten times more interesting. They wore what amounted to a uniform of pajamas supplemented by a strip of red turkey twill about the waist, high leather boots, a shady hat and a cotton vest. Often enough a brace of revolvers was thrust into the folds of the cummerbund; though some individuals were followed by native gun-bearers. There were Bill the Boozer and Greasy Bill, German Harry and Jimmy from Heaven. There was a short-tempered bully called The Dove. There were French Pete, Nick the Greek, Mick the Greek, Shark-eye Parkes and Yorky Booth. There were hundreds of them, transient, shifting. Dick Ede and Lobb discovered gold on Woodlark Island, and after that Samarai, the nearest port of call for overseas vessels, became a frontier metropolis.

Bill Whitten, who had come from England as one of Sir Peter Scratchley's bodyguard, went up to the Trobriands to fish for mullet, or rather to buy the native catch, sun-dry it, and sell it to the miners for food for themselves and their native workers. But when he came to the Trobriands he found the natives eating oysters. They were small oysters, a couple of inches across, flourishing in shallow muddy water no more than two fathoms deep, and they looked quite unlike the gold-lip, the black-lip and the paka shell, valuable to commerce. They formed an important item in native diet; but to Whitten's interest and amazement, the diners were frequently put to the inconvenience of spitting out true pearls.

In that season, Whitten filled a pickle bottle with pearls as big as peas or bigger, and sold them for a fortune at Thursday Island. From his profits he started a store which developed into a chain of stores, a vast holding of plantations and a fleet of trading schooners; and he brought his younger brother Bob from England to share in the wealth.

In his Samarai store he sold alcohol — it was the nearest approach to a hotel the island had seen. Around the building was a long roofed balcony open at the sides. Every evening a large supply of bottles was left on a center table and the customers came in and helped themselves. In the morning the empty bottles were collected from the surrounding lawns, and their retail value totted up. An equal proportion was charged against each man who was known to have visited the establishment, however briefly, on the previous evening. The mere desire to pay for no more than his share kept each man drinking to his capacity. Such trading was simple and profitable. Within a year or two, three hotels came to Samarai. One was shipped from its foundations in Cooktown, then in process of becoming a ghost town in the north of Australia. Half a century later, at the beginning of the Pacific war, it was still in good condition, an imposing two-storied building typical of its epoch, and unique by reason of its profitable service in two countries; but it was demolished as part of the crazy "scorched-earth" policy adopted, heaven knows why, from the example of the Russians. That was Clun's Hotel. The others were the Cosmopolitan and the Old Samarai.

For Whitten couldn't preserve the secret of his fortune. The traders swarmed to the Trobriands, which they had previously known only as a recommended place for the seizure of native women. And with their competition the prices they paid for the gems reached such heights that little profit remained. The natives were so well provided with trade goods that within eighteen months of the beginning of the rush, in 1898, German Harry was buying back steel axes, knives, hoop-iron, adzes, cloth, looking-glasses, tobacco pipes and trade handkerchiefs from the phlegmatic natives for tobacco, and selling the goods at a profit to the European miners on Woodlark.

Some of the traders have left a name and a memory which persists to this day. After the first discovery the more notable rewards of the life were not monetary, but some men, by good management, good fortune, or a ruthless pursuit of money managed to be comfortable in their retirements. The most eminent of these in this area was Sam Brudo, a Trobriand pearl trader who had little commerce with the other Europeans on the island. In the season he made his purchases, and out of season (for diving was limited to a single monsoon) he traveled to India, to North Africa and Europe, selling his exquisite gems personally to the rajahs, the nabobs, the emirs and the rest.

Brudo, married to a native woman and fathering his small family with the domestic instincts he had inherited from his Belgian forebears, exerted a considerable influence for good upon the natives; and his memorial is principally an amazing development in wood sculpture. After buying the carvings in common use upon the island, he set the men to producing other artifacts — imitations of the Sepik carving of ceremonial tables, for example — and his intervention released the imaginations of the carvers, so that their scope increased. He was one of the few who exerted positive good for the benefit of natives.

At the opposite end of the scale was Nick the Greek, Nicholas Minister, for long a legendary figure in the records of the South Seas. Nick's stamping ground was the Louisiade Archipelago, but in each southeast monsoon he sailed to the Trobriands pearl-buying. He died there one day in 1915, and I have visited his grave, marked with rough coral blocks, in the little cemetery at a place called Losuia.

Of Nick the story has been written that, sailing out of Cooktown in Australia with a Binghi (Thursday Island) crew and a cargo that was largely rum, he was, for his excesses, attacked and frightfully slashed by his men, who, when he shammed dead, threw him overboard. He dived for the keel and let it run past him until he felt the rudder, upon which he drew himself up. He sat on it under the shelter of the counter, maintaining a precarious balance. Meantime the crew broached the rum.

When night fell Nick climbed on board, stabbed the helmsman, and with a tomahawk killed all seven of the remaining men as he lured them, one at a time, on deck. Thereupon he set back to Cooktown alone, and reported his crew to be "bobbing about in the water by the Barrier Reef."

A sequel to this has been told by ex-New Guinea magistrate C. A. W. Monckton, in his book *Some Experiences of a New Guinea Resident Magistrate*. It stated that "being sick and disgusted with men, he shipped and trained a crew of native women, with whom he sailed for many years; in fact I think," says Monckton, "until the day came when Sir William MacGregor appeared on the scene and passed the Native Labour Ordinance which, amongst other things, prohibited the carrying of women on vessels."

Nicholas Minister was once sought by a warship sailing upon the occasions of His Majesty Edward the Seventh; and being made aware of the fact addressed the crew of his own schooner. His father, he said, had died in Greece. Furthermore, it was the custom in Greece as in many parts of New Guinea that when a man died his name was spoken no more. His father's name had been Nicholas, the same as his own. "So there will be no more

Nicholas," Nick the Greek said. "Nicholas is dead and Peter the Pilot comes in his stead."

When the warship caught up to him he denied his identity and the crew confirmed it. "Nick the Greek is here no longer," the men said.

Nick thoughtfully offered, as a man who knew the islands well, to lead the search for himself, and his offer was accepted. He lived comfortably in the warship's wardroom, and wherever they went the natives in politeness and sympathy said, "Nick the Greek was here, but is no longer," and gave the greetings of old acquaintance to Peter the Pilot. It is said he was handsomely rewarded when the search was called off.

He gained another reward from the British Navy for a less amusing episode. A diver named T. E. Craig was walking the bottom in his diving suit when his native crew cut his airline, raided the cargo and scuttled the ship. The government offered £100 for the arrest of the ringleader. Nick went to the village from which the crew had been recruited and, lying in the bushes on the outskirts, shot everything that moved, including four women, and a number of boys little more than children. When all was quiet he inspected the dead and found the right man. He cut off the head, for the body was too much to carry, delivered it to the warship, and collected the reward.

Monckton invests this incident with the aura of romance, and depicts Nick as something of a hero. In actual fact he was a little man, very tough, very dirty. Habitually he went shoeless, but he wore thick woollen socks which were never washed. The soles of them used to shine from their accumulation of polished dirt, and from a habit he had of spitting on the floor and rubbing away the stain, as a neighbor of his, George Munt, a highly respected trader, remembers very well to this day.

Nick always wore a thick woollen jersey in spite of the tropical climate. He was crippled with arthritis; his hands were twisted and useless in his declining years. Yet even then he would sometimes have himself carried aboard his schooner *Progress,* have the sails set, and make his own way, single-handed, through the maze of islands.

As a leader in the tortoise shell trade, Nick was ruthless. He would leave natives on small islands for six months. They were waterless, foodless islands; and if no turtles came ashore the boys perished. Frequently, before this happened, they would have made a killing; and in that case Nick would pick up the collected shell and leave the hunter's carcass where it lay.

His first wife was a native woman he called Wire, because she was thin; his second another native called Gilam, a very intelligent girl who saved his life on occasions of native revolt. After his death she told a story of him that was verified by others of his crew members.

He was sailing for Duau through uncharted seas to the eastward of Normanby Island, and had shipped a local pilot who claimed to know the location of the reefs. Nick was taking some refreshment, sitting on a chair on the cabin top, when dead ahead he saw the peculiar luminescence which signaled "reef."

It was, in fact, the Gallows Reef off Duau, and if the

Progress had held her course she must have run on it.

Nick therefore jumped on the boy who was acting pilot and laid him out. He hauled in the line which was always trolling from the stern, thrust the big hook into the shoulder of the now conscious pilot, threw him overboard, and towed him till he drowned.

Nick had a brother named Solon Minister, who strangely enough was a good and kindly man, an honest citizen and a fair trader who through his descendants contributes still to the development of New Guinea. Solon married a Tewa Tewa woman, and his children and grandchildren may be encountered today round Port Moresby.

In the year of Whitten's discovery of pearls, "Saligigi" Bromilow, who five years before had founded the first Methodist mission upon Dobu Island, halfway between Samarai and the Trobriands, set up a Trobriand branch at the village of Oiabia on the island of Kiriwina, a village fronting the oyster-filled lagoon. A year later he was joined, temporarily, by an assistant, Miss J. Tinney; Miss Tinney and Mrs. Bromilow were the first white women Trobrianders had seen (though many of them had complexions just as fair).

White women were not at this time welcome in the European settlements in the islands surrounding New Guinea. The men, soldiers of fortune all, recognized each one of them, no matter what the state of her morals or the extent of her complacency, as a harbinger of order, a warranty of restrictions to come. Each man had a native woman or a native harem to perform the functions of the female, a woman who kept house, cooked meals, mended clothes and came readily enough from her sleeping place on the palmwood floor to share her consort's bed for a few brief moments in the steaming tropic night. And a native woman could be summoned, dismissed, bought, sold, given away, replaced or persuaded to share her status with a sister or a covey of sisters. Many were shot when their exploiters tired of them, and many more were simply thrown off the schooners into deep water far at sea.

Mission women avoided, as a rule, the centers of European society. They were admirable in their sincerity, but frequently misguided, as I judge them, in the methods they used to bring about their desired ends. Something of their state of mind is revealed in the diary of Miss Tinney, extracts from which are preserved in the mission at Oiabia today. Her first assignment in the Pacific was among the savage natives of Dobu, as bloodthirsty a community as existed in that wide ocean. Her mistake, and the mistake of her co-workers, was to believe that nothing in the life of the Dobuans was worthy of retention, or even of study. This she wrote, on native medicines:

"May 23, 1892. Paid a visit to some of the villages with Mrs. Bromilow and Miss Walker. In one village saw a man who was sick and looking the picture of wretchedness and misery. A native doctor was performing the obaoba. He had given something (most likely water) in a coconut shell, over which he was saying his incantations. We made him laugh during the performance, but do not know whether that broke the charm or not. After awhile this medicine (?) was given to the patient and the doctor went away. This is one of the customs we have to fight."

There was no question in the mind of Miss Tinney, or that of any of her associates, that everything unknown was something that they had to fight. Not once did they seek to ascertain the virtue of the treatment, although native doctors were capable of making cures. Nor did they find out whether the words spoken were in fact "incantations" or words of prayer or thanksgiving for past favors. They also displayed other aspects of this arrogance:

"July 17. Josiah has been having a fight with the people to get them to build the church without pay, but he has won, and a start has been made with the building."

And: "August 11. Last Wednesday Miss Walker and I and eight of the native girls climbed the mount in the middle of the island. He is about 900 feet high and very steep, being almost perpendicular in places. We had a big girl for each hand and four to look after the luggage. It is grand climbing mountains in that way with one pulling in front and one helping from behind. We had no chance to fall if we wanted to."

One of the anomalies of missionary thought was that while they roundly condemned any native usage of magic, they did not hesitate to employ it themselves, wherever they thought it might extend their influence. *Vide* Miss Tinney:

"July 9. After the service the feast was divided, and

by special request Mr. Bromilow took out his teeth to show the people. His native name is 'Saragigi, the Taker-out of Teeth.' "

But with all their shortcomings and their lack of understanding, the missionaries were brave, stouthearted, and capable of displaying their courage to the finest advantage. The emergencies in which they found themselves were sometimes desperate, and the people of Dobu were as savage as the worst of seafaring tribesmen anywhere:

"December 4, Tubetube. . . . When the Tubetubeans brought back their enemies to kill them they tied a man's hands together round the trunk of a tree. Then they put a burning coconut leaf between the man and the tree. This soon burnt down and then they would substitute another, the man all the time dancing round the tree in an agony. They would do this until the man was unable to move about any more, when he would be put aside to finish off afterwards, and another person would be treated as he had been."

Though traders who had little or no incentive to convert the natives to a new way of life sometimes displayed a little more interest and understanding than the missionaries, the basic pattern of intrusion was a contempt for the indigenes and a tendency to obliterate whatever knowledge was in the trust and keeping of the native community. The intruder was not here dependent upon the natives, as he was dependent in all the great land masses. He brought his own transportation, his own means of subsistence, and it was unnecessary for him to study native ways of life. In contradistinction, an explorer in Central Australia depended upon his relationship with the natives not only for his success but for the maintenance of life itself.

Moreover, in none of the European encroachments upon the Pacific, whether official, religious, or conducted for private profit, was there any cohesion, any single purpose or belief tending to produce an apparently united front or a believable example for the natives to follow. The missionary was at odds with the trader, and both incited the antagonism of the government representative. Missions of various denominations plotted against one another. Emissaries of competitive nations seemed alike to the indigenes, but issued contradictory edicts. The British, the Russians, the French, the Spaniards, the Dutch and the Americans crisscrossed the broad waters and left confusion in each wake.

The whole history of European development in the area is, in the main, one of utter disregard for its people; and one can only imagine that this has always been so, long, long before the Spaniards and the Portuguese first tried to take it in a pincer grip. The older histories survive but fragmentarily, in traditions and legends and stories and the tattered remnants of beliefs, with only here and there an isolated artifact to support their evidence. The Pacific's history as we know it testifies to nothing more than the growing ability of man in this area to record and preserve; all else is conjecture.

But there will yet be discoveries made here that will cast a new light upon the history of the world as an entity. Someone will yet solve the mystery of the dingo. Someone will discover the source of Ptolemy's confident assumption of a Great South Land. Perhaps someone will uncover traces here of the Phoenicians who, seven centuries before Christ, are said to have circumnavigated Africa, and were certainly equipped, both with the instruments and tools of marine propulsion and the mental approach to the adventure of living, to penetrate the great ocean.

The discoverers face one major problem: each wave of humanity from the beginnings of time until the present century has, of deliberation or by neglect, obliterated much of the history, the memories, the traditions and the beliefs of those they found awaiting them. The contempt of the roving man for the established man, long sedentary in ancient communities, is notorious; the effects of this contempt have maintained our knowledge of Pacific man at a level not far upraised from rudimentary conjecture.

The New World was a single island once, not long ago; most people see it now as the great connected continents of the Americas, from Alaska to Cape Horn, from the tropics to the polar regions. A truer concept includes, as I think, the continent of Australia, and the great islands of New Guinea and New Zealand; a New World centered upon the mighty spaces of the Pacific as the Old World once was centered upon the Mediterranean, looking inward from the seacoasts of Africa and Asia and Europe. There are signs that the concept is still enlarging, that the New World of the near future will include the island groups of the Philippines and Japan; that the thrusting, probing, growing cultures born of new approaches to new problems will find sure converts here, so that the New World will advance to the bastions of ancient Asia; and the startling advance in human communications which has paralleled the development of New World countries has made such enlargement practical and desirable.

But the New World of today as I see it consists of the three continents and the islands sheltered in their linking sea. It has been lately fashionable to describe Australia as an outpost of Asia, from what evidence I do not know. Alliance and eventual integration is always good, provided the alliance is sincere; but alliance comes most easily between nations formed of similar elements, holding comparable ethics and desires, born and nurtured in circumstances that are similar, struggling against like restraints and difficulties, inspired and inflamed by a common love of freedom.

Over the centuries ahead the whole human race will work towards a total integration, with disruptive elements ever creating new alliances and swift separations, with each fresh movement offset by the culture-pendulums of the differing sects, each retrogression countered again by the rebel who is natural man. But in the proximate millennium the physical camps of the New World and the Old will gather strength; the communications of which man makes insistently greater use seem to give inevitability to this projection.

In this New World the components are lands we inherited from sea adventurers; and as far as we can trace, the indigenes they partly despoiled and displaced came likewise by their holdings. The slow march overland by which the human race spread from the place of its development to dominate the ancient lands came to a halt at the edge of the ocean. It was, or it must have been, an infinitesimal progression from established centers. The seacoast developed a particular kind of adventurer, and when he set out upon his incredible voyages, he left his traditionalist brothers behind him.

He was motivated by greed as well as adventure, by greed and curiosity, and perhaps the threat of known disaster of potential recurrency behind him. But he was, he must have been, the type of man prepared to face the unknown, ready to learn, and, learning, to adjust his attitudes. He must have been attuned to nature, and confident in that sympathy and in his strength; and his seed carried the strain.

He must have left plenty of his like behind him, established on good land in good circumstances; but his companions were all of his kind. The old breed in the old place kept developing its explorers and its innovators, but the new men made a new race, with a greater consciousness of past venture, and the knowledge that others of their blood had succeeded. Their tradition was a tradition of change and uprooting; their aims had altered with their exodus.

That is conjecture, but it is more than a hazard that in the Old World today there is a different feeling, a more cautious approach, a more controlled rebellion against the past.

The New World is a world of strong relationships.

Sydney and San Francisco are more alike than cities on the same continent, though not even their latitudes correspond. They were born of gold and greed and the necessity for trade; they developed after a pattern that was evolved in the hearts of men who thought similarly.

The nerve center of the great hemisphere is, as I believe, in the Pacific Ocean, in the wildness of waters, in the great reaches where less than a century ago men could still escape from the conventions and the laws.

18

Ruy Faleiro the astronomer, dubbed conjurer and charlatan by his fellow-countrymen, withdrew from the Court of Portugal to the Court of Spain, and there became closely associated with Fernando de Magalhães, known as Magellan, another who had found contempt in Portugal.

These two together presented a plan to Charles the Fifth of Spain to sail the American coast southwards until they discovered a passage, traveling if need be to the seventy-fifth degree of latitude; and thence reaching the Spice Islands from the west. The voyage would complete a circumnavigation of the world, break the Portuguese threat of a European monopoly in spices, and justify Spain's assumption of sovereignty over certain Spice Islands under the terms of the Treaty of Tordesillas, which confined Spanish expansion to lands westward of a line running north and south three hundred and seventy leagues west of the Cape Verde Islands.

Faleiro signed the agreement as a joint captain-general of the proposed expedition, but when the five ships set forth from the mouth of the Guadalquivir, he stayed behind, having cast his horoscope to arrive at the disconcerting conviction that he would sacrifice his life if he sailed.

In the event, his fears had some confirmation. A certain San Martino of Seville went as astronomer in his stead. When Magellan, having accomplished the major part of his purpose and having additionally converted the King of Cebu to a brief Christianity and to a temporal alliance with the King of Spain, took arms against his heathen neighbor, Cilapolapu of Mactan, and was killed, San Martino made one of the party which foolishly (for the Spaniards had demonstrated the inferiority of their forces) went to treat with the victors for the body of their captain. He lost his life.

But if Ruy Faleiro had looked deeper into the stars he might have perceived that the memory that forever marks him is that of a man who refused his fate and turned his back on destiny, a man who traded away a permanent glory for an ignominious preservation. In another temper he might, indeed, with his influence over Magellan and an equal authority, have dissuaded him from the unnecessary campaign which clouded the success of the expedition. He might have changed the known history of the world, and he and his heirs established an aristocracy of the conqueror in the islands of the Pacific, according to his contract with the king.

Faleiro feared his stars, and many another man with him. There were others who did not, and it is in this circumstance that the inheritors of the New World tradition will glory when that tradition comes to be firmly established at its ultimate of expansion. Men will be proud then that their leaders, the penetrators, the explorers and those who closely followed were men who, of deliberation, chanced their hands against the unknown terrors. Venture and Adventure built the New World; its symbol should be the presentiment of naked man, alone, independent and erect; its banner a device of stars, its sanctuary the omnipresent sea.

There have been times when, in obedience to an exhortation of the spirit, conjured by omens, perhaps, that work in secret on the senses, I have left my house to walk in solitude upon a windswept beach, perhaps to watch the sun rise and hear the cry of a gull, a lorn, lost sound surmounting the swelling cadenzas of thunderous waters; to walk in seeming solitude and feel the rapturous buffeting of the racing, rising gales, and smell the salt and taste the oils of seaweed in the great cold draughts of air that set my blood hurrying from my lungs to tingle my skin and warm my spirit and occupy my mind with nothing more than a vast appreciation of these physical joys.

It is then I sometimes find myself in the good company of the army of my ancestors, in the kindly presence of approving ghosts, faceless, formless, known to me only by an assurance of their proximity. They stand behind me, as I in centuries to come will stand with them behind some familiar stranger, on some related strand between the unchanging sea and the tamed and tempered shore. It is then I find myself possessed of their beliefs, their simple aims; strengthened by their resolve which, equally with any act of mine, put me in this place at this time, facing the things I have to do, equipped with these sinews, these brain cells, these genes and chromosomes.

Without question and without thought I accept then the actuality of the beings who personify the waves and the tempests. I see the beauty of the sirens and remember the strength of the demi-gods. I joy to the achievements of the heroes and fear the gods. If this be madness I remain safe; the sour sanity of disbelief is quick enough to return; and I have no witnesses, for at such moments I have no desire to break down the intimacy of such a close-knit brotherhood.

I feel the presence of my father there. We walk together still, as when I was a child. I have no need now, nor desire, to take his hand and turn my face into the skirts of his coat as I did then, for comfort and protection and encouragement; he is a companion, equal in his inheritance, sharing the thought that in his lifetime he was slow to express.

Sometimes I am aware of that grandfather I never knew, who preached his Calvinistic creed to the heathen; staunch in his faith and confident in his mission even after he joined the rush for gold, his fingers coarsened with the work of pick and shovel, gold-pan and cradle, but tender still with the pages of the Bible in his Sunday pulpit.

It is not a time to think, alone between the sea and the land; it is a time to be infused and freshened with the surge of life, the acceptance of its continuity. But after I return and am sheltered and protected from the elements which are my friends, my mentors and my examiners, I sometimes envy the now vanished men of that good company for some of the very possessions that we, in our advance, have examined and rejected, and with which we are no longer armed. I envy them their heroes and their demi-gods, and much more; I am jealous of the strength they drew from thoughts no longer potent.

For the demi-god was more than the hero of a tale for children. He was a constant inspiration and example to the youth of the tribe; he was a man born of a human mother who could do the impossible; and it has always been imperative, throughout this human history of ours, that men come forward to attempt the impossible. It was thus we crossed the oceans; thus will we reach the stars.

The demi-god was, typically, a man born of a woman impregnated by a god; by the sun or the moon or the winds or the seas or the earth itself; it is good that individual man should, in moments when the delirium of ambition holds him in sway, harbor the possibility that his ancestry might have coupled the safe and sane attributes of humanity with the illimitable powers of the gods; that he is related to the origins of life itself; that the oceans in their power are his brothers, or that he has a consanguinity with the stars.

3 3 7

It was in some such delusion grown to faith that the rebel ever broke the bonds with which his tribe was self-enchained; it was the denial of limits recognized in the habit of ages that gave a constant impetus to man's progress from his beginnings. And the spirit of rebellion born to fruition in a strong and intelligent personality has been the most important single factor recurring in the recorded accomplishment of each change for the better that man has made.

Such an individual was truly an inheritor of godly traits; in the language of art he was a demi-god.

Maui, of the Polynesians, numbered among his feats the taming of the sun. In the light of the probable migration of that people from cold regions near the Arctic Circle to island homes where climatic conditions were at an optimum, it is a fairly simple assumption that before the stories grew, he was a man of the tribe who led his people on the great migration. It matters little whether the journey was accomplished in a generation or over a thousand years; for each contributing leader could well have been known by the style and title of the first.

Maui fished up New Zealand from the sea. But before the Maoris reached New Zealand, their Ao-tea-roa, their "Land of the Long White Cloud," Maui, in earlier versions of the story, fished up, with a combination of magic and skill, other island homes of the people, the Tongan group for example.

Again the translation could well be that he was the discoverer of these lands, or that the people discovered them because of the impetus that Maui gave to their migrations. Indeed, in the stories, he made the division of the lands and allotted appropriate sections to his brothers the chiefs. More and more, as you dwell upon the tales, you tend to substitute a rational explanation for what seem at first like wild conceits.

Maui brought fire from the underworld. Maui was mischievous. Maui was capable of failure, was given to rage, brooked no excuses. In the far northland from which his people may have come was Loki, the God of Fire, a mischievous and malevolent god, given somewhat to rage. Even their names are alike: Loki was called "Lowe" by the Scots. You could adduce from these circumstances wedded to others, as MacMillan Brown, for one, has done, that these brown people of a Caucasian inheritance came from the same stock as Norsemen and shared a re-membered tradition. But then again, Mala, of the Siassi people who are unrelated to these others, being Mela-nesian, was a demi-god of a similar character. Of course, he could well have been patterned upon Maui.

There are a thousand explanations of the story, and of all the stories. The most direct one is that they fulfilled an important tribal function: while the laws were invio-late and the customs sacred, the will to break new ground, to strike out beyond the known and close hori-zon, even the capacity for rebellion which is such a precious attribute of the human race, was kept refreshed by the story of the demi-god.

The story is the receptacle of racial wisdom. Among the people of every race a thousand stories are added to the common store in every generation; a thousand ver-

sions of the old stories or stories new from the consciousness of thinking man. There are stories which are dropped
from circulation; but there are also stories which persist,
and of most of these it may be truly said that they are
those with the greatest content of wisdom; stories which
the elders can produce from memory in the comparative
tranquillity of age to prove a point or to point a moral, to
indicate a course of action or to provide warnings against
the consequences of ill-considered deeds.

Such stories as serve these purposes stretch so far into
the past that some of them are common to almost all the
races upon earth. One such is the story of rebuilding, of
development from a time of chaos — the story of the
Tower of Babel.

In whatever version you find it, the era pre-dating the
time of chaos was a bright and wonderful period of advancement; so that one of the functions of this story is to
provide a stimulus for progress, a recapture of paradise
on earth. Thus it points the way for communal and individual effort, and promotes a cohesive solidarity for
the tribe. It has, indeed, many functions which old men,
as they near the end of life, would understand.

It is quite possible that the differing versions have no
common origin. For the history of advancement in every
tribe must be punctuated with periods of chaos, from
which a still more ancient time looked golden indeed.
And it would be against the preceding period of chaos
that each advance would be remembered. Indeed, an
over-hasty appraisal would leave the impression that a
period of chaos is essential to advancement; a proposition

with which I do not agree, for there are examples to the contrary. Nevertheless, chaos does provide the opportunity for leadership; and from its bloody battleground a victor of unusual capacity may construct the foundations of a national security.

But now that our stories no longer depend on the tenacity of the human memory, the simplifications which ensured them life and meaning have disappeared. The hero is no longer fashionable and has become the protagonist; the storyteller makes apology for his weakness, offsets his strengths, and in a fashion which must surely change some day, tends to make him indistinguishable from the others of his community.

From the greatest wars in history, no figures of legend have come down. The heroes of the probes into space are examined and studied, flayed of the blinding cloaks of their glory so that they show as no bigger, no braver, no better constituted for leadership than that other man who watches them upon a television screen. They have no magnificent vices; their rages are controlled; they have become insipid.

Moreover, they no longer stand alone. They are supported and accompanied by a thousand others, each painted as of nearly equal stature — the men who make the instruments by which they navigate their courses, the planners and plotters, the generals and statesmen, all the specialized and circumscribed divisions of the team. By the adoption of this attitude we have destroyed a great source of national and cosmic inspiration.

When, some day, I join that company of ancestors that

crowds my occasional solitude, I expect to find that they will have made their judgments of my generation upon factors which are unchanged throughout the ages. They will be unmoved, I think, by the vast quantity of manufactured material at our disposal, by our ability to fly, and to talk the world around, to send pictures by the airwaves with the speed of light, to calculate to a known degree of accuracy our chances of reaching the stars.

There are men among them who, like Pánfilo de Nárvaez upon the coast of Texas, melted the metal parts of their horse furniture to make the tools for boatbuilding, and flayed the horses themselves to make the bellows for the forges, and a necessary substitute for planks. There are men who learned by trial and error to bend the elements to their will; men who evolved the methods of navigation from their personal experience and left their maps for others yet to come; men reduced, in the extremity of their hardships, to eating leathers, to moistening parched mouths with their own urine, to tapping the blood of spent horses to assuage their thirsts; and still unwilling to turn back from the course that destiny indicated.

Yet the capacity to cope with turbulence, to tame rebellious animals with muscle intelligently applied, to bullock through a fury of elements, to retain a hold on life against the attacks of a blistering sun or a blizzard cold as death, to meet in good heart an enemy with superior arms, to watch through jungle nights, to dare the supernatural and flaunt authority long established was coupled in these men with other traits.

They knew of their own observation the nature of plants; they came to a strange country and found its edible foods. They made substitutes for spices and knew the values of herbs. They could cool a fever and hearten a failing spirit. From the ends of the earth they brought conceits of beauty: flowers pressed in books and the magic of an alien art. To the ends of the earth they took their ideals.

They knew the ways of animals and learned from them. They watched as a dog watches, from the ridges fringing the untraveled plain. They bridged the chasms like the spiders, and hoarded against the seasons like the squirrels. They raided the honey stores of ants and bees. They made friends with the dog and utilized his capacities — did not Balboa exact a man's share of booty for the services of his warrior-dog Leoncico, sired by Ponce de León's famous hound? There was nothing in nature they did not conceive it their duty to know and to learn from; there was not a cloud in the sky that did not merit, for however small a space, their unalloyed attention.

They could think and they could contemplate and they could learn. The birds and the animals told them what fruits were poisonous; the birds and the clouds indicated a way for them to follow over the sea. Every sound on the airwaves carried them a meaning they translated; they followed every strange scent to its source. They learned for the sake of learning, and they loved their world.

Above all they could love; they could love even that which they destroyed. Of their regard for humanity and its continuance they composed their codes of ethics and invested their gods with a consideration related to their own. They tried to shape a future to benefit a kindred they would never know; and if they left them nothing else but pride and confidence, that was a fortune large enough.

A man would hold his fellow humans in great contempt and little love did he not realize that among the company of his ancestors were lesser men: cautious men and cowards, wicked and evil men, the great aggregation of the nondescripts, and the mentally halt and lame and blind. But it is not they who set the standards by which we live; we rise in the tradition of the heroes, and will so continue.

When I was enlisted in the service of the king, I served for a long time as a noncommissioned officer; but by reason of my duties as a captain of aircraft found it necessary, from time to time, to give orders to commissioned officers in less responsible positions. I was not commissioned, because I could not see the necessity for much that I was asked to do — I found no merit in performing antics under orders in a gymnasium, for example, and therefore was absent, and frequently without excuse, from all the physical training periods. When I went on leave, if I happened to be enjoying myself, I did not report back to my station on time. Nor did I see any virtue in holding men I outranked to a regime I did not follow myself. It followed that my record was fairly black; though this did not apply to the time I spent with aircraft, when I gave of my best.

Sometimes, because of hot temper or an impatience

with stupidity, I spoke my mind to commissioned officers. There came a day when a very senior man, a group captain with rather less experience than mine in operational flying, used my aircraft and showed some disrespect for the guns on which, from time to time, the lives of my crew were dependent. I spoke to him on the subject without regard to his rank, and within minutes found myself closeted with my own commanding officer.

"I ought to crime you for what you said," he told me. "But from another point of view you're to be commended for looking after your gear. Nevertheless, I am not going to have my officers spoken to in that way by noncommissioned men; therefore, you are going to go up for a commissioning interview."

It was perhaps unfortunate that I was turned down on my record of poor discipline. The commanding officer was furious, but secured me another interview, this time with an air commodore. I traveled half a day to see him, and when I eventually entered his office found him sympathetic. He told me to sit down; that first he wanted to talk things over. We discussed the fishing trade, which to my surprise he knew as well as I. We talked at length about gold mining, in which I had dabbled — not as much as he — and about the timber game. We discussed deer stalking and the handling of cattle; and he probed into recesses of my career that I had forgotten. He knew a great deal, that air commodore, and I wish that I could remember his name.

Finally, after half an hour of this, he said, "Now this is the score. Forget about your record; that won't count in this interview. I am going to ask one question, and only one, and if your answer is correct you will, in my opinion, make a proper officer. If you give me the wrong answer, you haven't a hope in hell."

"Suits me, sir," I said.

"Right. Stand up," he ordered, reverting suddenly to discipline. "Put out that cigarette. Stand to attention."

He leaned over the desk.

"You've had a crack at a lot of things, and you've always been broke. What kind of a bloody life do you think you've had?"

"A good one, sir," I answered, and he relaxed.

"Right. You're in. You've made it. And now that's all. Dismiss."

He was right, of course. And I am proud of being invested with His Majesty's commission, but even prouder of winning it in the way that I did. And among the silent brotherhood of the sea storm I can sense approval. It is an attitude they understand.

When it is time to go I stand, for a moment, on the hard wet sand, and look to where the rising moon lays its path of enticement across the tossing restless waves, the implicit promise never changed from when the old ones sailed the easting down to bring me here; the skies wild with the wind that filled their sails, the same air throwing the same spray into my face as soaked their beards. What kind of a life did they have? I know the answer.

45643

PR
6035
U45
Z53

RUHEN, OLAF

DATE DUE

GAYLORD

PRINTED IN U.S.A.